SPIRITUAL WARFARE

terms of engagement

DR. DAVID JEREMIAH

with Dr. David Jeremiah

Edited by William Kruidenier
Unless otherwise indicated, Scripture verses quoted are from the NEW KING JAMES VERSION.

Printed in the United States of America.

CONTENTS

ABOUT
DR. DAVID JEREMIAH
AND TURNING POINT

D r. David Jeremiah is the founder of Turning Point, a ministry committed to providing Christians with sound Bible teaching relevant to today's changing times through radio and television broadcasts, audio series, books, and live events. Dr. Jeremiah's common-sense teaching on topics such as family, prayer, worship, angels, and biblical prophecy forms the foundation of Turning Point.

David and his wife, Donna, reside in El Cajon, California, where he serves as the senior pastor of Shadow Mountain Community Church. David and Donna have four children and eleven grandchildren.

In 1982, Dr. Jeremiah brought the same solid teaching to San Diego television that he shares weekly with his congregation. Shortly thereafter, Turning Point expanded its ministry to radio. Dr. Jeremiah's inspiring messages can now be heard worldwide on radio, television, and the Internet.

Because Dr. Jeremiah desires to know his listening audience, he travels nationwide holding ministry rallies and spiritual enrichment conferences that touch the hearts and lives of many people. According to Dr. Jeremiah, "At some point in time, everyone reaches a turning point; and for every person, that moment is unique, an experience to hold onto forever. There's so much changing in today's world that sometimes it's difficult to choose the right path. Turning Point offers people an understanding of God's Word as well as the opportunity to make a difference in their lives."

Dr. Jeremiah has authored numerous books, including *Escape the Coming Night* (Revelation), *The Handwriting on the Wall* (Daniel), *Overcoming Loneliness, Grand Parenting, The Joy of Encouragement, Prayer—The Great Adventure, God in You* (Holy Spirit), *When Your World Falls Apart, Slaying the Giants in Your Life, My Heart's Desire, Sanctuary, Searching for Heaven on Earth, The Secret of the Light, Captured by Grace, Grace Givers, Signs of Life, What in the World Is Going On?, The Coming Economic Armageddon, I Never Thought I'd See the Day!,* and *God Loves You: He Always Has— He Always Will.*

ABOUT THIS
STUDY GUIDE

The purpose of this Turning Point study guide is to reinforce Dr. David Jeremiah's dynamic, in-depth teaching and to aid the reader in applying biblical truth to his or her daily life. This study guide is designed to be used in conjunction with Dr. Jeremiah's *Spiritual Warfare: Terms of Engagement* audio series, but it may also be used by itself for personal or group study.

STRUCTURE OF THE LESSONS

Each lesson is based on one of the messages in the *Spiritual Warfare: Terms of Engagement* compact disc series and focuses on specific passages in the Bible. Each lesson is composed of the following elements:

- *Outline*

The outline at the beginning of the lesson gives a clear, concise picture of the topic being studied and provides a helpful framework for readers as they listen to Dr. Jeremiah's teaching.

- *Overview*

The overview summarizes Dr. Jeremiah's teaching on the passage being studied in the lesson. Readers should refer to the Scripture passages in their own Bibles as they study the overview. Unless otherwise indicated, Scripture verses quoted are taken from the New King James Version.

- *Application*

This section contains a variety of questions designed to help readers dig deeper into the lesson and the Scriptures, and to apply the lesson to their daily lives. For Bible study groups or Sunday school classes, these questions will provide a springboard for group discussion and interaction.

- *Did You Know?*

This section presents a fascinating fact, historical note, or insight that adds a point of interest to the preceding lesson.

Using This Guide for Group Study

The lessons in this study guide are suitable for Sunday school classes, small-group studies, elective Bible studies, or home Bible study groups. Each person in the group should have his or her own study guide.

When possible, the study guide should be used with the corresponding compact disc series. You may wish to assign the study guide lesson as homework prior to the meeting of the group and then use the meeting time to listen to the CD and discuss the lesson.

For Continuing Study

For a complete listing of Dr. Jeremiah's materials for personal and group study call 1-800-947-1993, go online to www.DavidJeremiah.org, or write to: Turning Point, P.O. Box 3838, San Diego, CA 92163.

Dr. Jeremiah's *Turning Point* program is currently heard or viewed around the world on radio, television, and the Internet in English. *Momento Decisivo*, the Spanish translation of Dr. Jeremiah's messages, can be heard on radio in every Spanish speaking country in the world. The television broadcast is also broadcast by satellite throughout the Middle East with Arabic subtitles.

Contact Turning Point for radio and television program times and stations in your area. Or visit our website at www.DavidJeremiah.org.

SPIRITUAL WARFARE: TERMS OF ENGAGEMENT

INTRODUCTION

The sad legacy of the American War Between the States, or Civil War, was more than 1.1 million dead and wounded. And more than 20,000 of those casualties occurred at one time: the Battle of Antietam—September 17, 1862, near Sharpsburg, Maryland. This 12-hour battle ranks as the bloodiest day of the five-year-long struggle between North and South.

Militarily, neither side won a decisive victory, though General George McClellan, leader of the Union forces, was able to stop the Confederate advance into Maryland and force General Robert E. Lee's forces back across the Potomac. In retrospect, historians and analysts consider Lee to have been a better tactician and leader than McClellan. So how was McClellan able to thwart Lee's advance? It was only possible because two Union soldiers discovered a misplaced copy of Lee's battle plans and delivered them to McClellan before the fighting began. By knowing the Confederate strategy, the Union general was able to mount defenses and attacks that proved decisive.[1]

When it comes to spiritual warfare, something similar has happened: God has given us proprietary information about our enemy and his strategy. We know who he is (his origin and history), what his nature is, what his strategies are, and what the final outcome of his efforts will be. But best of all, God has provided explicit directions on how to mount our defenses against his attacks. With such information, there is no reason we should ever lose a spiritual battle.

But before getting into those details, most Christians face a greater challenge: acknowledging the seriousness, maybe even the existence, of something called "spiritual warfare." In the early days of the Civil War, many Northern civilians packed picnic lunches and sat on hillsides to watch what they thought would be entertaining defeats of the upstart Rebel forces. But the blood-stained battlefields and agonizing screams of the wounded quickly told a different story: This is war! And it is serious.

Many followers of Jesus Christ are suffering needlessly because they don't realize they are part of a war in which they are suffering consistent defeat. But they don't have to. Based on the information God has provided in Scripture about spiritual warfare, no Christian need suffer at the hands of Satan. If the Union general, McClellan, had not studied and responded to the Confederate battle plans he received, he would have suffered serious defeat.

Satan, our enemy, is much stronger and more powerful than any individual human being. But when we, by faith, put on the Lord Jesus Christ (Romans 13:14), we clothe ourselves with His strength, His armor, as Paul calls it in Ephesians 6:10-18. Then, the tables are turned: ". . . because He [Christ] who is in you is greater than he [Satan] who is in the world" (1 John 4:4). The whole armor of God—five defensive pieces and one offensive piece—is given in Christ to every believer: truth, righteousness, peace with God, faith, salvation, and the Word of God. With the defensive armor, we are able to resist Satan's attacks. With the offensive weapon of the Word, we are ensured that Satan must flee from the authority of God's truth.

Spiritual Warfare—Terms of Engagement is your guide to studying spiritual warfare and each piece of the armor God has provided for every believer. Even if we agree that we are in a war and that God has given us protective armor, it is still up to us to clothe ourselves with it—first, through faith in Christ as Savior and then in continual submission to Him as Lord. Only by living a life continually clothed with Christ will spiritual victory be ours.

1. Thomas Bailey and David Kennedy, *The American Pageant*, ninth edition (D. C. Heath, 1991), 456-457. Cited in *More Perfect Illustrations for Every Topic and Occasion* by the editors of PreachingToday.com (Wheaton, IL: Tyndale House Publishers, Inc., 2003), 269.

ARE WE REALLY IN A WAR?

Ephesians 6:10-18

In this lesson we are introduced to the reality of spiritual warfare and how God has provided for our protection.

OUTLINE

There are two dimensions to winning any war: engagement and armament. Even though they are in a spiritual battle, too many Christians are not engaged spiritually or intelligently. And still fewer know the intimate biblical purposes of the armor God has given for their protection.

I. The Call to Battle
   A. A Word of Encouragement
   B. A Word of Explanation

II. The Covering in Battle

OVERVIEW

The brightness and clarity of a morning in July 1861, did not foretell how the day would end. For that to have been true, the day should have dawned with thunderstorms and lightning strikes. For Manassas Junction, Virginia, about 25 miles outside Washington, D.C., was to be the site of the First Battle of Bull Run early in the American Civil War.

Most folks did not think the War Between the States would last long—the blue-coated Northern soldiers would quickly drive the Southern "Rebels" back into the South, and the secession movement would be squashed. So the hills and roads around Manassas Junction were filled with gaily-dressed spectators who had come out to watch the two armies meet. Ladies with parasols settled themselves onto blankets and opened the picnic baskets they brought.

But it's likely their appetite for food and entertainment was soon sated by the sight of blood and guts. A genuine battle took place before their eyes—fighting, shooting, screaming, and dying. By the end of the day, hundreds lay dead and thousands lay wounded. And suddenly the folks in Washington, D.C., realized a serious war was beginning. It would not be fun or glorious; but like all real wars, there would be winners, losers, and casualties.[1]

People often think of war as glamorous until they, or someone they know, becomes a casualty. That's the way too many Christians think about spiritual warfare. It's a great subject for conferences, movies, lectures, books, and preaching, but not so much for personal involvement. The truth is that every Christian is a participant in a spiritual war. Everything looks like it's going fine on the outside, then we find ourselves suffering spiritually and we don't know why. We didn't know that spiritual warfare could actually invade our personal lives.

Research shows that many professing Christians don't believe in spiritual warfare (in biblical terms) because they don't believe in an actual devil or demons. Others believe the devil exists, but they don't know how to relate their personal struggles to the larger reality of spiritual warfare. Spiritual battle is real, and we are responsible to defend ourselves using the spiritual defenses God has provided. Ephesians 6:10-18 will be our key text, for within it we will find the Bible's "terms of engagement" for victory in spiritual warfare.

THE CALL TO BATTLE (EPHESIANS 6:10-12)

There was a day in our society when the population in general had a greater sense of good versus evil in the world—two world wars provided opportunity to reflect soberly on the reality of conflict. The population at large believed God and heaven were good and Satan and hell were bad and that most conflicts could be traced back to that larger division.

Today, things are different. Many professing Christians have little sense of conflict in their life. They go through their day-to-day activities, attend church on Sunday, and live quiet and orderly lives as good citizens. They live without any awareness of the great spiritual conflict taking place all around them and how it might be impacting their personal life. But in Ephesians 6:10-12 Paul issues a call to battle: ". . . be strong . . . Put on the whole armor of God . . ." Every Christian is called to be aware of and participate in the spiritual warfare that surrounds us. But the call to battle is not just in Ephesians 6—it's throughout the New Testament: 1 Corinthians 16:13; 1 Timothy 1:18; 6:12; 2 Timothy 2:3-4. Christianity is nothing if it is not a fight, a battle, a war. Why else would Paul's opening words on this subject be, "Be strong"?

A Word of Encouragement (Ephesians 6:10-11)

Even soldiers need to be encouraged—and especially when preparing for battle. Paul gives us two reasons to be encouraged in the face of spiritual warfare.

1. Your Power Is a Gift (Ephesians 6:10)

First, we are not to be strong in our own strength but in the strength that comes from knowing Him: "Be strong in the Lord and in the power of His might." God does not call us into His service without giving us the strength and resources we need to be victorious.

We know God has not given us a spirit of fear but of power (2 Timothy 1:7)—the same power to which Paul refers in "power of His might." It is the same power that raised Jesus Christ from the dead (Ephesians 1:19-20). Not even death can overcome the power of God. And it is this power that gives us ability to stand firm in the face of attacks by the enemy. And that power is appropriated by us when we don the armor Paul goes on to describe. To put on the armor of God is to be dressed in God's power, ready for conflict and victory.

We are not being dressed for battle by someone unfamiliar with war. God presents Himself as a Warrior-God in the Old Testament doing battle against unrighteousness and evil in the earth: "He shall strike the earth with the rod of His mouth, and with the breath of His lips He shall slay the wicked" (Isaiah 11:4-5). Paul even borrows from these Old Testament images to create a description of the Christian's spiritual armor (Isaiah 11:4-5; 59:17). Because we are being asked to do everything in battle that God does, we are given the same armor and protection that He has: namely, His righteous power and might.

The charge we are given—"be strong"—is the same one given to Joshua (three times) by God when he assumed leadership of the nation of Israel to settle the Promised Land (Joshua 1:6, 7, 9). Joshua's charge to "be strong and courageous" in the face of his physical enemies is the same charge we are given by Paul as we face spiritual enemies. That must tell you something: the reality behind physical conflicts is first spiritual. Preparing for both is the same: standing in the gift of God's power and might.

J. C. Ryle wrote these words about the Christian's obligation to fight the good fight:

> The true Christian is called to be a soldier and must behave as such from the day of his conversion to the day of his death. He is not meant to live a life of religious ease, indolence, and security. He must never imagine for a moment that he can sleep and doze all the way to heaven.[2]

Sadly, a lot of modern preaching has a goal of making Christians more comfortable rather than more clothed in the armor of God. Conflict (discomfort) is not something to be engaged and defeated but something to be avoided as one does a nuisance of any kind. We hear very few calls from the pulpits in America for "Christian soldiers" to fall into formation and prepare to stand firm against the attacks of the evil one. Think what a difference it would make in the spiritual health of the Church of Jesus Christ if every believer was dressed every day in the full armor of God and was standing victorious against the enemy's attacks. As a preacher and pastor, the goal of my ministry is to equip the saints (Ephesians 4:11-12) so thoroughly in the truth of God's Word that they are able to live and serve victoriously. Properly equipped and full of God's power and might, the Christian is able to live a victorious life.

2. Your Perseverance Is Guaranteed (Ephesians 6:11)

The second bit of encouragement Paul gives is that we will "be able to stand against the wiles of the devil"—guaranteed! The word "wiles" was used in the older King James Version of the Bible but is not often heard in conversation today. It means organized conduct, plans, strategies, or methodologies—especially relating to war. And against whom do you suppose Satan is putting together such plans and strategies? That's why we need to live in the armor of God. Satan is planning attacks against all who oppose His work or promote God's work.

I grew up with a father who was president of a small Christian college. And I recall one particular year it seemed nothing but bad things happened. There were problems with students, financial problems, problems with some citizens criticizing the college, problems with the college's religious affiliation—problems in every direction. And I recall asking my father one night, in short, "Why is it that we're trying to serve the Lord and having such a hard time of it when others have life so easy?" And I'll never forget my father's counsel in reply (paraphrasing): "If I were Satan, I would do anything I could to disrupt the impact of a Christian college like this. We are training hundreds of future leaders for Christ, have many effective faculty members, and alumni serving Christ all over the world. I think Satan would be happy to disrupt what is going on here at this school. And I think he's giving us his best shot this year. He's not bothering the people who aren't making an impact for Christ, but the ones who are!"

I personally believe Satan has "wiles" (strategies and plans) in place for every Christian who is living for Christ. Why else would Paul direct every Christian to put on the whole armor of God? Four times in Ephesians 6:11-14, Paul refers to the Christian's "stand" against the evil one. Why would we need to stand were we not under relentless attack? We are told to "stand" (a defensive posture) rather than "attack" because the battle has already been won. Satan is trying to take from us the certainty we have in Christ. So our stand is one of holding on to what Christ secured for us by His death and resurrection. But just as lions take plenty of time to position themselves perfectly to make a lethal strike on their prey, so Satan takes all the time needed to set up an attack on the Christian (1 Peter 5:8).

If we don't stand our ground, we are giving that ground to the enemy. Every time we compromise our spiritual standards or fail to walk in righteousness, we are giving ground to the enemy. We are allowing him to have a bit more influence in our life than before. Our task is not to defeat him—Christ already defeated him at the empty tomb. Our task is to stand firm against his attempts to destroy our credibility or God's credibility in our sight. Anything he can do to weaken or destroy our influence for Christ, he will do. But our perseverance—if we are standing firm in the armor of God—is guaranteed.

Naturalist Craig Childs explains what it means to stand one's ground when he was confronted by a mountain lion:

> Mountain lions are known to take down animals six, seven, eight times their size. Their method: attack from behind, clamp on to the spine at the base of the prey's skull and snap the spine. The top few vertebrae are the target, housing respiratory and motor skills that cease instantly when the cord is cut. Mountain lions have stalked people for miles. . .

> I hold firm to my ground and I do not even intimate that I will back off. If I run, it is certain I will have a mountain lion all over me. If I give it my back, I will only briefly feel its weight on me against the ground. The canine teeth will open my vertebrae without breaking a single bone. The mountain lion begins to move to my left, and I turn, keeping my face on it, my knife at my right side. It paces to my right, trying to get around on my other side, to get behind me. I turn right, staring at it. My stare is about the only defense I have.

[The lion] does the same thing. He just keeps staring at him, continues to try to provoke him to run, turning left and right, back and forth, again and again, now just ten feet away. Finally, the standoff ends. The lion turns and walks away, defeated by a man who knew what and what not to do in his presence.[3]

That's what we must do when confronted by (the "roaring lion") Satan: stand our ground on the authority of God's Word.

A Word of Explanation (Ephesians 6:12)

A word of explanation is in order: Against whom, exactly, are we fighting?

1. The Common Struggle Denied (Ephesians 6:12a)

Paul begins with a negative—he defines who we are *not* fighting against: "For we do not wrestle against flesh and blood . . ." Paul could have chosen any athletic metaphor he wanted (like box or race), but he chose "wrestle" because of the intensity it calls to mind. Athletic wrestlers strain every muscle in close "combat" with their opponents, never being able to relax until the match is over. Spiritually, Paul sees Christians the same way—in an always-on wrestling match with the devil and his evil forces.

I said earlier that physical conflicts have spiritual roots. Thus Paul says we don't wrestle against "flesh and blood"—human beings. Even if we are being attacked by a human being, the warfare we're experiencing is not human, it is spiritual. Even though our spiritual enemies were "disarmed" at the cross (Colossians 2:15), they are still on the attack. Their work begins in the spiritual realm even when it is manifested in the physical. We must look beyond people in order to see what Satan is doing in the spiritual realm.

2. The Cosmic Struggle Declared (Ephesians 6:12b)

We don't wrestle with human beings, but we do wrestle with "principalities, against powers, against the rulers of the darkness of this age, against spiritual hosts of wickedness in the heavenly places." The great Welsh minister, Dr. David Martin Lloyd-Jones wrote,

> The great trouble with the world today, and with the church unfortunately, is that they know so little about the devil and his principalities and powers. Much teaching concerning holiness and sanctification never even mentions the devil and these powers at all. The problem is regarded solely as something confined to ourselves.[4]

Satan commands a vast force of fallen angels who have different levels of authority and responsibility under his leadership. His forces are organized and hierarchical; and you, if you are a Christian, fall somewhere in his plans. Your defeat is part of his strategy. The cosmic battle in which we are engaged is no haphazard event. If it appears that way, it is only because we are oblivious to what the Bible says about it.

THE COVERING IN BATTLE (EPHESIANS 6:13-18)

There is definitely a war going on all around us. Our greatest comfort as we play our role in this combat is that we are not unprotected. Not only does God provide power and might by which to stand, but He covers us in His armor. In this study guide we will look at each part of the armor—what it means to God and what it means to us. And most importantly, how it protects us from the "fiery darts of the wicked one" (verse 16). God provides the armor, but we provide the putting on of the armor. Not even God's armor can be a defensive weapon if we go into battle without it. When we make every provision called for by God's armor, we will be protected. God's part in spiritual warfare is to ensure the victory which He has done through Christ and to provide armor for our protection. Our part is to glorify God by donning the armor and refusing to yield to Satan's attempts to discredit God and discourage us. God has done His part. Hopefully this study guide will equip you to do yours.

A pastor friend and I were talking once about why so few Christians have never studied the Book of Revelation, and why so few pastors preach on it. "I think Satan keeps them from studying it or preaching it," my friend said.

"Why would Satan do that?" I asked.

He answered, "Well, how eager would you be for your enemies to study a book that spells out your ultimate defeat?"

He made an excellent point. The Bible tells us Satan loses and we win in the end. But in the interim, he is on the attack. All we have to do is be alert and wear the armor God has provided in order to make it safely through.

Notes:

1. From Stu Weber, *Spirit Warriors* (Sisters, OR: Multnomah Publishers, 2001), 9-10.

2. J. C. Ryle, *Holiness* (United States of America: Jay P. Green Sr., 2001), 33.

3. Craig Childs, *The Animal Dialogues* (New York: Little, Brown and Co., 2007); *The Week* (2-8-08), 40-41.

4. D. M. Lloyd-Jones, *The Christian Warfare* (Grand Rapids, MI: Baker Book House, 1977), 20-21.

1. In terms of spiritual warfare, how would you interpret and apply the four admonitions given by Paul in 1 Corinthians 16:13?

   a. Watch. (See 1 Peter 5:8.)

   b. Stand fast in the faith. (How does Satan attack your faith?)

   c. Be brave. (Why? What does that suggest?)

d. Be strong. (Why can spiritual warfare result in weakness?)

e. What other key admonitions could you suggest (in addition to Paul's four) for living a protected, defended spiritual life?

f. What do these kinds of words and terms suggest to you about the nature of the spiritual life? (Peaceful? Dangerous? Explain.)

2. Read 1 Timothy 1:17-20.

   a. To what event is Paul probably referring in verse 17? (See 2 Timothy 1:6-7.)

   b. What is Paul's objective for Timothy's life? (verse 18b)

   c. What key word does Paul use in verse 18b that connects his words to Ephesians 6:12-18?

d. In verse 19, what would be the evidence of waging the "good warfare"? (verse 19a)

e. And what would be the evidence of not waging the "good warfare"? (verse 19b)

f. Why is "the faith" (verse 19b) Satan's main target? Why does he want us to question or doubt our faith?

g. How would you best explain Paul's actions toward Hymenaeus and Alexander? (verse 20; see 1 Corinthians 5:1-5, especially verse 5)

h. What did Paul teach was the ultimate goal for one who was defeated in spiritual warfare and had given in to persistent sin? (See 2 Corinthians 2:5-11.) How would this action be a great defeat for Satan?

3. Based on what you have learned so far, put Paul's words to Timothy ("Fight the good fight of faith") into your own words of exhortation for being victorious in spiritual warfare. (1 Timothy 6:12)

a. Why is "confession" of our faith so important on an ongoing basis?

b. How can we "confess" our faith in ways besides (in addition to) the formal creeds of the church?

DID YOU KNOW?

W hen we hear the word "armor" today, we often think first of large medieval suits of armor that covered a soldier from head to toe—and weighed more than 50 pounds. That is obviously not what Paul had in mind in Ephesians 6. What he describes is not armor in the medieval sense at all, but a collection of six independent pieces of protective gear, five defensive (belt, breastplate, shoes, shield, and helmet) and one offensive (sword). The image Paul is using is obviously a Roman soldier dressed for battle, which would have been very similar to what Paul has described (with the addition of a spear, which Paul doesn't name).

IDENTIFYING THE ENEMY

Ephesians 6:10-12

In this lesson we prepare for spiritual victory by getting to know our enemy.

OUTLINE

Knowing one's opponent or enemy is one of the secrets to victory on the playing field or the battlefield. So coaches and generals spend hours studying their opponents' game and battle plans. The study of Scripture is the best way for a Christian to learn the ways of Satan.

I. **Satan's Personality**

II. **Satan's Position**
   A. He Is a Prince
   B. He Is a Ruler
   C. He Is a God

III. **Satan's Power**

IV. **Satan's Purposes**
   A. He Is the Great Deceiver
   B. He Is the Great Divider
   C. He Is the Great Destroyer

In the days leading up to the Six-Day War in June 1967, Aharon Yariv, head of Israel's military intelligence, knew that Israel was vastly outnumbered. Those arrayed against Israel held a 2:1 advantage over Israel in manpower, 2:1 in tanks, 3:1 in aircraft, 4:1 in warships, and 7:1 in artillery. Yariv needed to know everything possible about his enemies—especially about Egypt, the largest in military terms.

To that end, Yariv's spies infiltrated every level of Egypt's armed services, especially the air force. The spies provided complete information about pilots, commanders, schedules, radar, battle codes and communication networks, and the personal schedules of senior Egyptian air force officials—when they were most likely to be away from their posts and unable to coordinate operations.

The result? Swift, decisive victory of Israel over Egypt. Israel launched a surprise attack on the Egyptian air force in pre-dawn hours of June 5, striking 18 of Egypt's air force bases—blowing up airplanes and runways and destroying support facilities. The Egyptians lost over 300 of their 420 combat aircraft and 100 of their 350 combat pilots. By June 10—six days later—Israel dominated their enemies, capturing the Gaza Strip, the Sinai Peninsula, the West Bank of the Jordan River, and the Golan Heights in northern Israel as a defensive buffer against Syria.[1]

No matter how well one knows his enemy, most major wars between nations last longer than six days. But without knowing one's enemy, they could last much longer. When it comes to spiritual warfare, too many Christians live in spiritual defeat because they don't know their enemy and his strategies for defeating them—if they even believe in him, that is. Satan loves to convince Christians that he is a harmless myth, a legend uncovered in the sands of time. In an April 2009 survey by the Barna Research Group, 60 percent of self-identifying Christians said the devil was symbolic, not real. Yet 64 percent believe that a person can be under the influence of spiritual forces like the devil and demons.[2] There was obviously some overlap between those who don't believe in the devil and those who believe a person can be under his influence. That kind of double-mindedness comes from not knowing what the Bible says about the devil, the Christian, and spiritual warfare.

While in Germany, I visited the Wartburg Castle where Martin Luther lived, for safety's sake, from May 1521 to March 1522.

(Luther posted his "95 Theses" against the established church's practice of indulgences in October 1517.) While living in Wartburg Castle, tradition says that Luther, during a bout of spiritual conflict, threw an inkwell at the devil. There is even a dark stain on the wall in Luther's room where the inkwell supposedly hit and splattered. The authorities on site said, No, the inkwell event never happened. But it could have. Martin Luther, based on his writings, was well familiar with the devil's tactics. He even wrote, "When I go to bed, the Devil is always waiting for me. And when he begins to plague me, I give him this answer: I say, Devil, I must sleep. That's God's command. Work by day, sleep by night. So, go away."[3] To Martin Luther, the devil was a real being, not an abstract idea.

Five times in Ephesians 6:12, Paul uses the word "against" in describing our spiritual warfare. We are battling "against" real beings: principalities, powers, rulers, and spiritual hosts of wickedness. When we think of "against" we think of force, of someone or something pushing back against us. That is the nature of spiritual warfare— real beings pushing against one another, Satan against Christians. Paul's exhortation to the Ephesians to "be strong in the Lord and in the power of His might" (verse 10) is so they can enter this very real spiritual battle that is ongoing for all who follow Christ. There is a real "devil" (verse 11), a "wicked one" (verse 16), who shoots "fiery darts" (verse 16) at Christians. Those who believe what the Bible says on this point can learn to defend themselves against the devil. Those who believe the devil doesn't exist will have to explain the "fiery darts" in their lives some other way.

SATAN'S PERSONALITY

Satan is given many names in Scripture, the following being just some of them: your adversary (1 Peter 5:8); the accuser of the brethren (Revelation 12:10); the angel of light (2 Corinthians 11:14); the deceiver (Revelation 12:9); the destroyer (Revelation 9:11); the evil one (John 17:15); the liar (John 8:44); the murderer (John 8:44); the prince (John 12:31, 14:30, 16:11; Ephesians 2:2); the serpent (Genesis 4:3; Revelation 20:2); and the tempter (Matthew 4:3). All the names given to him represent various facets of his personality and strategies.

Satan originated in heaven as a wise and beautiful angel (Isaiah 14:12; Ezekiel 28:12, 14-15). Isaiah tells us that while he was named Lucifer, the son of the morning, and served in God's court, pride rose up in Satan's heart and he purposed to become like God

(Isaiah 14:12-14). When Lucifer challenged God's supremacy in heaven, God cast him out of heaven, down to earth. Lucifer and all the angels had free will just as we do, and the exercise of Lucifer's will—and that of many angels who rebelled with him—cost him an honored place in heaven. The first sin we know about in the universe was Lucifer's sin of pride (1 Timothy 3:6).

C. S. Lewis wrote, "The essential vice, the utmost evil is pride. Unchastity, anger, greed, drunkenness, and all of that are mere fleabites in comparison: it was through Pride that the devil became the devil. Pride leads to every other vice. It is the complete anti-God state of mind."[4]

SATAN'S POSITION

There are three positions that Satan legitimately fills at the present time: prince, ruler, and god.

He Is a Prince

The Bible calls Satan "the prince of this world" three times: John 12:31; 14:30; 16:11 (NIV). He is also called the "prince of the power of the air" in Ephesians 2:2. As the prince of this world, Satan is in charge of evil men; as the prince of the power of the air he is in charge of evil spirits. In other words, Satan is the leader of evil whether on earth or in heaven.

He Is a Ruler

First John 5:19 tells us that "the whole world lies under the sway of the wicked one." In other words, he is the ruler of the world system in which we live—the world of power, lust, ambition, greed, and lies. Satan has a kingdom just like God has a kingdom (Matthew 12:26). First and foremost, a kingdom is the authority to rule, not just a set of geographical boundaries. And Satan has a kingdom he rules—a kingdom of darkness (Colossians 1:13) in which he rules over angelic (demonic) beings (Matthew 25:41) and some human beings who have given themselves over to the powers of darkness. The principalities, powers, rulers, and hosts to which Paul refers in Ephesians 6:12 represent hierarchical levels of authority within Satan's kingdom—perhaps as many as a third of the created order of angels who rebelled against God and went with Satan to earth (Revelation 12:4).

He Is a God

In 2 Corinthians 4:4 Paul refers to Satan as "the god of this age" ("god" with a lowercase "g") with the power to blind the minds of the unbelieving to the light of the Gospel. We normally associate a "god" with a religion, and that is perfectly appropriate here. Satan definitely has his own religion. He has his own church (Revelation 2:9; 3:9), his own gospel (Galatians 1:8), his own ministers (2 Corinthians 11:15), his own doctrines (1 Timothy 4:1), and his own communion table and cup (1 Corinthians 10:20-21). His goal is to counterfeit everything God does so as to lead astray the unwary—and his religion serves that purpose.

SATAN'S POWER

This may be the question most Christians have about Satan: How powerful is he? Does he have the power to hurt us as well as harass us?

For starters, 2 Thessalonians 2:9 says that Satan's works are often accompanied by "all power, signs, and lying wonders." So he does have supernatural power—as well as the power of death (Hebrews 2:14) and the power of a stalking lion (1 Peter 5:8). There is no question that Satan has power, but we should not make the mistake of thinking he has power equal to God. Satan is not the equal or opposite of God in position nor in power. (Michael, the archangel [Jude 9] is Satan's opposite, both being created beings.) God is infinite and eternal; Satan is a created, limited angel.

The best way to remember Satan's limited power is by remembering 1 John 4:4: "He who is in you is greater than he who is in the world." Satan's power is great compared to ours, but not even in the same league as God's power. God has Satan on a leash (Job 1-2) and there he remains, in spite of appearances, until he will be cast into the "lake of fire" where he will live in torment forever (Revelation 20:10).

SATAN'S PURPOSES

There are many action verbs attached to Satan's activities in Scripture. I will summarize them by focusing on three that serve to reveal his purposes: Satan deceives, divides, and destroys.

He Is the Great Deceiver

In a conversation with religious leaders, Jesus set the record straight about Satan's character: "[Satan] was a murderer from the beginning, and does not stand in the truth, because there is no truth in him. When he speaks a lie, he speaks from his own resources, for he is a liar and the father of it" (John 8:44b). In Revelation 12:9, Satan is identified as the one "who deceives the whole world."

Satan began sowing seeds of deception in the Garden of Eden when he twisted the words God spoke to Adam and Eve (Genesis 3:1-4). As a deceiver, Satan is also a counterfeiter—one who always has a slightly different (and wrong) take on God's words and actions. Almost everything Jesus was and did, Satan tried to copy. For instance, Jesus was the light of the world (John 9:5), so Satan disguised himself as an angel of light (2 Corinthians 11:14). Satan always mixes enough truth with error to make it attractive and enough error with truth to make it deadly. He knows the Bible well and can misquote it or take it out of context at will. He loves to ask us, "Has God indeed said . . .?" (Genesis 3:1)

The greatest defense against Satan the deceiver is a thorough, working knowledge of the Word of God.

He Is the Great Divider

The first thing Satan did after rebelling against God was to divide the hosts of heaven, the other angels, into two camps: those loyal to Satan and those loyal to God. And he's never stopped dividing. He instigated a division in the early church in Jerusalem by promoting dishonesty by a member (Acts 5:1-11). Ananias wanted to be recognized for giving a financial gift to the church, but lied about the amount of the gift. It wasn't that he held back some money for himself that was the problem; it was that he created the impression for the apostles that he had given it all.

Satan is still sowing seeds of division in the Body of Christ through lies, jealousy, pride, power, and finances. When "two or three are gathered in [Jesus'] name," He is there to join with them in fellowship (Matthew 18:20). But Satan is also there looking for an opportunity to divide those two or three, to break up their unity. And often he uses the tongue—that human organ that "is set on fire by hell" (James 3:6).

He Is the Great Destroyer

Satan uses two means to destroy the people of God (see Revelation 9:11, "destroyer"): adversity and direct attacks.

1. He Attempts to Destroy Us Through Adversity

There is no question about Satan's ability to hinder, delay, or frustrate our lives. The great apostle Paul was not immune to such harassment as he told the believers in Thessalonica: "Therefore we wanted to come to you—even I, Paul, time and again—but Satan hindered us" (1 Thessalonians 2:18). It is an arresting insight for young Christians to gain: God does not always protect us from the difficulties of life, even when we are doing our best to serve Him. And that includes difficulties that are orchestrated by Satan himself.

Satan's goal in creating adversity, of course, is to discourage us to the point that we will at least give up serving the Lord if not give up the faith altogether. There is an end-game to Satan's strategies of which too many Christians are unaware.

2. He Attempts to Destroy Us by Direct Attack

Ephesians 6:16 makes a clear reference to the direct attacks from Satan we are likely to experience: "the fiery darts of the wicked one." I believe one of Satan's most oft-used direct attacks is that of discouragement, for this reason: If Satan can discourage us, it means we have lost hope. And if we have lost hope, then we have lost faith in God and His promises. And if we lose faith in God, we make God look bad. And that is Satan's ultimate goal—to make God look bad in the eyes of all Creation. So, while Satan's attacks are often directed at us, they are ultimately directed at God. The worse we do as Christians, the worse God looks as the One in whom we place our faith and to whom we direct our hope.

I read a story once about Satan going out of business, selling all his tools at a diabolical type garage sale. Hate, envy, jealousy, greed —all his tools were spread out on a table to be examined. Off to the side lay a small, wedge-shaped tool that was more expensive than all the rest. When asked why the small tool was the most expensive, Satan replied that the tool was discouragement. He explained that he could use discouragement to pry open a human heart better than any other tool. Once discouragement gets inside, the devil said, all the other tools can do their work.[5]

Unfortunately, Satan has not gone out of business and will not until God puts him out of business at the end of time. Until then, he is walking about seeking whom he might devour. The believer is helpless against the devil except when he or she is clothed in the armor of God. We cannot defend ourselves against his direct or indirect attacks in our own strength. It is only as we are "strong in the Lord and in the power of His might" (Ephesians 6:10) that we can walk in the victory God has planned for us.

Martin Luther, besides being the father of the Protestant Reformation, was a great lover of music as part of his defense against the devil:

Music is a fair and lovely gift of God which has often wakened and moved me . . . Music drives away the devil and makes people [happy] . . . Next after theology I give to music the highest place and the greatest honor . . . Experience proves that next to the Word of God only music deserves to be extolled as the mistress and governess of the feelings of the human heart. We know that to the devil music is distasteful and insufferable. My heart bubbles up and overflows in response to music, which has so often refreshed me and delivered me from the plagues of the enemy.[6]

As evidence of his love of music and his deep understanding of the theology of spiritual warfare, Luther penned some of the most powerful and accurate words ever written on the subject in his hymn "A Mighty Fortress Is Our God." He wrote, "For still our ancient foe doth seek to work us woe; his craft and power are great and armed with cruel hate, on earth is not his equal." He then goes on to clarify that we cannot defeat Satan on our own: "Did we in our own strength confide, our striving would be losing; were not the right Man on our side, the Man of God's own choosing; dost ask who that may be? Christ Jesus it is He; Lord Sabaoth, His Name, from age to age the same, and He must win the battle."[7]

Notes:

1. Adapted from Gregory Elder, *Intelligence in War: It Can Be Decisive* (Central Intelligence Agency). See https://www.cia.gov/library/center-for-the-study-of-intelligence/csi-publications/csi-studies/studies/vol50no2/html_files/Intelligence_War_2.htm (accessed 23 September 2010).

2. Barna Group, "*Most American Christians Do Not Believe That Satan or the Holy Spirit Exist,*" April 10, 2009, http://www.barna.org/barna-update/article /12-faithspirituality/260-most- american-christians-do-not-believe-that-satan-or-the-holy-spirit-exis, (accessed 31 August 2010).

3. Roland Herbert Bainton, *Here I Stand* (Peabody, MA: Hendrickson Publishers, 1950), 375-376.

4. C. S. Lewis, *Mere Christianity* (San Francisco: HarperCollins, 1952), 121.

5. Robert Jeffress, *The Divine Defense: Six Simple Strategies for Winning Your Greatest Battles* (Colorado Springs: Waterbrook Press, 2006), 35.

6. Bainton, 351-352.

7. Martin Luther, trans. by Frederick H. Hedge, *A Mighty Fortress Is Our God*, <http://www.hymnsite.com/>, (accessed 30 August 2010).

1. Read Isaiah 14:3, 12-17.

   a. Who is this lengthy portion of Scripture describing in historical terms? (verse 3)

   b. How is Babylon ultimately connected in Scripture to opposition to God? (Revelation 14:8)

   c. Where did "Lucifer, son of the morning" dwell originally? (Isaiah 14:12a)

   d. And to what realm was he banished? (verse 12b)

   e. How might Luke 10:18 possibly relate to Isaiah 14:12?

   f. What were the five statements (the five "I will's") Satan made against God? (verses 13-14)

      1. "I will _____."

      2. "I will _____."

      3. "I will _____."

      4. "I will _____."

      5. "I will _____."

g. How does Satan's last statement summarize what was at the heart of his rebellion?

h. How did Satan use this same line of thinking when he attacked God in the presence of Adam and Eve? (Genesis 3:5)

i. How did the first of the Ten Commandments address the issue of "other gods"? (Exodus 20:3)

j. How was the notion of "one God" incorporated into Israel's life and worship as a nation? (Deuteronomy 6:4, in the context of 6:4-9)

k. How does Satan tempt Christians today to establish other "gods" in their life? To what kinds of "gods" (idols) would you be attracted if you were not spiritually careful?

l. Describe the ultimate demise of the king of Babylon.
   (Isaiah 14:15-17)

m. How does his ultimate end parallel that of Satan's?
   (Revelation 20:7-10)

2. From the introduction to Jesus' parable in Luke 19:12, what do you learn about kingdom authority? Is a kingdom primarily a place or a right to rule?

a. From 1 John 5:19, how would you describe the kingdom over which Satan has authority?

b. What did Jesus, and John the Baptist before Him, announce at His first coming? (Matthew 3:1-2; 4:17)

c. In terms of kingdoms, what was Jesus' goal with reference to Satan's kingdom? (1 John 3:8)

d. How did Paul describe the increase of Christ's kingdom and the decrease of Satan's kingdom in Colossians 1:12-14?

DID YOU KNOW?

It is instructive to note that Paul doesn't exhort Christians to put on the "armor of God" but the "whole armor of God" (Ephesians 6:11, 13). Besides an occurrence in Luke 11:22 (ASV), the Greek word for "whole armor," *panoplia*, occurs only here in the New Testament. *Panoplia* was formed from two words: *pas* (all, whole) and *hoplon* (tool, implement, weapon). It was a word used to describe a fully-armored soldier, one who has taken up and put on all the various pieces of armor available to him. Thus, when Paul says to put on the "whole armor of God," the suggestion is not to pick and choose. Every piece of armor is important: belt, breastplate, shoes, shield, helmet, and sword.

THE GIRDLE OF TRUTH

Ephesians 6:14

*In this lesson we learn the importance
of truth in spiritual warfare.*

OUTLINE

The mind is the primary battlefield on which spiritual warfare is
waged. Therefore, our spiritual defense comes down to what we
believe and think. If our mind is filled with truth about God,
ourselves, and our enemy, then we will be prepared to withstand
the lies and deceit of Satan.

I. **The Purpose of the Girdle of Truth**
    A. It Was Important for Advancing
    B. It Was Important for Attacking
    C. It Was Important for Awarding

II. **The Power of the Girdle**
    A. The Truth of God
    B. The Truth in Us

When the former Soviet Union began to crumble, those leading its dissolution relied not on explosive arms for victory but on the explosive power of truth. Dissident leaders like Vaclav Havel and Aleksandr Solzhenitsyn were convincing their followers that truth was more powerful than the sword. Christian author and philosopher Os Guinness describes their methods:

> Aleksandr Solzhenitsyn in his Nobel speech wrote, "One word of truth outweighs the entire world." You see, as Solzhenitsyn and the leaders of the Velvet Revolution knew with clarity, chiseled in courage, there were only two ways for them to bring down the might of the Soviet tyranny. One was to trump their force physically. But they had no way to do that; that was impossible. The other was to counter physical force with moral, staking their stand on the conviction that truth would outweigh lies and the whole machinery of propaganda, deception, and terror would come falling down around them. As you know, if you've studied history at all, they chose the latter and the unthinkable happened. One night, they won.[1]

We have seen already that Satan is the father of lies—that he relies on lies and deception to accomplish his ends. He deceives and divides in order to destroy. Therefore, it should come as no surprise that the first of the six elements of Christian armor listed by Paul is the belt of truth. Only by knowing and standing in the truth can we detect the devil's lies and stand against his attempts to divide and destroy.

As we get further into the details of the Christian's armor, it will become apparent that to put on the armor of God is to put on the Lord Jesus Christ Himself. Paul wrote in Romans 13:14, "But put on the Lord Jesus Christ, and make no provision for the flesh, to fulfill its lusts." Everything the armor represents, Christ is: truth, righteousness, peace, faith, salvation, and the living Word of God. The seven verses describing the armor of God (Ephesians 6:11-17) are a commentary on the first seven words of Romans 13:14. Clothed in the Lord Jesus Christ, we are clothed in the armor of God. But it is our responsibility to make sure that we have put on Christ, put on the armor, and that we stay clothed continually in order to remain protected.

THE PURPOSE OF THE GIRDLE OF TRUTH

We would not normally consider a leather or linen belt as a piece of armor since it is not made of metal. And the Roman soldier might not have either since it was a common piece of apparel worn by almost all Romans. The girdle, or belt, served three purposes in the dress of a Roman, and likewise as part of a soldier's apparel.

It Was Important for Advancing

If a Roman needed to move quickly, he gathered up the folds of his long robe and tucked them under the belt he wore around his waist. And the soldier would do the same, making sure that his robe or toga did not impede his progress. The process would have been known as "girding up one's loins" to free them from obstacles. And for a spiritual application Peter wrote, "Therefore, gird up the loins of your mind . . ." (1 Peter 1:13). That is, get rid of those things that clutter the mind and distract it from the task of knowing and applying the truth. And Paul is saying that the belt of truth is what removes all impediments from Satan (lies, deceit) as he attacks the believer —in the sense of Hebrews 12:1 (NIV): "Therefore, . . . let us throw off everything that hinders and the sin that so easily entangles . . ."

It Was Important for Attacking

Girding up one's robe allowed for advancing—a prerequisite for attacking. The belt not only held the soldier's robe out of the way, it held his sword or quiver of arrows as well. It is no accident that the believer's one offensive weapon—the sword which is the Word of God—is connected to the belt of truth. The Word is the believer's only weapon when it comes to attacking the lies of Satan as we will see below.

It Was Important for Awarding

When a Roman soldier was rewarded for valor in battle, he was given a medal, or pin, that would be affixed to his belt—much as today's military personnel wear ribbons on the left-breast area of their shirt or jacket. Those awards were a sign of the soldier's prowess in battle. That he was alive to display his medals was a testament to his skill over the enemy. While we don't wear medals for Bible memory on our sleeve as Christians, we do know that storing up the Word in our heart is a sure defense against sinful temptations (Psalm 119:11).

THE POWER OF THE GIRDLE

There are two aspects of the power of the belt of truth. First, it is God's truth; and second, it is God's truth *in us.*

The Truth of God

The debate for truth is raging in our world today. Again, I turn to Os Guinness to delineate three ways truth is viewed. The first view is the traditional view that says truth exists independently and is waiting to be discovered. The second view is relativism—truth is defined by each individual as he sees it. The third view is the postmodern position that truth doesn't exist, it must be created by each individual.[2]

Obviously, Christianity relies on the first view: Truth is objective, eternal, and independent of man's interpretation. Truth comes from God; Jesus said, "I am the . . . truth" (John 14:6). Man's opinion about truth changes nothing about truth since truth originates in God and is eternally true. We can discover, but not create, truth. Truth remains truth regardless of our opinion of it.

Some people think it is arrogant for Christians to speak of truth as absolute and revealed through the living and written Word of God —Jesus Christ and the Scriptures. But it is not arrogant; we are simply taking God at His Word. There is great importance in educational circles today about the pursuit of the truth wherever it may be found. Like Solomon of old, Christians welcome the exploration of God's creation, but for a different reason: We pursue knowledge believing it will confirm the truth of Scripture; we are not looking for new or alternate sources of truth.

I have chosen to be a teacher and preacher of the Word of God because I believe truth is what the human race needs more than anything else. People don't need warm and fuzzy; they need truthful and accurate. They need to know exactly who they are and who God is and how they can be brought back into a relationship with Him. And they need to know the truth about Satan and spiritual warfare so they can understand the things that happen in their lives. Our world today is full of confusion, missteps, and false starts—because people don't know the truth; they don't know how to interpret, discern, and understand what is happening to them and to our world.

The systematic study of biblical doctrine is the lifelong task of the Christian. When we know truth, then we will be prepared to defend ourselves against the attacks of Satan just as Jesus did in the wilderness (Matthew 4:1-11). When tempted by the devil, Jesus resisted the temptations on the basis of truths from Deuteronomy that He quoted. It was His knowledge of truth that allowed Him to recognize and resist what Satan was offering.

In his book *Spirit Warriors*, Stu Weber describes what it means to know the truth in a practical way:

> The Christian soldier must possess a strong, unshakeable conviction in the reliability of Scripture and in its living power to impact the battlefield. You must not allow yourselves to drift in your thinking, especially in this postmodern world that sees truth as individually centered, and fluid, and culturally constructed. You must also demonstrate a facility with Scripture, becoming conversant with its pages and principles on a level that is wholly involved in the dailyness of life. Every good spirit warrior constantly asks himself this question: What does the Bible say about this? About that? About anything?[3]

Throughout the four Gospels and Acts we find Jesus and the apostles demonstrating a ready facility with the Word of God. They apparently had committed much of it to memory so they were able to quote it in teaching or ministry moments. We may never memorize the entire Bible, but we need to be intimately familiar with all of it so we either know, or know how to find, God's perspective on the situations we encounter in life. If we don't know the truth of Scripture we are victims waiting to happen; we are prime targets for Satan to tempt us through lies and deception.

In order to gain that kind of knowledge we have to become students of the Word: in church, in small groups, in personal Bible study, through reading books based solidly on Scripture, through memorization, and other means. Our mind must be filled with God's truth so the Holy Spirit can quicken that truth to our hearts in a moment of need. If our mind and heart are a vacuum, Satan is ready and waiting to fill it with the opposite of God's truth.

Why did the apostle Paul write his letters? Certainly to address particular questions and circumstances in the churches. But above all, it was so the new Christians in the churches could be firmly grounded in the truth! Paul knew their best defense against opponents of the Gospel would be a thorough knowledge of God's truth. And the same is true for us today. Churches that do not consistently teach their members the truths of God's Word are doing them a great disservice. Within the covers of the Bible is everything we need to know to be victorious in spiritual warfare. Knowledge of Scripture is the foundational cornerstone of a victorious life in Christ.

The Truth in Us

So far, the truth I've been talking about is truth "out there"— the objective Word of God which is the truth of God. But there is another dimension to truth: the truth "in here"—the (more) subjective reality of truthfulness in our lives as the truth of God is lived out through us. To reflect this second dimension of truth we might read Ephesians 6:14 this way: "Stand therefore, having girded your waist with truth . . ." In other words, has the truth about God we have acquired from Scripture caused us to become truthful people, people of integrity? If we give the devil any place in our life (Ephesians 4:27), we are giving him opportunity to gain influence. And we give him a place in our life when we harbor and embrace something in our heart, mind, or life that is contrary to God's truth. If we are not allowing the Word of God to displace all carnal or fleshly attitudes and beliefs, we are giving place to the devil and setting ourselves up for defeat. It is no surprise that the apostle John wrote, "I have no greater joy than to hear that my children walk in truth" (3 John 4). (Note: He didn't say "know the truth"; he said "walk in truth.")

When we do battle with Satan, we cannot be a pretender. We cannot act like we are righteous when we know there is unconfessed sin in our life. It is that unconfessed sin that becomes a "place" (Ephesians 4:27) for the devil. Many who have been Christians a long time, or perhaps grew up in a Christian home and church environment, can walk the Christian walk and talk the Christian talk on cue. They can put on a convincing Christian face when needed. They can even quote the truth of God since they have heard it all their life. But that doesn't mean they are living truthful lives, lives transformed by the truth of God.

When my youngest son, Daniel, left home and went off to college, he went to a mid-size college in the South to play on their football team for a couple of years. When he arrived on campus and got to know the rest of his teammates, he discovered that he was the only Christian on the team—which was a surprise to him. He assumed in the South—part of the Bible Belt—that there would be other Christians. There was one other fellow on the team who professed to be a Christian. In fact, he was the head of the campus organization of Christian athletes. At first, Daniel really looked up to this older student—he knew the Bible well and attended a local Baptist church in town each Sunday. But after being on campus for a while and developing a relationship with this young man, Daniel discovered the guy was living together with his girlfriend outside the bonds of marriage. You can image what happened: Discovering this inconsistency completely deflated Daniel's admiration for his teammate. The person he thought was deserving of honor and respect turned out to be living a double-minded life: professing Christ on the one hand but living in sin on the other. Daniel's disappointment wasn't a matter of him judging the other student; it was a matter of using the student's own testimony and profession of spirituality as the benchmark, as well as his unwillingness to leave a sinful living arrangement. We cannot profess to be walking in the truth while living a lie (1 John 1:6).

In a conversation with Jewish religious leaders in His day, Jesus asked, "Which of you convicts Me of sin?" (John 8:46a). And the answer was, "No one." There was no place in Jesus' life where He could be accused of inconsistency or untruth. When He said, "I am the . . . truth" (John 14:6), He also proved it by living truthfully—living with integrity and honesty and transparency. Jesus was girdled with the truth; He lived with a clear conscience. A half-dozen times in his letters, Paul addressed the importance of a clear conscience. We cannot enter spiritual battle with a guilty conscience by which Satan can hold us hostage.

David, the psalmist and king of Israel, took the "truthfulness" approach to his life, possibly after being called to account for covering up his dual sins of murder and adultery. In Psalm 139:23-24 he wrote this prayer: "Search me, O God, and know my heart; try me, and know my anxieties; and see if there is any wicked way in me, and lead me in the way everlasting." He wanted God to uncover and reveal whatever hidden sins might be in his heart. He knew he couldn't fulfill the responsibilities of his life if he wasn't living a truthful life. That is a good prayer for every follower of Christ to pray on a regular basis: "Show me, Lord, what I cannot see with my own eyes."

God is looking for people throughout the earth whose hearts are loyal to Him (2 Chronicles 16:9), people on whose behalf He can show Himself strong, people who are sincere—a word made from two words that originally meant "without wax." When a piece of pottery had a crack, an unscrupulous merchant would fill the crack with wax. Honest merchants would advertise their pottery as being "Sine Cereus" (sincere)—without wax. That meant it had no deficiencies or flaws. And we should be the same way. That doesn't mean perfect—it means honest before God about our failures and flaws, seeking His forgiveness and cleansing (1 John 1:9).

It is no coincidence that, of the six elements of spiritual armor, only one is offensive—the sword, which is the Word of God—and that it would have hung from the soldier's belt, or girdle. So Paul establishes an intimate connection between truth and the Word of God. It's not enough to have a sword (the Bible). We have to have a belt of truthfulness that allows us to take the sword with us wherever we go and implement that truth in and through our life.

We will talk more in this study guide about where the battlefield in spiritual warfare actually exists—usually the battlefield is our mind (2 Corinthians 10:3-5). Therefore, the primary weapon is truth by which our mind is renewed and strengthened against the attacks of the enemy (Romans 12:2).

Notes:

1. Os Guinness, *Time for Truth: Living Free in a World of Lies, Hype and Spin* (Grand Rapids, MI: Baker Books, 2000), 10-11.

2. Ibid., 12.

3. Stu Weber, *Spirit Warriors* (Sisters, OR: Multnomah Press, 2001), 166.

1. Read Ephesians 1:15-19.

    a. What does Paul pray that God would give to the Ephesian Christians? (verse 17)

    b. What do the words "wisdom" and "revelation" suggest about what it takes to "know Him"? (verse 17)

    c. What needs to happen to the "eyes of [our] understanding"? (verse 18)

    d. What does "enlightened" mean with regard to truth? What impact did our salvation have on the darkness we were living in? (Colossians 1:13)

    e. How would "the hope of his calling" be important in spiritual warfare? What happens to hope when we get discouraged? (Ephesians 1:18)

f. How can certainty of the riches of our inheritance in Christ be a defensive measure in spiritual warfare? (verse 18)

g. Why is a knowledge of God's power important in securing victory in spiritual warfare? (verse 19; see also 1 John 4:4)

h. If Paul "did not cease" (Ephesians 1:16) praying for these things for the Ephesians, what does that say about the ongoing responsibility to acquire knowledge and truth about God?

i. How might you use Paul's prayer for the Ephesians to pray for yourself?

j. What evidence would you find in your life that God was answering that prayer?

2. Read Proverbs 2:1-8.

   a. What do the three occurrences of "if you" suggest about what's being said in this passage? (verses 1, 3, 4)

   b. How does the word "then" in verse 5 bring the result that is expected from the "ifs"?

   c. Summarize what our responsibility is in seeking truth and knowledge of God. (verses 1, 3, 4)

   d. Summarize what will happen if we do what verses 1-4 advise. (verse 5)

e. From where do wisdom and knowledge (truth) come? (verses 6)

f. How are verses 7-8 a complement to 2 Chronicles 16:9?

3. What do Ephesians 1:15-19 and Proverbs 2:1-8 suggest to you about the acquisition of truth and knowledge of God?

DID YOU KNOW?

The maintenance of truth in the spiritual realm is mirrored by the maintenance of truth (standards) in the physical realm. There are hundreds of organizations all around the world that monitor various kinds of technical and scientific standards. When it comes to weights and measures (What is a true inch? What is a true pound? What time is it exactly?), the National Institute of Standards and Technology (NIST) is the U.S. governmental agency charged with maintaining "truth" when it comes to U.S. standards. NIST employed nearly 3,000 technical workers who operated on a budget of just under one billion dollars in 2009. Whether in the spiritual or physical realm, establishing and maintaining "truth" calls for serious effort.

THE BREASTPLATE OF RIGHTEOUSNESS

Ephesians 6:14

In this lesson we explore how righteousness protects the believer from Satan.

OUTLINE

Police and military personnel are wearing increasingly high-tech versions of a bulletproof vest—lighter, stronger, and more protective —to protect their vital organs. Just so, the Christian needs to wear the breastplate of righteousness continually to protect his most vital organ: the heart.

I.   **The Breastplate Symbolizes Christ's Righteousness**

II. **The Breastplate Symbolizes the Christian's Righteousness**

III. **The Breastplate Symbolizes Consistent Righteousness**

IV. **The Breastplate Symbolizes Controlled Righteousness**

The late theologian Francis Schaeffer (d. 1984) was among the first to observe that America has become a post-Christian nation. Though America has been called a Christian nation almost since its founding, that is no longer a widely held view. I don't know where the line between Christian and post-Christian should be drawn exactly, but I know it occurred sometime during my lifetime.

Things are very different in America now than when I was growing up in the 1950s and even later. There is now a general antagonism toward Christianity in our nation that seems to be on the increase. Christianity is publicly attacked and ridiculed in unprecedented ways, with attempts made to marginalize its meaning and its influence. There has never been a time in America when it has been more necessary to understand the principles of spiritual warfare.

The question is, Are Christians prepared for the battle? Are they wearing the spiritual armor outlined in Ephesians 6? In the previous lesson we studied the first piece of armor Paul mentions: the belt of truth—objective truth and subjective truthfulness, knowing the Word of God and then living the Word of God. Unfortunately, there are many who claim to be committed to the Word but who are not yet ready to live lives of spiritual integrity, honesty, and transparency. They are not sure they want to commit to defending themselves against the attacks of Satan.

The question every Christian needs to ask is, Am I living a life that makes me prepared to engage with Satan and defend the Gospel I claim to believe? In other words, Am I dressed with the breastplate of righteousness—the second piece of the armor of God?

When I was a brand new pastor of a group of seven families that wanted to start a new church, I suddenly realized I needed to begin winning people to Christ if our church was to grow. One problem: I didn't know how. I was a Bible college and seminary graduate but had never been taught how to do personal evangelism. So I began studying the evangelism materials compiled by Dr. D. James Kennedy, materials eventually published as *Evangelism Explosion*. In those materials Dr. Kennedy discussed a survey in which Christians were asked why they don't witness to others about Christ. He thought the top three answers would be (1) fear, (2) lack of training, and (3) lack of exposure to non-Christians. But to his great surprise the number one reason Christians gave for not sharing their faith was because of the life they lived. In other words, they didn't think it was right to talk about believing in Christ when they weren't living for Christ themselves. These Christians perfectly illustrate the need for the breastplate of righteousness.

The breastplate worn by a Roman soldier covered the front of the torso from the neck down to just below the waist. Without a breastplate a soldier could take an arrow to the heart and be killed instantly, or a sword thrust to the stomach, injuring vital organs. The breastplate was a critically important piece of armor for a soldier, and it is for the Christian as well. The breastplate of righteousness communicates four symbolic messages for the believer.

THE BREASTPLATE SYMBOLIZES CHRIST'S RIGHTEOUSNESS

When we put on the full armor of God, we are putting on Jesus Christ—and vice versa. Just as He is the truth, He is also our righteousness. In 1 Corinthians 1:30, Paul writes that Christ "became for us wisdom from God—and righteousness and sanctification and redemption."

Paul is referring to the second of two things that happened on the cross. First, Christ took upon Himself all our sin—He became sin for us. Second, for those who believe in Him and embrace His sacrifice in our place, He imparts to us His righteousness—He is our righteousness; the reason God no longer holds our sin against us but views us as His righteous, redeemed children. So Christ became righteousness for us—and not just because He was the Son of God. He chose to live a sinless, obedient life as the human Son of God so that He might earn a righteous standing before God that could be given to those whose sin He took upon Himself. It is because of what happened at the cross that Paul would write to the Philippians, ". . . not having my own righteousness, which is from the law, but that which is through faith in Christ, the righteousness which is from God by faith" (Philippians 3:9). In short, a Christian is a person to whom has been imputed the righteousness of Jesus Christ in the sight of God.

When you put on the breastplate of righteousness through faith in Christ, it symbolizes that you are protected by the righteousness of Christ. Protected from what? From the accusations of Satan before God about your sin, your faithless life, your faults, your lack of commitment. Satan is the "accuser of [the] brethren" (Revelation 12:10).

He comes before God to accuse you, just as he accused Job (Job 1:9-11; 2:4-5), of being unworthy of God's favor. But thankfully, we have "an Advocate with the Father, Jesus Christ the righteous" (1 John 2:1). And because we have been given Christ's righteousness, He is able, as our Advocate, to defend us before the Father, to defend us from the attacks of Satan. When God looks at us He doesn't see our sin. Instead, He sees the righteousness of Christ imparted to us, and our sin having been paid for by Christ.

I don't have to worry when Satan accuses me before the Father —and neither do you if you belong to Christ. Our "positional righteousness"—credit for having lived the righteous life Jesus lived —is what saves us. Practically, yes we sin; yes we are unrighteous. But positionally, we are righteous. That does not mean we are free to live unrighteously, for then we give the devil a "place" in our life (Ephesians 4:27) from which to legitimately attack and accuse us. Thankfully, our protection does not ultimately depend on our practical righteousness but on the righteousness of Christ which we put on by faith in Him.

So first, the breastplate symbolizes the righteousness of Christ that is made available to all who believe in Him.

THE BREASTPLATE SYMBOLIZES THE CHRISTIAN'S RIGHTEOUSNESS

In 1 Corinthians 1:30, Paul said that Christ had become not only our righteousness but our sanctification—a big word that simply means to become more in practice what you are in position. It means to become *actually* more righteous instead of just positionally righteous in a legal sense before God. So the breastplate symbolizes the Christian's ability to withstand the temptations of Satan to sin and actually become a righteous (holy, set apart) person for God.

It is our responsibility to "put on" the breastplate of Christ's righteousness in a practical sense; to resist the devil (James 4:7); to take the ways of escape from sin that God promises always to provide (1 Corinthians 10:13). The Scriptures affirm this responsibility by continually exhorting us to pursue righteousness (1 Timothy 6:11). Positional righteousness is not all we need in spiritual warfare; we need practical righteousness as well. Indeed, the apostle John writes that "whoever does not practice righteousness is not of God . . ." (1 John 3:10). Thomas Merton puts the pursuit of righteousness and spiritual warfare into perspective by saying that "the enemy is more easily overcome if he is not suffered to enter the door of our hearts, but is resisted without the gates at his first knock."[1]

In Ephesians 4:24, we are exhorted to "put on the new man which was created according to God, in true righteousness and holiness." That is a foreshadowing of the righteousness—the linen, white garments (Revelation 19:14)—in which we will be clothed in heaven for all eternity. And while we will not become perfectly righteous in this life, our responsibility is to be continually living "on earth as it is in heaven" (Matthew 6:10). In response to Christ securing righteousness for us, God asks us to live as righteous people.

Apart from your righteousness, positionally in Christ and practically in life, you have no defense against Satan. He can feed you lie after lie and if you are not dressed in the breastplate of righteousness, you have no authority to resist him. Indeed, the people who said they couldn't witness about Christ because of their own life are examples of how this works. Satan has convinced them that they are hypocrites for living like they do while wanting to tell others about Jesus. Without the breastplate of righteousness— positionally and practically—Satan is right! It is only when we have been granted righteousness in spite of our sins (Christ took our sins on the cross, remember) that we can say to Satan, "I'm not telling people about Jesus because I'm perfect, but because Christ is. He has forgiven all the things that would make me look like a hypocrite." Paul explains this well concerning his own life in 2 Corinthians 6:3-10. He says he can commend himself as a "[minister] of God" because he has "the armor of righteousness on the right hand and on the left" (verse 7). As often as Satan tried to attack and derail Paul and his ministry through persecutions and hardships (read the complete list), Paul was never defeated because he was clothed with "the armor of righteousness."

The unrighteous Christian life is a powerless Christian life, a life based on a guilty conscience loaded down with shame and guilt: "A man who is conscious of being in the wrong is usually a coward. A man who knows that he is right can withstand a multitude, and he enters the conflict without fear."[2] If you are opposed and condemned by those who oppose Christ and His Gospel, including Satan, only righteousness—positional and practical—can give you a reason to stand firm. The breastplate of righteousness is not only a symbol of Christ's righteousness given to you but His righteousness expressed through your life on a daily basis.

THE BREASTPLATE SYMBOLIZES CONSISTENT RIGHTEOUSNESS

As with all the pieces of spiritual armor in Ephesians 6, and just as with a Roman soldier's armor, the pieces have to be worn consistently. The best armor in the world is of no use if it is not worn. Whereas the Roman soldier didn't necessarily go into battle every day, the Christian soldier does—spiritual warfare is 24x7x365, to use contemporary terminology. It is unrelenting and never-ending this side of heaven.

As for righteousness, it is not a Sunday-only requirement. Righteousness is not something we parade about piously on Sunday or at other times when we are in the presence of other Christians. Because spiritual warfare is consistent, wearing the breastplate of righteousness must be consistent as well. The moment we decide to take off the breastplate is the very moment Satan looks for—an opportunity to gain a "place" in our life (a "foothold," as the NIV puts it in Ephesians 4:27).

One thing I learned quickly in the early days of my pastoral ministry was that I could not traffic in second-hand truth. That is, I could not stand up and preach to people based on the experiences of others, or based on something I had read in a book. If I am not consistently living out in my life the very spiritual realities I am exhorting my congregation to pursue, my preaching will lack any power whatsoever. I would be like those who were afraid to witness for Jesus because of the quality of their spiritual life—I would be afraid to preach about Jesus because I would know how shallow my own life was. As a preacher-pastor, I am called to live out the very truths that all Christians are called to live, but to an even greater degree. There is increased accountability for any who would teach or exhort others toward righteousness (James 3:1).

My wife and I have enjoyed a private joke over the years regarding times when I may have been the primary cause of a disagreement between us. These disagreements don't happen much any more, but they have at times—and they never lasted long for this reason: I would leave home in the morning and arrive at the church and begin to study God's Word to prepare for my upcoming Sunday sermon. Invariably I would be immediately convicted by something in the passage I was studying. Suddenly, the spiritual power left my life. I would have to pick up the phone and call Donna and apologize for my insensitivity or outright sin. I learned that if I didn't deal quickly with any unrighteousness in my life that the rest of the day was wasted; I was only going through the motions, spinning my wheels and going nowhere. I can't stand in the pulpit and exhort others to live a righteous life if I am not living a righteous life myself.

Paul's practical way of illustrating this is to say, "'Be angry, and do not sin': do not let the sun go down on your wrath, *nor give place to the devil*" (Ephesians 4:26-27, italics added). Satan knows when you and I are living unrighteously, when our conscience is conflicted or unclear, when we cannot stand firm because of our sin, when we have removed the breastplate of righteousness. Inconsistent righteousness is an invitation to be attacked spiritually.

THE BREASTPLATE SYMBOLIZES CONTROLLED RIGHTEOUSNESS

Consider the spiritual implications of the following words:

I am your constant companion. I am your greatest helper or heaviest burden. I will push you onward or drag you down to failure. I am completely at your command. Half of the things you do you might just as well turn over to me, and I will be able to do them quickly and correctly. I am easily managed—you must merely be firm with me. Show me exactly how you want something done; after a few lessons I will do it for you automatically. I am the servant of all great people and alas, of all failures as well. Those who are great, I have made great. Those who are failures, I have made them failures. I am not a machine, though I work with all the precision of a machine plus the intelligence of a man. You may run me for profit or run me for ruin—it makes no difference to me. Take me. Train me. Be firm with me, and I will place the world at your feet. Be easy with me, and I will destroy you. Who am I? I am Habit! I am Habit![3]

We are to make a habit out of living righteously. We are to cultivate righteousness so we don't have to stop and decide which way to go at every crossroads we encounter. If we are still having the same internal discussions on matters of right/wrong, righteous/ unrighteous, sin/not sin that we had as brand new Christians, then something is wrong. We are to live a life under the control of the Holy

Spirit who will shape and direct our life "in paths of righteousness for His name's sake" (Psalm 23:3).

The secret to a controlled, righteous life is not to work or try harder. The apostle Paul tried that and met with utter failure as he describes in Romans 7 (see verses 15, 19). He wanted to do right (righteously) but found that he was unable with his own strength and resources to do so. The opposite of self-effort is to "let go and let God," which some people advocate. But what does that mean? Am I to do nothing while I wait for God to make me righteous? Neither of those approaches is biblical.

Think about what the breastplate covers—first and foremost, the heart. Police and military personnel today wear bulletproof vests for the same reason the Roman soldier did: to protect their heart. Spiritually, the heart is the seat of emotion and affection. The key to walking in the righteousness of Christ is to fall in love again—and remain in love with—Jesus. Instead of trying to *live* better, we need to *love* better. The more deeply our heart is following after Christ, the more righteousness will characterize our conduct and character.

Four aspects of righteousness—Christ's, ours, consistency, and control—are part of the breastplate of righteousness. With yours in place, your heart will be well-protected against the fiery darts of the evil one.

Notes:

1. Quoted in Robert Jeffress, *The Divine Defense* (Colorado Springs: WaterBrook Press, 2006), 110.

2. Charles Erdman, *Commentaries on the New Testament: The Epistle of Paul to the Ephesians* (Philadelphia: Westminster Press 1931), 124.

3. Jeffress, 121.

1. Read Hebrews 2:16-18; 4:14-16.

   a. Whom did Jesus come to earth to help? (verse 2:16)

   b. And who is included in the "seed of Abraham"? (Romans 4:16)

   c. How does "Therefore" connect Hebrews 2:16 and 2:17? (To save human beings, God sent His Son to earth as a _____ .)

   d. What was the central purpose of Christ's role as a human-divine high priest? (verse 2:17b)

   e. What kind of suffering is referred to in verse 2:18—suffering from physical abuse or spiritual suffering?

f. Given the fact that "being tempted" was a form of suffering for Christ, how does that cast a different light on the events of Matthew 4:1-11?

g. What kind of suffering do you imagine Christ endured in the wilderness when tempted by Satan?

h. How does linking suffering with temptation provide a new insight into spiritual warfare? How is spiritual warfare painful?

i. What is unique about Christ's response to the temptations He endured? (Hebrews 4:15b)

j. Explain how Christ's being tempted, yet without sin, becomes a benefit to us when we are being tempted or otherwise engaged in spiritual warfare. (verse 4:16)

k. What kind of "grace" should we expect from God when we approach His throne during a time of temptation? (verse 4:16; 1 Corinthians 10:13)

l. What should be your first response when experiencing temptation and spiritual warfare? (Hebrews 4:16)

2. Read Hebrews 5:7-10.

   a. How does Christ's experience (verse 7) suggest a context of spiritual warfare?

   b. Why did the Father hear Christ's prayers? (verse 7b)

   c. Why are "godly fear" (NKJV) and "reverent submission" (NIV) good synonyms for righteousness? (verse 7b)

d. What did Christ's experiences in spiritual warfare teach Him (train Him) to do? (verse 8)

e. What did His perfect obedience (righteousness) qualify Him to become? (verse 9)

f. If Christ suffered as the Son of God, what might you expect as a child of God as you seek to live a righteous life?

DID YOU KNOW?

Once when Swiss theologian Karl Barth was asked what he thought was the most important word in the New Testament, he answered, "The [Greek] word *huper*." *Huper* is a Greek preposition that occurs around 150 times in the New Testament, meaning "on behalf of" or "in place of." Barth cited that word because it represents the substitutionary work that Christ did for sinful human beings. He died "in place of" us on the cross at Calvary: "For He made Him who knew no sin to be sin for [*huper*—in place of] us" (2 Corinthians 5:21). In light of that, we have become "ambassadors for [*huper*—on behalf of] Christ" (verse 20). [From James Montgomery Boice, *Whatever Happened to the Gospel of Grace?* (Wheaton, IL: Crossway Books, 2001), 102.]

THE SHOES OF THE GOSPEL OF PEACE

Ephesians 6:15

*In this lesson we discover the role of peace
in spiritual warfare.*

OUTLINE

As hard as the world has tried to produce peace in our time, it has
failed. That is because the world has yet to submit itself to the
Author of peace who alone is able to calm the fears and anxieties
of individuals and nations. Satan has no power over those who are
at peace with God.

I. **The Relationship of the Shoes to Armor**

II. **The Requirement of the Shoes for the Armor**

III. **The Reasons for the Shoes as Armor**
   A. Without Shoes, You Are Ungrateful
   B. Without Shoes, You Are Unreasonable
   C. Without Shoes, You Are Unproductive
   D. Without Shoes, You Are Un-Christian
   E. Without Shoes, You Are Unprepared

IV. **The Requisitioning of the Shoes for the Battle**
   A. Meet the Author of Peace
   B. Meditate Upon the Prince of Peace
   C. Manifest the Spirit of Peace in Your Life
   D. Memorize the Word of Peace
   E. Measure Your Life by the Rule of Peace

S tu Weber is a pastor and former army Green Beret soldier who brings a unique perspective to the subject of spiritual warfare:

Historically, far more soldiers on the battlefield have been immobilized by foot problems than have gone down from bullets. This was certainly true in Vietnam. Many a platoon sergeant in those jungles felt the most critical part of his job was to be a foot-care specialist. Sometimes he felt more like a nurse or a mother than he did the leader of a lean, mean fighting machine. "Change your socks, boys," became the regular mantra. "Take your boots off. Dry your feet. Powder 'em up or you're no good to this unit."[1]

Who can imagine a soldier, whether in Roman times or Vietnam or Afghanistan, going into a serious battle barefooted? A soldier well-equipped in every other area would be sorely deficient without footwear of some sort. "However powerful your chest may be, however wonderful your loins, if you get wounded in your feet, if you slip and fall in the battle, you will be easy prey for the antagonist."[2] Roman soldiers wore thick-soled, leather sandals with hob-nailed soles that provided stability and traction. They were a far cry from the boots worn by modern soldiers, but were adequate for the day.

Since Paul is using a typical Roman soldier's armor as the model for the armor of God in Ephesians 6, what kind of shoes is Paul designating for the Christian going into spiritual warfare? He talks about having our feet "shod . . . with the preparation of the gospel of peace" (verse 15). It may seem odd that "shoes of peace" are given out to Christian soldiers preparing to go into war. What is the purpose of "peace" in spiritual warfare? Since shoes are the foundation on which the soldier stands, peace must have something to do with the steadfastness and firm foundation on which the believer stands in the face of Satan's lies and accusations.

It is the role of the peace of God in spiritual warfare—the peace that comes from the good news of the Gospel—that is the subject of this lesson. From what we have learned already, we can immediately see a connection: The last thing Satan brings is peace. He comes "to steal and to kill and to destroy" (John 10:10a) and to divide and deceive. Therefore, if you and I can maintain a perspective of peace in our lives *regardless of our circumstances*, we will establish a strong defense against the enemy's attacks.

THE RELATIONSHIP OF THE SHOES TO ARMOR

We began our study of the armor of God with the belt of truth and then looked at the breastplate of righteousness. In both cases, we put on truth and righteousness by putting on the Lord Jesus Christ. Christ is our truth and our righteousness, and He is also our peace: "For He Himself is our peace . . ." (Ephesians 2:14). By the time we have looked at all the components of the armor of God, we will have found that putting on Christ is how we put them on. Satan was never able to defeat Jesus—not once—and as long as we are found clothed with Him we will not be defeated either.

So far, the first three components of the armor follow a logical progression: Paul started with truth, the knowledge of which leads to righteousness in Christ, the effect of which is the peace of God in the believer's life. Romans 5:1 says, "Therefore, having been justified by faith, we have peace with God through our Lord Jesus Christ." We read the Bible (truth) and embrace Christ as Savior and Lord (righteousness) and receive peace with God as a result. The acquisition of peace suggests its prior absence—and it was absent! The Bible says that before coming to faith in Christ we were "enemies" of God (Romans 5:10; Colossians 1:21; James 4:4). But now, through Christ, we have peace with God.

Here's why peace is so important: As Paul says in 2 Corinthians 10:3-6, our battle is not against flesh and blood—"we do not war according to the flesh." As we have already seen, the main battlefield in spiritual warfare is the realm of the mind. Therefore, our challenge is to bring "every thought into captivity to the obedience of Christ" (verse 5). If, instead of peace, our mind is occupied with worry, anxiety, envy, hatred, unrest, confusion, and all the rest, we are prime targets for Satan. Therefore, the peace of God—a settled, content, peaceful mind and heart—is a key weapon in our defense.

Just as Winston Churchill's voice over the radio during the World War II air raids over London brought peace to the British people, so Jesus Christ brings peace to all who trust in Him. Churchill couldn't keep the German dive-bombers from attacking London, and Jesus doesn't promise that we won't be attacked by Satan. But in both cases, peace changes the outlook. Peace brings hope and certainty and confidence that victory is possible. Jesus comes to us in the midst of our battles and speaks peace to us: "Peace I leave with you, My peace

I give to you; not as the world gives do I give to you. Let not your heart be troubled, neither let it be afraid" (John 14:27). He also says, "These things I have spoken to you, that in Me you may have peace. In the world you will have tribulation; but be of good cheer, I have overcome the world" (John 16:33). And Paul wrote that it is the peace of God that "surpasses all understanding" and "guard[s] your hearts and minds through Christ Jesus" (Philippians 4:7).

So, truth leads to righteousness and righteousness leads to peace. And that is something Satan cannot destroy.

THE REQUIREMENT OF THE SHOES FOR THE ARMOR

Is peace really a requirement? Jesus said that in the last days "men's hearts [will be] failing them from fear and the expectation of those things which are coming on the earth" (Luke 21:26). We have a 2,000-year lead-time on the fact that things in the last days are going to be bad. So yes, peace is a requirement for all who do not want to be consumed by the fear that Satan will be promoting in the last days. Granted, the Church will not be on earth during the Great Tribulation when things will be at their worst. However, with the increasing instability in our world today, it is easy to yield to worry and anxiety. But the Christian with a foundation of peace does not have to yield to such temptations.

The key to protection from anxiety and worry is not more money or prescription sedatives from the doctor. It is having a reason not to worry about the future. And God, who holds past, present, and future in His hands, is that reason.

THE REASONS FOR THE SHOES AS ARMOR

There are five key reasons for making sure we have put on the shoes of the gospel of peace: gratitude, reason, fruitfulness, our testimony for Christ, and preparedness—all of which are based on Christ's teaching about worry in Matthew 6.

Without Shoes, You Are Ungrateful

In Matthew 6:25, after telling His listeners not to worry about food and clothing, Jesus asks a rhetorical question: "Is not life more than food and the body more than clothing?" Jesus is saying, "You can't live your life peacefully or be victorious in spiritual warfare if you aren't trusting God for the basic provisions of your life." We have much to be thankful for every day of our life. When we are in a state of anxiety or worry about the future, we are saying to the world, "God cannot be trusted." As I have said before, Satan's key goal in spiritual warfare is to make God look bad, to discourage us from trusting Him. So if we are worried and lacking peace, our actions say that God cannot be trusted. And they also say we are ungrateful for what God *has* provided.

Jesus' entire message in this portion of the Sermon on the Mount is that God can be trusted to provide for His creation. And the result of such trust is peace.

Without Shoes, You Are Unreasonable

In the next verse, verse 26, Jesus asks, "Are you not of more value than [the birds of the air]?" God provides for them, so it is only reasonable that God will provide for us.

There is a place for reason and logic in the kingdom of God, and here is an application: God's provision for those in creation who do not bear His image suggests that He also intends to provide for those who bear His image. How would it look throughout the earth if those commissioned as God's representatives (image-bearers) were left uncared for? How would it make God look as a loving, generous, and gracious God? It would make Him look unreasonable. And when we doubt that He will provide, and resort to anxiety, it makes us look unreasonable as well.

It's not reasonable for God to provide for birds and not for human beings. And when we live unreasonable lives, we lose our peace.

Without Shoes, You Are Unproductive

Continuing, Jesus asks in verse 27, "Which of you by worrying can add one cubit to his stature?" In other words, worry changes nothing! You can't add a single hour to your life or inch to your height (alternative renderings of verse 27) by worrying. I have discovered in my own life that about 90 percent of the things I am tempted to worry about are things I have no control over one way or another. Or they are things that never come to pass, things that get resolved in some unforeseen way. It's completely fruitless to worry about things you have no control over.

The one (negative) thing worry does accomplish, with which Satan is thrilled, is that it derails us; it keeps us from focusing on the things we can control—like work, ministry, good works, encouraging our family and friends, Bible study, or other worthy endeavors. If our heart and mind are preoccupied with worry, they cannot be occupied with good works of righteousness that flow from a life at peace with God and His plans for the future.

Without Shoes, You Are Un-Christian

Scripture does not say that a person who worries is not a Christian, nor do I. That is not the point of Jesus' words in verse 32: "For after all these things [food and clothing] the Gentiles [pagans] seek." But He is saying that we act like a person who doesn't know God when we live a worry-filled life.

"Gentiles" in the Bible is used to refer to pagans—people who don't know God. A person who doesn't know God has every reason to be anxious about the future. And when we, who claim to know God, act like those who don't, we violate what we profess to believe: God is good and will provide for those who belong to Him. We need to take to heart Joshua's question to the Israelites: We need to decide whose side we are on—God's or the world's (Joshua 24:15). If we say we are on God's side, then we need to live like it—which means living in peace. That is Jesus' recommendation, of course. It is what separates us from the world: peace that also protects us from Satan.

Without Shoes, You Are Unprepared

Finally, without peace we are unprepared. In Matthew 6:33-34 Jesus reminds us that "sufficient for the day is its own trouble." Every day of our life brings new and unexpected challenges—plenty for any person to deal with. We do not need to add to that daily menu of concerns matters that lie in the future, about which we can do little. That doesn't mean we shouldn't be wise and plan for the future (Proverbs 6:6-11). But it does mean we shouldn't *worry* about the future, especially with regard to things God has promised to provide. If our feet are not shod with the peace of God, we will take onto our daily plate things we have no business worrying about.

In Psalm 55:22 David wrote, "Cast your burden on the Lord, and He shall sustain you; He shall never permit the righteous to be moved." And the apostle Peter quoted the same verse in his first epistle (5:7-8) as a prelude to his word about Satan, our enemy: "Be sober, be vigilant; because your adversary the devil walks about like a roaring lion, seeking whom he may devour." So Peter makes a connection between the peace of God and attacks from the enemy—a connection we would also do well to make.

Those are five good reasons to make sure that our feet are shod with the peace of God that comes from receiving the "gospel of peace." To receive Christ's gospel is to receive Christ. And to receive Him is to go into battle clothed with His divine protection.

THE REQUISITIONING OF THE SHOES FOR THE BATTLE

We know how to find and purchase the shoes we need for daily life, but what about spiritual shoes? How do we get the peace of God that will protect us from the attacks of Satan? Let me suggest five ways: meeting the Prince of Peace, meditating upon the Prince of Peace, manifesting the Spirit of peace, memorizing the Word of peace, and measuring our life by the rule of peace.

Meet the Author of Peace

We meet the Author of peace when we meet Christ, the One who established peace between God and man by His substitutionary sacrifice on Calvary's cross. Once we know the Author of peace, "the peace of God, which surpasses all understanding, will guard [our] hearts and minds through Christ Jesus" (Philippians 4:7). Many other Scriptures testify to God being the Author of peace (1 Corinthians 14:33; Philippians 4:9; 1 Thessalonians 5:23; 2 Thessalonians 3:16; Hebrews 13:20).

The important question for you to ask and answer is this: Have I met the Author of Peace? There can be no peace without that meeting taking place.

Meditate Upon the Prince of Peace

As with all relationships, it takes time and communication for them to grow as they should. Once we meet the Author of peace we must grow in our relationship with Him in order to walk in His peace as Isaiah 26:3 says: "You will keep him in perfect peace, whose mind is stayed on You, because he trusts in You." Meeting and meditating upon Christ through prayer and the study of His Word is crucial to keeping our mind "stayed on Him" and knowing His peace.

Manifest the Spirit of Peace in Your Life

The third way to acquire and keep peace is by being filled with the Holy Spirit (Ephesians 5:18). Peace is part of the fruit of the Spirit (Galatians 5:22), the fruit of the Spirit being the manifestation of Christ in us (Galatians 2:20). When we allow the Holy Spirit to control our thoughts and actions, then peace will be part of the result. Just as Christ was filled and empowered by the Holy Spirit (John 3:34) and manifested victory over anxiety and worry in His own life, we can do the same.

Memorize the Word of Peace

Unfortunately, the older most Christians get, the less they seem interested in Scripture memory—maybe because memory becomes more of a challenge the older we get! But remember how Jesus defeated Satan in the wilderness (Matthew 4:1-11)? It was by quoting Scripture to correct the lying temptations Satan was shooting at Him like fiery darts. It is the Word of God against which Satan has no power, no rebuttal. And if we are to resist Him, we will do it only on the basis of the authoritative Word of God. So please—regardless of your age—continue to meditate on and to memorize the Word of God.

Measure Your Life by the Rule of Peace

Finally, "let the peace of God rule in your [heart]" (Colossians 3:15). In other words, let peace guide your decisions and choices in life. Remember that peace is the fruit of the Spirit. If you don't have peace about something you're considering, it may not be from God. He is perfectly capable of communicating His peace to you if you will wait upon Him for it.

If you need His peace today, follow the reasons and requisites outlined in this lesson and you will have it.

Notes:

1. Stu Weber, *Spirit Warriors* (Sisters OR: Multnomah Press, 2001), 171.

2. D. M. Lloyd-Jones, *The Christian Soldier* (Grand Rapids, MI: Baker Book House, 1977), 270-271.

1. What does Paul say God "is" and "isn't" in 1 Corinthians 14:33?

   a. When confusion and disorder appear in the life of a church or individual, what does that say about the presence of God in that situation?

   b. Why does confusion present such a ready opportunity for Satan to attack?

2. Read Philippians 4:8-9.

   a. List the virtues Paul recommends in verse 8.

   b. What does he say to "do" concerning these virtues? (verse 8b)

   c. What is the connection between this list and Paul's exhortation in verse 9? (How does this list describe what the Corinthians learned from Paul?)

d. If the Corinthians follow through on Paul's advice, what will be the result? (verse 9b)

e. How much of modern culture and media could be described by the words in verse 8?

f. If we "meditate" on the confusion and discord in modern culture (through various media), what effect might that have on our personal peace?

g. How does Satan use modern, worldly events and media to tempt people to find peace through worldly solutions? What kind of solutions?

3. Sanctify means becoming in practice what we are in position. What is our position with regard to peace with God? (Romans 5:1)

a. Explain in your words how your life should reflect the sanctifying work of "the God of peace." (1 Thessalonians 5:23)

b. Give examples of how a lack of peace can impact one's "spirit, soul, and body." (verse 23)

- spirit:

- soul:

- body:

4. Who is "the Lord of peace"? (2 Thessalonians 3:16)

a. How is He qualified to give peace to those who need it? (Hebrews 4:15)

b. When Jesus returned to heaven who did He send to help His followers live in peace? (John 14:26-27)

5. How would you summarize your responsibility to walk in peace based on Romans 12:18; 14:19 and Hebrews 12:14?

DID YOU KNOW?

There is a significant lack of peace in America. As of 2007, 13.3 percent of adults ages 18-54 (19.1 million people) have some kind of anxiety disorder. Anxiety disorders cost more than 42 billion dollars annually. People with an anxiety disorder are three-to-five times more likely to visit a doctor and six times more likely to be hospitalized for psychiatric disorders than those without. Common anxiety disorders are obsessive compulsive disorder (3.3 million people), panic disorder (2.4 million), post traumatic stress disorder (5.2 million), and social anxiety disorder (5.3 million). Two of the top medications prescribed for anxiety disorders are number seven and eight among the top 10 drugs prescribed in the U.S. (See http://www.healthyplace.com/anxiety-panic/main/anxiety-disorders-statistics-and-facts/menu-id-69/)

THE SHIELD OF FAITH

Ephesians 6:16

*In this lesson we discover the priority of faith
in spiritual warfare.*

OUTLINE

Whether one is a soldier, athlete, carpenter, or shop owner, various pieces of equipment are critical to accomplishing one's mission. And that is true of the believer engaged in spiritual warfare. Of all the elements of the armor of God, faith is the most fundamental and important.

   I.   **The Priority of the Shield of Faith**

  II.   **The Purpose of the Shield of Faith**

 III.   **The Potential of the Shield of Faith**

  IV.   **The Protection of the Shield of Faith**

   V.   **The Possession of the Shield of Faith**

  VI.   **The Principles of the Shield of Faith**
        A. Focus on the Source of Your Faith
        B. Fortify the Strength of Your Faith

We come in this lesson to the fourth part of the armor of God described by the apostle Paul: the shield of faith. Perhaps more than any other part of the armor, a shield strikes us as being the best part of our defense. A shield is something you can hold up and put between yourself and any incoming danger. If it's large enough, the shield can protect your whole body. And if it's strong enough, it can deflect all manner of danger. In movies that depict warfare in ancient or medieval times, we often see a phalanx of advancing soldiers, creating a wall in front of them and a ceiling over them by interlocking their body-sized shields together as they slowly march forward. A barrage of arrows loosed by their opponents is the signal to raise and interlock the shields providing protective cover from the incoming darts.

So it is the image of a shield—perhaps the ultimate defensive, protective piece of a soldier's armor—that Paul creates for us in Ephesians 6:16: "Above all, taking the shield of faith with which you will be able to quench all the fiery darts of the wicked one."

Our question is this: Why does Paul assign faith to the shield? Why is faith perhaps the best defense we have against the fiery darts of Satan? Why is faith so necessary for victory in spiritual warfare? Faith is obviously a central theme in Scripture from Genesis to Revelation. As far back as Genesis 15:6 we find faith being the bridge between God and man: "And [Abraham] believed in the Lord, and He accounted it to him for righteousness." And it was that belief in the Lord that Satan challenged in the Garden of Eden: "Has God indeed said . . . ?" (Genesis 3:1). If we define faith as confidence in what God has said (confidence in God and His Word), then it stands to reason that Satan would be out to shake the foundations of our faith. Conversely, it stands to reason that our faith is what will allow us to brush off the attempts by Satan to discredit God and His Word in our sight.

Our entire Christian life is lived by faith: ". . . the life which I now live in the flesh I live by faith in the Son of God" (Galatians 2:20b). Faith is not our own faith—it is the faith given to us as a gift by God. We walk by faith, not by sight (2 Corinthians 5:7). Faith is what keeps us in step with God, and it is what keeps us from yielding to the temptations of Satan.

Every element of the armor of God is important and indispensable, but faith is at the center of our defense. Just as the soldier's shield was the largest part of his armor, so faith occupies the largest place in our spiritual defense against Satan.

THE PRIORITY OF THE SHIELD OF FAITH

Paul places a priority on faith by saying, "Above all, taking the shield of faith . . ." (verse 16a). Faith is the key part of our spiritual armor against Satan.

Ahab was a king in the Old Testament who went out to do battle against the Assyrians. He was wearing body armor, but an arrow shot at random by an Assyrian soldier "struck the king of Israel between the joints of his armor" and he died (1 Kings 22:34). Ahab no doubt had all the requisite pieces of armor on but, he was still killed. If there had been a shield in place, the arrow would never have found an entry point between the joints of his armor.

I believe Satan attacks the same way, looking for "chinks" in our armor where he can aim one of his fiery darts. But with the shield of faith in place, we add a second layer of defense. That is why Paul says, above all, to take up the shield of faith.

THE PURPOSE OF THE SHIELD OF FAITH

Helpfully, Paul tells us exactly what the purpose of the shield of faith is: "to quench all the fiery darts of the wicked one." "Fiery darts" in Paul's day could refer to poison-tipped arrows or to arrows whose pointed heads were dipped in pitch and set ablaze. Poison would kill even if the arrow only wounded the soldier, and flames could set on fire tents or anything else they struck if they missed hitting a soldier—lethal in any case.

New Testament scholar Peter O'Brien helps us to understand Paul's words:

> The burning arrows depict . . . every kind of attack launched by the devil and his hosts against the people of God. They are as wide ranging as the insidious wiles that promote them, and include not only every kind of temptation to ungodly behavior, every kind of doubt, and every kind of despair, but also external assaults like persecution and false teaching.[1]

Pastor Stu Weber makes an important point about the strengthening of faith by being part of a community of faith:

> Do you see the critical point here? This is the shield of faith, which by design, is interlocked with the soldier next to you. This is the shield of faith utilized in community, the community

of faith. I would say in small groups we are linking our shields together to protect ourselves from the enemy. In our spiritual battle, as is true in any combat environment, there is no room for lone rangers. If you expect to be protected, you've got to stick with a group, march with a unit, and live like a family.[2]

Faith protects us individually and it protects us as a community of followers of Jesus. The more of us who have our faith linked together with others, the stronger our defenses will be—individually and corporately.

THE POTENTIAL OF THE SHIELD OF FAITH

If I believe in the divine inspiration of Scripture (and I do), then I have to take note of even the smallest words in the text—such as "all" in verse 16. Paul doesn't say we can quench "some" of the fiery darts of the enemy, but "all" his fiery darts. In Greek and in English, "all" means all! In our modern world, armies would be clamoring for a defensive weapon that was able to neutralize "all" the bullets and bombs of the enemy. But that's what "all" means—a powerful notion when it comes to spiritual warfare. There is not an attack from Satan you can imagine that cannot be neutralized by faith. (But remember: Satan's goal is to discredit God. Having faith doesn't mean that we will never experience hardship. But it will mean, as seen in Job's life, that Satan's goal of turning us against God will be defeated.)

Author and pastor emeritus R. Kent Hughes has written,

> It is no exaggeration to say that during earthly life multiple thousands of deadly blazing arrows are launched at the Christian warrior by demons and by demon-oppressed culture. But the answer is faith. The apostle John wrote: "And this is the victory that has overcome the world—our faith" (1 John 5:4, NASB). Why? Because faith binds us in vital, deep union with God. Faith is not just belief; it is belief plus trust. It is resting in the person of God and His Word to us.[3]

THE PROTECTION OF THE SHIELD OF FAITH

In order to understand how the shield of faith protects us, we must know the kinds of fiery darts the enemy is firing at us. There is no better place to begin than with Satan's first involvement with humanity in the Garden of Eden. There, the first dart Satan fired at Adam and Eve was doubt: "Has God indeed said, 'You shall not eat of every tree of the garden?'" (Genesis 3:1). Satan's goal is always to get human beings to doubt the integrity of God.

When Eve answered Satan by quoting what God had said, Satan used his next dart, denial—"You will not surely die,"—directly contradicting what God had said (Genesis 3:4). Notice that he uses doubt to create questions in Eve's mind before coming out with a flat denial of the truth. He finishes his attack with the dart of deception: "For God knows that in the day you eat of it your eyes will be opened, and you will be like God, knowing good and evil" (Genesis 3:5).

Doubt, denial, and deception regarding the words God has spoken and regarding God's integrity. After all, if God has told us things that aren't true, He can't be a God of integrity. Satan's goal is not necessarily to hurt you physically (although see Job 1-2), but in the process of your circumstances to cause you to doubt who God is and what He has said. From that perspective it is easy to see why faith is so important. If we stop believing who God is and what He has said, we have little reason to persevere in the Christian life.

Hebrews 11 is the great chapter in Scripture on faith—God's "Hall of Faith"—where the names of many in the Old Testament who exercised faith are recorded. Noah is mentioned because he took God at His word and built an ark to prepare for a flood in a world that had never even seen rain (Hebrews 11:7). Noah no doubt encountered great criticism from those around him who thought he was foolish. But Noah's shield of faith extinguished those fiery darts because He trusted in God and His promises. Noah could easily have chosen to doubt what God had said, but his faith remained strong.

Abraham is mentioned (Hebrews 11:8)—he who left his homeland in Mesopotamia to go to a new land following God's direction: "And he went out, not knowing where he was going." He didn't know *where* he was going, but he did know *why*: Because he had faith in God's promises. Abraham's wife, Sarah, is recognized for her faith for ultimately (after initial disbelief) believing God's promise to give her and Abraham a child in their old age (Hebrews 11:11). Abraham is cited again for his faithful obedience to God when he was instructed to offer his son, Isaac, as a sacrifice (Hebrews 11:17). Abraham could easily have doubted that he heard God clearly and correctly: Kill my son, Lord? But he chose to walk in faith toward that goal until God Himself stepped in to stop the sacrifice.

Moses is mentioned (verses 24-27) for choosing by faith to identify with his afflicted kinsmen in Egypt rather than spending his life in luxury in the royal household of Pharaoh. I can only imagine the kinds of doubts Moses entertained when he considered giving up his place of wealth and privilege and identifying with his poverty-stricken brethren in the mud pits of Egypt. And then there was Joshua, who ran the risk of looking like a fool when he announced and carried out his plan of attack on Jericho: March around the city, blow the trumpets, and shout—and the walls will come down. But, "By faith the walls of Jericho fell down after they were encircled for seven days" (Hebrews 11:30). Joshua had to explain to his army what must have seemed like a strange directive, but he did it—by faith.

I alluded in a previous lesson to Jesus' temptation by Satan in the wilderness, which He overcame by faith in the words (the Word) of God in Deuteronomy. Professor Howard Hendricks asked a telling question based on Jesus' faith: "If your spiritual survival depended on how well you knew the book of Deuteronomy, how long would you last?"[4] That's a powerful reminder that, "All Scripture is given by inspiration of God, and is profitable for doctrine, for reproof, for correction, for instruction in righteousness" (2 Timothy 3:16).

THE POSSESSION OF THE SHIELD OF FAITH

How do we acquire such devil-defeating faith? How do we acquire such faith? First and foremost, we have to take up the shield ourselves. Yes, faith is the gift of God. But it's a gift we have to put to use ourselves. The accounts in Hebrews 11 as well as from Jesus' experience in the wilderness prove that point.

The word of God referred to in Ephesians 6:17 as our offensive weapon is not the Bible, the *logos* of God, but the *rhema*, the truths or sayings of God. We don't throw the Bible at the devil in spiritual warfare, but we defeat Him by our faith in the revealed truth of God needed for that particular situation. The Bible is the "armory" of God where all the weapons are stored. But the sword of the Spirit is each individual truth of God (found in the "armory") that we use to defeat Satan in a given setting.

When we use the shield of faith, we exercise faith in the area of our vulnerability. When Satan attacks, we defend ourselves by faith in a particular truth of God. That is consistent with what Paul wrote about faith in Romans 10:17, "So then faith comes by hearing, and hearing by the word [*rhema*] of God." The secret to gaining a larger and stronger shield of faith is to memorize Scriptures that address the "chinks" in our armor—the places in life we are most vulnerable spiritually and emotionally. Then, when attacks in those areas come, we have the *rhema* of God in hand to defeat the enemy. Whether your areas of vulnerability are worry about finances, anger, envy, lust, discouragement—whatever they are—God has a word for that area toward which you can direct your faith.

The late pastor and author Ray Stedman gives us practical direction:

> Faith is not simply a passive idea; it is acting upon belief. Faith is decision and action and resolution. Faith is saying, "Yes, I believe Christ is the truth. He is my righteousness. He is my peace. Therefore, this and this and this and this must follow." When you say "therefore" you move from belief into faith. Faith is particularizing; it is taking the general truth and applying it to specific situations and saying, "If this is true, then this must follow." And that is the shield of faith.[5]

In order to hold up the shield of faith, you must know what you believe. And that kind of faith comes from knowing "the word [*rhema*] of God" (Romans 10:17).

THE PRINCIPLES OF THE SHIELD OF FAITH

I believe there are two principles bound up in this idea of a shield of faith: focusing on the source of your faith and the strength of your faith.

Focus on the Source of Your Faith

Faith is not in faith! Faith is in the integrity and the promises of God. As Hebrews 12:2 puts it, we are to "[look] unto Jesus, the author and finisher of our faith." Faith is only as good as the object toward which it is directed. In the case of our Christian faith, the object is Jesus Christ, the Son of God, who has promised never to leave us nor forsake us (Matthew 28:20; Hebrews 13:5).

If you and I went to Minnesota during the winter and went ice fishing on a frozen lake, we would need to know the answer to this question: Would you rather have a lot of faith in a thin sheet of ice or a little faith in a very thick sheet of ice? The answer is the latter because our faith is not in faith. You can have great faith in thin ice and it will still break. But even a little bit of faith in thick ice will keep you high and dry—even faith like a tiny mustard seed, Jesus said (Luke 17:6). It is not our great faith that saves us, but the object of our faith.

Fortify the Strength of Your Faith

Strengthening anything—body, mind, spirit—is accomplished the same way: exercise! Author and Christian philosopher Dallas Willard has written:

> A baseball player who expects to excel in the game without adequate exercise of his body is no more ridiculous than a Christian who hopes to be able to act in the manner of Christ when put to the test without the appropriate exercise in godly living.[6]

We have no shortage of opportunities to trust God in moments of spiritual challenge. Our challenge is to exercise our faith in God and His Word. No soldier's shield will accomplish its purposes unless it is taken up and put to use.

Notes:

1. Peter T. O'Brien, *The Pillar New Testament Commentary: The Letter to the Ephesians* (Grand Rapids, MI: Wm. B. Eerdmans Publishing Co., 1999), 480.

2. Stu Weber, *Spirit Warriors* (Sisters, OR: Multnomah Publishers, 2001), 172.

3. R. Kent Hughes, *Ephesians: The Mystery of the Body of Christ* (Wheaton, IL: Crossway Books, 1990), 235-236.

4. Robert Jeffress, *The Divine Defense: Six Simple Strategies for Winning Your Greatest Battles* (Colorado Springs: Waterbrook Press, 2006), 160.

5. Ray Stedman, *Spiritual Warfare* (Waco, TX: Word Books, 1978), 86.

6. Dallas Willard, *The Spirit of the Disciplines: Understanding How God Changes Lives* (San Francisco: HarperCollins, 1988), 4-5.

1. Abraham rescued his nephew Lot and recovered goods stolen from Sodom. Read what happened in Genesis 14:18-15:1.

   a. What did the king of Sodom offer to Abraham? (verse 21)

   b. What was Abraham's response? (verses 22-23a)

   c. What was Abraham's reason for declining the treasure? (verse 23b)

d. What might Abraham have been tempted to do that would have profited him greatly?

e. Following this event, what did God promise to Abraham in a vision? (verse 15:1)

f. What do you think the connection was between "shield" and "reward"? (How are "protection" and "provision" related? Can we be tempted to get a good thing in a bad way?)

g. What promise had God made to Abraham about his provision and prosperity in Genesis 12:1-2?

h. How was Abraham displaying faith by not accepting the king of Sodom's offer in light of God's promises?

i. Why would Satan tempt us to gain provision and prosperity in an illegitimate way? How would that make God look?

j. Describe a time you were tempted (or might have been) to pursue something legitimate in a way that would dishonor God. How did you resolve the temptation? How did your choices affect your faith?

2. Read Acts 5:1-11.

   a. What did Ananias and Sapphira do that was dishonest? (verse 2)

   b. What favor were they seeking? (See Acts 4:36-37.)

   c. To what does Peter attribute their poor judgment and carnal motivation? (verse 3a)

   d. What was their true sin—greed or deceit? Were they free to keep the money? What did they do that was wrong? (verse 4)

e. If Ananias and Sapphira had exercised faith, how would their actions have been different?

f. How might faith in Old Testament passages like Psalm 23:1 and Psalm 15 have guided their choices and decisions?

g. How was this experience bad for Ananias and Sapphira (verses 5, 10) but instructive for the church? (verse 11)

h. What can you learn from this experience about the danger of yielding to Satan's temptations to deceive?

DID YOU KNOW?

There was more than one size shield in the Roman army's armory. The *aspis* was small and round—not mentioned in Scripture —and the *thureos* was large, four-cornered and rectangular, or shaped like a door (the meaning of *thureos*—"like a door"). In the Old Testament, fancy gold and bronze shields, sometimes captured from an enemy, were displayed as the spoils of war (2 Samuel 8:7) or as displays of wealth and craftsmanship (1 Kings 10:17). It is the *thureos* shield that Paul refers to in Ephesians 6:16, the only place it is mentioned in the New Testament. Paul intends for faith to be large enough to "quench all the fiery darts of the wicked one" (Ephesians 6:16).

THE HELMET OF SALVATION

Ephesians 6:17

*In this lesson we learn of the protection provided
by the helmet of salvation.*

OUTLINE

Ideas and thoughts have consequences. Because the battlefield of
spiritual warfare is the mind, the believer's thoughts are of central
importance to victory. The helmet of salvation provides the believer
with the mind of Christ and the wisdom of God as he enters the battle.

I. **Understanding the Helmet of Salvation**
   A. The Helmet of Salvation Is Personified in Jesus Christ
   B. The Helmet of Salvation Is a Prerequisite to Any Kind
   of Ministry
   C. The Helmet of Salvation Is the Power of God in Your Life
   D. The Helmet of Salvation Is Produced by Reading
   God's Word
   E. The Helmet of Salvation Is Possible Through Prayer
   F. The Helmet of Salvation Is the Promise of Hope

II. **Using the Helmet of Salvation**
   A. The Helmet of Salvation Is Useful for Defending
   Ourselves in a Hostile World
   B. The Helmet of Salvation Is Useful for Demolishing
   Strongholds of the Mind and Heart

The Ephesians who first read Paul's letter would have pictured immediately each part of the believer's armor since they were used to seeing Roman soldiers throughout the Mediterranean world. For us, "helmet" suggests images of a football helmet or a military helmet, but the Roman helmet Paul speaks of was different. It was more like a leather cap, reinforced with metal plates for protection and ornamented with a plume on top.[1]

The helmet of salvation is more than simply knowing one is a Christian—the idea that such knowledge or assurance would be a defense against Satan's attempt to make us doubt our salvation. While that explanation is no doubt true, there is more to it than that. The helmet of salvation is bigger than assurance. It encompasses the totality of our experience—past, present, and future—as a child of God. When we put on the helmet of salvation we are equipping ourselves with "the mind of Christ" (1 Corinthians 2:16), the wisdom of God that is personified in the person of Jesus Christ (1 Corinthians 1:24, 30; Colossians 2:2-3).

Old Testament scholar Tremper Longman gives us an excellent summary of the biblical concept of wisdom:

> Wisdom is the skill of living. It is a practical knowledge that helps one know how to act and how to speak in different situations. Wisdom entails the ability to avoid problems, and the skill to handle them when they present themselves. Wisdom includes the ability to interpret other people's speech and other people's writing so that we can react correctly to what they are saying to us.[2]

If there is anything we need in being victorious in spiritual warfare it is skill—that is, wisdom. Satan is crafty and cunning. He has been studying human weaknesses for thousands of years. He knows how to set snares and traps for the unwise and unwary. But with God's wisdom—the skill of living according to His precepts —we can avoid Satan's entanglements. Because traps are often a surprise, another helpful definition of wisdom is "doing the right thing without a precedent." The person who can react to an unexpected temptation or change in circumstances in the same way Jesus Christ would is a person who has biblical wisdom, who has the mind of Christ.

UNDERSTANDING THE HELMET
OF SALVATION

Following are six truths about the helmet of salvation we must understand in order to gain its protection.

The Helmet of Salvation Is Personified in Jesus Christ

"Christ the power of God and the wisdom of God." So wrote the apostle Paul in 1 Corinthians 1:24. As I have already noted in previous lessons, putting on the spiritual armor of God is putting on Jesus Christ. When we clothe ourselves in Him through faith in Him as Savior and submission to Him as Lord, we have God's spiritual armor in place. Truth, righteousness, peace, faith, salvation, and the Word of God—all are personified in Jesus Christ.

When Christ was on earth teaching and ministering in the power of the Spirit—revealing to people the nature of the kingdom of God—the individuals and crowds were continually astonished at His wisdom. It started when he was only 12 years old (Luke 2:41-52), amazing the Jewish scholars in the temple in Jerusalem. He "grew in wisdom and stature" (verse 52, NIV) until He began His public ministry, announcing that a wisdom "greater than Solomon" had appeared in Him in Israel (Matthew 12:42). People were amazed that a carpenter from Nazareth had the kind of knowledge and wisdom that Christ had (John 7:15, 46).

Without question, the two wisest people ever to inhabit planet earth were Solomon and Jesus of Nazareth—and Jesus was the wiser of the two. It is the wisdom of God in Christ that we put on when we put on the helmet of salvation.

The Helmet of Salvation Is a Prerequisite to Any Kind of Ministry

A number of years ago, my wife Donna, my oldest daughter, and I visited the Dominican Republic. While there, we took time to tour the locale using rented motorbikes—the most common form of transportation on the island. We did not wear helmets since they weren't required by law and didn't think too much of it until that evening. At dinner, a native of the Republic told us it was not uncommon for 20-25 fatalities *per day* to occur due to motorbike crashes. Had we known that statistic ahead of time we would definitely have worn helmets! I don't know the policy on wearing helmets in the Dominican Republic today, but I hope they have turned an option into a prerequisite for riding motorbikes on the island.

Wearing the helmet of salvation is not optional for anyone involved in Christian ministry (and that should be every Christian). Wisdom is a prerequisite for living victoriously in the Christian life, and it is definitely not optional for those under the pressure of leadership in vocational ministry. When the early church needed to select men to serve the church in Jerusalem, the apostles advised them to choose seven men "who are known to be full of the Spirit and wisdom" (Acts 6:3, NIV).

Leaders of churches are on the front line of counteracting the influences of worldly culture in the lives of Christians. I can tell you that Christian leaders are facing new questions and challenges for which no guidebook exists. The wisdom of God is our only hope for knowing how to navigate the treacherous waters of this world where Satan's influence is widespread. And the helmet of salvation is our only hope.

The Helmet of Salvation Is the Power of God in Your Life

There are two kinds of wisdom (skill) in life: the wisdom of God and the wisdom of men. And that which is accomplished for God can only be accomplished with His wisdom. The apostle Paul wrote to the Corinthians that he did not minister among them with "persuasive words of human wisdom, but in demonstration of the Spirit and power." He did not want the Corinthians' faith to be in "the wisdom of men but in the power of God" (1 Corinthians 2:3-5).

Paul said, "I did not come to you with my own concepts, my own thinking, my own program, or my own methods. I came to you equipped with a helmet of salvation protecting my mind that I would not be tempted to minister with the wisdom and power of men but with the wisdom of God." Being clothed with Jesus Christ and filled with His Spirit results in the power of God being released through our life.

The Helmet of Salvation Is Produced by Reading God's Word

Paul's words to his young protégé in ministry, Timothy, point out the connection between the Scriptures and the wisdom that leads to salvation; the connection between the Word of God and the helmet of salvation: ". . . from childhood you have known the Holy Scriptures, which are able to make you wise for salvation through faith which is in Jesus Christ" (2 Timothy 3:15).

Timothy had been taught the Scriptures from childhood by his mother Eunice and his grandmother Lois (2 Timothy 1:5). From them he gained the wisdom needed to commit himself to Christ and then to follow Paul in the ministry of spreading the Gospel and leading churches. This is a testimony to the living nature of the Word of God—it is "living and powerful . . . and is a discerner of the thoughts and intents of the heart" (Hebrews 4:12). God said, through the prophet Isaiah, that His Word always accomplishes the purpose for which it is sent (Isaiah 55:11). The impact of the Scriptures on a child like Timothy was profound. He gained wisdom to believe in Christ and wisdom to follow God's call into ministry. Every believer who desires to grow wise in the spiritual life must immerse himself in the Scriptures.

The Helmet of Salvation Is Possible Through Prayer

There is no more clear statement in Scripture about how to get wisdom than James 1:5: "If any of you lacks wisdom, let him ask of God, who gives to all liberally and without reproach, and it will be given to him." How does one get wisdom? Ask for it! And the context of James' promise is the context of falling into "various trials" (James 1:2)—a context that sounds suspiciously like that of spiritual warfare. When we are attacked by our spiritual enemy and need skill to handle our defense, we need only to ask God for wisdom.

When someone asks me for counsel on how to handle a situation in his life, I try not to get too deep into the discussion before asking, "Have you asked God about this?" That should be step number one when we find ourselves in uncharted territory dealing with an unprecedented situation. Yes, God can give me wisdom to give to you, but James didn't say to ask your pastor when you lack wisdom. He said to ask God yourself. As believer-priests, every Christian has been given freedom to go boldly before the throne of grace to seek "mercy and find grace to help in time of need" (Hebrews 4:16). No Christian needs to go through a middleman to get wisdom from God.

The helmet of salvation is the wisdom of God in Christ Jesus, and it is available to every Christian who will ask God for it.

The Helmet of Salvation Is the Promise of Hope

Finally, the helmet of salvation is a picture of the promise of eternal hope: "But let us who are of the day be sober, putting on the breastplate of faith and love, and as a helmet the hope of salvation" (1 Thessalonians 5:8).

How does the helmet of salvation provide hope? By reminding us that spiritual warfare is only temporary, that the day is coming when all struggles will be over and we will inherit our eternal promise of salvation in Christ. At the moment when the battle is raging intensely, we wonder if it will ever subside. We wonder whether we will have the strength to carry on with wisdom and skill into the future. And the answer is, Yes!—if we have put on the helmet of salvation.

The wisdom of God reminds us that we are fighting a battle the outcome of which is settled. When we are standing firm in our faith and being buffeted by Satan, we can remain standing because we know the outcome of the battle is not in jeopardy. We know that Christ is the Victor and Satan is the defeated foe. We know that we are called to defend the name of God in the earth as His image-bearers as Satan tries to cast aspersions on His name and cause His people to lose confidence in Him. We know that Satan's motive in attacking us is to tempt us to "curse God and die" (Job 2:9). And we know that we do not have to give in. We know our enemy and his strategy; and with the armor of God in place, we can stand firm.

Pastor John MacArthur has well said, "Living without hope is like running a race without a finish line. It's ridiculous for someone to say, 'Start running for the rest of your life. There's no finish, but give it everything you have.'"[3] There is a finish line and we have been shown it in Scripture. So we are not standing firm without hope —we are standing firm in the "hope of salvation" that the helmet of salvation provides.

Now that we understand the helmet of salvation and its role in spiritual warfare, we need to know how to use it, how to wear it faithfully and to its full advantage.

USING THE HELMET OF SALVATION

It is important to recognize and remember that ideas have consequences. Ideas can sway nations as history has demonstrated over and over. Our world today needs men and women who are equipped in their minds to do battle against ideas and ideologies that Satan is sowing into the political, moral, and economic landscape of this world. Those who are not equipped to withstand his deception need those of us who are equipped to be sources of light and wisdom in an increasingly dark world. The ideas of the kingdom of God— ideas protected and promoted by the helmet of salvation—have the kind of consequences our world needs.

The Helmet of Salvation Is Useful for Defending Ourselves in a Hostile World

The world has always been hostile toward Christianity but never so much as today. Jesus told His disciples that they would be brought before authorities on account of their faith. They should not fear such situations because "it will be given to you in that hour what you should speak; for it is not you who speak, but the Spirit of your Father who speaks in you" (Matthew 10:18-20).

That is not a promise allowing ministers for Christ to exempt themselves from the hard work of study and sermon preparation. It refers (as I have already mentioned) to those unprecedented times when you find yourself in an unforeseen situation and you need wisdom on what to do or say. Because you have on the helmet of salvation, you have the mind of Christ, you will know what to say and do. God will give you what you need in those moments. This was demonstrated by the apostles often in the early chapters of Acts when they were hauled before the Jewish authorities for preaching the Gospel in Jerusalem. And the leaders "marveled" at the words the apostles offered in their own defense (Acts 4:13). These were "untrained" men (Peter and John) who spoke with boldness and clarity —words they had not prepared but were given in the hour of need. The apostle Paul, though educated and articulate, still found himself in new situations continually (Acts 22, 23, 24, 25 for example), and he testified to the grace of God, using the power and wisdom given him at the moment.

In short, we are to "always be ready to give a defense to everyone who asks you a reason for the hope that is in you, with meekness and fear" (1 Peter 3:15). We are to study and know the truth, of course. But we are to rely on the helmet of salvation to give us the specific way(s) necessary to defend the Gospel and our own testimony in unprecedented situations.

The Helmet of Salvation Is Useful for Demolishing Strongholds of the Mind and Heart (2 Corinthians 10:4-5)

Finally, we turn to Paul's words to the Corinthians for counsel on making our own thoughts captive to Christ. Remember: the battlefield for spiritual warfare is in the mind. We who once lived in the world need the discipline of tearing down the strongholds and arguments that once ruled our lives, and submitting them to the authority of Christ and His Word. A stronghold is a fortress in the physical realm and takes on that quality in our mind—a fortress Satan loves to build and make permanent; a fortress of thoughts that must be torn down and replaced with God's Word. Giving Satan a "place" (Ephesians 4:27) is to allow him access to our mind—something the helmet of salvation will prevent.

Can Satan establish a stronghold of lies and deception in the mind of a Christian? Yes, if he is allowed. It is our responsibility never to allow that to happen; to take every thought captive, measure it by the Word of God, and reject all that is not consistent with the glory and wisdom of Christ. We tear down strongholds by replacing carnal thoughts with the pure Word of God through meditation and memorization —and by resisting the devil and his thoughts whenever they appear in our mind (James 4:7). It is by depending on the *rhema* of God (the specific words of Scripture), by employing the sword of the Spirit (Ephesians 6:17b).

This lesson concludes our study of the defensive dimensions of the believer's spiritual armor: truth, righteousness, peace, faith, and salvation. The helmet of salvation guards our mind by filling it with the wisdom of Christ for every situation, the skill to defend ourselves against the attacks of the enemy. Those who have put on Christ by faith and are living in submissive obedience to Him have the helmet of salvation in place. But it needs to remain in place—the responsibility of the believer. Make sure today that you have put on the Lord Jesus Christ and that you are bringing every thought captive to Him and to His Word.

Notes:

1. D. M. Lloyd-Jones, *The Christian Soldier* (Grand Rapids, MI: Baker Book House, 1977), 309.

2. Tremper Longman III, *How to Read Proverbs* (Downers Grove, IL: InterVarsity Press, 2002), 14.

3. John MacArthur, *How to Meet the Enemy: Arming Yourself for Spiritual Warfare* (Wheaton, IL: Victor Books, 1992), 123.

APPLICATION

1. Read 1 Corinthians 2:1-16.

   a. What did Paul not take with him when he visited the church in Corinth? (verse 1)

   b. What was the sole reality that he wanted the Corinthians to see in his life? (verse 2)

   c. What insights do we get about Paul, the man, from verses 3-4a?

d. If that was true of Paul in his "natural self," what do you think accounted for the impact of his ministry? (verse 4b)

e. Why was Paul happy for there to be a stark contrast between his natural abilities and his ministry for Christ? (verse 5)

f. How did Paul reinforce this contrast with the account recorded in 2 Corinthians 12:7-10? (especially verse 10)

g. What are the two kinds of wisdom Paul mentions in 1 Corinthians 2:6-7?

h. What kind of wisdom and reasoning did those who crucified Christ exhibit? (verse 8)

i. What does verse 9—the reference to "eye" and "ear"—say about the limitations of man's wisdom?

j. How does man come to understand the truth of God? (verse 10a)

k. What new reality is possible for those who have been given the Spirit of God? (verse 12)

l. How does the natural man view the truth of God? (verse 14a)

m. What does "spiritually discerned" mean? (verse 14b) How does one become spiritually discerning?

n. Why should we not be intimidated by those who would judge us for our Christian stand regarding truth? (verse 15)

o. Does that same defense apply when Satan judges us and intimidates us for our stand for Christ? Why?

p. Explain in your own words what it means that we have "the mind of Christ." (verse 16b)

2. When we put on Christ through faith in Him, to what do we gain access? (Colossians 2:3)

   a. If wisdom means "skill," what does Paul mean when he says Christ is the "wisdom of God"? (1 Corinthians 1:24) What "skill" did Christ demonstrate?

   b. Explain in your own words the benefit(s) of the helmet of salvation.

DID YOU KNOW?

The Hebrew word for wisdom is *hokmah* which literally meant "skill." It occurs, along with its verb and adjective forms, more than 300 times in the Old Testament. It was used to describe craftsmen who built the tabernacle (Exodus 28:3; 35:35), a "crafty" person (2 Samuel 13:3), a "charmer" (Psalm 58:5), animals like ants, badgers, locusts, and spiders (Proverbs 30:24-28), makers of idols (Isaiah 40:20), and ship captains (Ezekiel 27:8). Not all these would be considered "wise" as we normally think of wisdom, but they were all skillful in their particular area of life. These uses provide insight into wisdom being the "skill of living." [From Kenneth Boa and William Kruidenier, *Living What You Believe—Wisdom from the Book of James* (Colorado Springs: NavPress, 2000), 18.]

THE SWORD OF THE SPIRIT

Ephesians 6:17

In this lesson we discover how to use
the sword of the Spirit.

OUTLINE

An armory is a depot or facility where weapons are stored. In that sense, the Bible is an armory in which are stored many individual truths that can be used as a weapon—a sword of the Spirit—to defeat the temptations and attacks of the enemy if we will learn to use them.

I. **The Explanation of the Sword of the Spirit**

II. **The Emphasis of the Sword of the Spirit**

III. **The Example of the Sword of the Spirit**
   A. Temptation Number One: The Lust of the Flesh
   B. Temptation Number Two: The Lust of the Eyes
   C. Temptation Number Three: The Pride of Life

IV. **The Effect of the Sword of the Spirit**
   A. This Truth Explains the Dynamic of Preaching
   B. This Truth Encourages the Discipline of Reading the Bible Through Systematically
   C. This Truth Exhorts Us to the Diligence of Memorizing Key Passages of God's Word

OVERVIEW

The Christian apologist Ravi Zacharias tells a story about a pastor in a small Midwestern community who heard a disturbance in his yard on a Sunday afternoon. The sound was of arguing between youngsters—and he recognized his own son's voice as part of the melee. Hurrying over to the window, he saw his little boy in the backyard with his fist clenched, staring down the neighborhood bully who had come into the backyard. Before he could run to his son's rescue, he heard him scream at the top of his lungs in what sounded like a war cry, "I come to you in the name of the Lord Almighty, the God of the armies of Israel." Thoroughly surprised by such a terrifying threat, the bully turned tail and fled the scene. The family laughed together later when they realized the little boy's Sunday school lesson that morning had been on David and Goliath, and he decided to apply the same formula to the giant who had invaded his yard.[1]

The little boy in that story serves as a good example of what we will find in this lesson: a word from God is enough to cause our spiritual enemy, Satan, to flee from us. I don't mean that in the sense that a Bible verse is a magical charm that can cause a powerful spiritual being to cower in our presence. I mean it in the spiritual warfare sense: the Word of God—the sword of the Spirit (Ephesians 6:17)—is the one offensive weapon God has given us to use in our battle against the devil and his demons. Satan has no authority when it comes to the Word of God. The authority of the Word is the authority of God Himself and is to be used by believers to counter the lies and deception Satan tries to get us to believe.

Defensive armor—truth, righteousness, peace, faith, and salvation—can keep us from being hurt by the devil. But the sword of the Spirit—the *rhema* (truth) of God—is the one offensive weapon we can use against Satan.

The word for sword Paul uses is not the word for a large broadsword, often swung with both hands. It was the word for a much shorter sword—akin to a dagger. Six to 18 inches long, this sword was carried in a scabbard on the soldier's hip and was used in hand-to-hand combat. It was the sword carried by those who came to arrest Jesus in the Garden of Gethsemane (Matthew 26:47) and is the sword used by Peter to cut off the ear of the high priest's servant on the same occasion (Matthew 26:51). It was also the sword used to kill James, brother of John, by order of King Herod (Acts 12:2).

So the sword we have been given is one that we can use when we are face-to-face with the devil—as Jesus was in the wilderness when He used the Word of God to turn back Satan's temptations (Matthew 4:1-11). While Ephesians 6:17 is our primary text for this sword as part of our spiritual armor, we will also look at several other passages of Scripture that illustrate the power of the Word of God.

THE EXPLANATION OF THE SWORD OF THE SPIRIT (EPHESIANS 6:17)

There are two Greek words for "word": *logos* and *rhema*. *Logos* is used to describe Jesus Christ as the Word (John 1:1) and the entire corpus of God's revelation to us in the Bible (as in Hebrews 13:7). But *logos* is not used in Ephesians 6:17; the word for "word" in that verse is *rhema*. *Rhema* doesn't refer to the entirety of the Word of God; it refers to the truths or sayings of God contained in the Bible. *Logos* refers to the whole, while *rhema* refers to the parts. Thinking of how our modern Bibles are arranged, the Bible is the *logos* while the verses are *rhema*. *Logos* is the armory where the swords are kept while *rhema* is the swords themselves. The *logos* is filled with individual *rhema* (or *rhemata*, plural). So Paul is saying that we are to take up the sword of the Spirit which is the sayings or truths of God.

Let me clarify an important point: Some theologians espouse the neo-orthodox view that the Bible is just a book until it speaks to us, at which point it becomes the Word of God to us. Not true! The entire Bible is the inspired, inerrant Word of God, from Genesis to Revelation, both in its entirety (*logos*) and its parts that we use as the sword of the Spirit (*rhema*).

THE EMPHASIS OF THE SWORD OF THE SPIRIT (HEBREWS 4:12)

Hebrews 4:12 tells us that "the word of God [*logos*—the entire Bible] is living and powerful, and sharper than any two-edged sword, piercing even to the division of soul and spirit, and of joints and marrow, and is a discerner of the thoughts and intents of the heart." This verse says the entire Bible is alive—and the same will obviously be true of all the verses that make up the whole. The Bible is unlike any other book in the world in that regard. The Word of God is a living armory from which we take living swords when forced into combat with our spiritual enemy.

THE EXAMPLE OF THE SWORD OF THE SPIRIT (MATTHEW 4:1-11)

There is no better example in Scripture of how to use the sword of the Spirit than Jesus' encounter with Satan in the wilderness. Jesus turned back all three of Satan's temptations by using the *rhema* of God.

It is important to notice what comes just before this incident. In Matthew 3 Jesus is validated as God's Son by the Father speaking from heaven when Jesus was baptized by John the Baptist: "This is My beloved Son, in whom I am well pleased" (Matthew 3:17). Immediately, Satan tries to separate Jesus from that title. If Satan can lure Jesus into ignoring God's will, Jesus would have disqualified Himself to be the redeemer of mankind. The second Adam (1 Corinthians 15:45) would have failed just as the first Adam did.

It is also important to note that the Holy Spirit led Jesus into the wilderness where the confrontation with Satan would take place. It was necessary for Jesus to pass this test before He began His public ministry: "Then Jesus was led up by the Spirit into the wilderness to be tempted by the devil" (Matthew 4:1).

In this encounter with Jesus, Satan used the three basic temptations that he always uses when tempting the people of God: the lust of the flesh, the lust of the eyes, and the pride of life. These are the three ways he lured Adam and Eve into ignoring the will of God for their lives, choices which plunged the entire human race into sin: the fruit was pleasing to look at (eyes), it was good to eat (flesh), and it would make them like God (pride).

Temptation Number One: The Lust of the Flesh (Matthew 4:1-4)

Fasting for 40 days, Jesus was hungry when the devil came to Him. So Satan tempted Him to turn stones into bread so he could relieve His hunger. Satan was saying, "If you are indeed the Son of God, there is no reason you should be hungry. Exercise your power and prerogative and create some bread for yourself. What could be wrong with that?"

The point of the temptation was to get Jesus to act independently of the Father, to do what He wanted instead of what the Father wanted for Him, to work a miracle for His own good instead of for the glory of the Father. But Jesus came to earth to serve, not to be served (Mark 10:45). He came to earth to do the Father's will, not

His own (John 6:38). On the night of His arrest, Jesus could have called for "more than twelve legions of angels" to free Him from His captors, but He didn't—it wasn't the Father's will (Matthew 26:53). No faithful Son acts independently of His Father. Jesus would have negated His role as the Son if He had turned stones into bread to satisfy His hunger. The entire redemptive ministry of Jesus would have stopped before it ever got started if He had yielded to Satan's temptation.

Jesus answered Satan: "It is written, 'Man shall not live by bread alone, but by every word [*rhema*] that proceeds from the mouth of God'" (Matthew 4:4, quoting Deuteronomy 8:3). Jesus pulled a sword from the armory of Deuteronomy to defeat this first of three temptations: the lust of the flesh.

Temptation Number Two: The Lust of the Eyes (Matthew 4:5-7)

Undeterred, Satan again appealed to Jesus' Sonship, taking Him to the "pinnacle of the temple" in Jerusalem: "If You are the Son of God, throw Yourself down" and let the angels of heaven catch you before You hit the pavement below.

There was a rabbinic tradition in Jesus' time that when the Messiah came to deliver the Jews from their oppressors, He would descend from the pinnacle of the temple into the temple courts. So if Jesus jumped from the pinnacle and landed unhurt in the temple courts below, it would have proven that He was the Messiah, at least in terms of the rabbinic tradition believed by the Jews.

Since Jesus had refused to act independently of the Father in the first temptation, Satan tempted Him now to work in concert with the Father—let God's angels catch You; let God prove that You are His Son by protecting Your life. But this would have amounted to presumption on Jesus' part, a test for the Father. The Father had not told Jesus to jump off the temple, so it would have been presumptuous for Jesus to assume the Father would intervene to save Him.

So Jesus pulled another sword from the armory, this time from Deuteronomy 6:16: "It is written again, 'You shall not tempt the Lord your God'" (Matthew 4:7). This was the temptation of the lust of the eyes—a chance for Jesus to show off in the eyes of the Jewish people in Jerusalem. There is an important lesson here: It is biblical to believe in miracles; it is not biblical to schedule them based on our desires.

It's also important to note that since Jesus rebuffed Satan with Scripture in the first temptation, Satan used Scripture in the second temptation (Psalm 91:11-12; Matthew 4:6). Satan knows the Bible and will twist it and take it out of context with us just as he did with Eve in the Garden of Eden and with Jesus in the wilderness. It's another powerful reminder of why we need to know the Word of God so we, like Jesus, can recognize when it is being taken out of context by Satan for his purposes.

Temptation Number Three: The Pride of Life (Matthew 4:8-11)

The final of the three temptations was an appeal to Jesus' human pride—to become ruler of "all the kingdoms of the world" (verse 8). Satan showed Jesus the kingdoms of the world and said they could be His if He would just fall down and worship Satan.

Yes, Satan had a right to make such an offer since he is the ruler of this world (1 John 5:19). Not an absolute ruler, of course—he is a ruler on a short leash held by God. But the kingdoms of this world are under his sway and influence, and he was offering that influence to Jesus in exchange for Jesus worshipping him. In essence Satan was offering Jesus a shortcut to becoming ruler of the world. Why not set up Your kingdom now, Jesus? Why wait and go through the pain and suffering of the cross? I'll hand over the kingdoms of this world now and You can make them Your own. Satan was trying to keep Jesus from going to the cross and accomplishing the redemption of mankind. If he could keep that from happening, God's plan of redemption would be foiled.

Again Jesus went to the armory and pulled out a sword from Matthew 4:10: "Away with you, Satan! For it is written, 'You shall worship the Lord your God, and Him only you shall serve'" (verse 10). And with that third and final answer, "the devil left Him, and behold, angels came and ministered to Him" (verse 11).

This event in Jesus' life is a perfect illustration of James 4:7: "Therefore submit to God. Resist the devil and he will flee from you." We get a textbook example from Jesus Himself on how to wield the sword of the Spirit and cause the devil to flee. The Holy Spirit brings to our mind a portion of Scripture that fits exactly the circumstance we are in. That is a *rhema*, a teaching, that we use to defeat the devil's temptation when we stand firmly on it. That is the power of God's living and active Word in spiritual warfare.

THE EFFECT OF THE SWORD OF THE SPIRIT

There are three effects of the sword of the Spirit on our life: the dynamic of preaching, the discipline of reading, and the diligence of memorization.

This Truth Explains the Dynamic of Preaching

When preachers proclaim the truths of the Word of God, the living and active swords of the Spirit are flung from the pulpit toward those who are listening. It's a dangerous thing to sit under the preaching and teaching of the Word of God if you are not a Christian or a Christian living in sin who refuses to get right with God. Eventually, one of those swords is going to prick your heart and you are going to have to deal with the truth.

I met a man years ago who told me an amazing story. He had messed up every area of his life and was without hope—he had decided to take his own life to put an end to his misery. He was going to run his truck into a tree and end it all. Just as he was about to put his truck in gear, my voice came over his radio saying, "Some of you out there may be thinking about taking your own life. Don't do it. God loves you and sent Jesus Christ to be your Savior. God has a plan for your life." That truth shocked the man so that he didn't go through with his plan. He accepted Christ, got involved with a church, and began growing in the Lord.

That was a *rhema*—a truth of God that penetrated that man's heart and brought about an immediate result. That's how powerful the sword of the Spirit is in our life and in spiritual warfare.

This Truth Encourages the Discipline of Reading the Bible Through Systematically

How do you think Jesus knew what to say to Satan when He was tempted in the wilderness? Because He knew the book of Deuteronomy from start to finish. He knew the progression of the content—what Moses wrote and why. It shows that the Old Testament books we tend not to read as often are full of swords of the Spirit! And that is an argument for reading the Bible systematically—that is, using a reading plan that covers *all* the books of the Bible instead of just our favorite books.

Remember: the whole Bible is the armory (*logos*) of God in which are stored the swords of the Spirit (*rhema*). But if we're not reading the whole Bible, we'll overlook some powerful swords to use against the enemy in spiritual warfare.

This Truth Exhorts Us to the Diligence of Memorizing Key Passages of God's Word

Finally, Jesus' experience—as well as that of the apostles—teaches us the necessity for committing the Word of God to memory. I don't think Jesus had a scroll of Deuteronomy in the wilderness in which He looked until He found the verses He needed to counter Satan's temptations. Instead, He knew those verses by heart; He had committed them to memory.

I have found that I am rarely tempted by Satan when I am reading my Bible. Rather, temptations come when I am away from the Word and forced to rely on the verses I have committed to memory. We must have the Word of God committed to memory so the Holy Spirit can bring those verses to our mind when we need them.

The truth of God is the sword of the Spirit—but only if it has become part of our life.

Notes:

1. Ravi Zacharias, *Cries of the Heart: Bringing God Near When He Feels So Far* (Nashville, TN: Thomas Nelson, 2002), 5.

1. In John 4:34, how did Jesus describe the food that He lived on?

   a. How is this answer consistent with the answer He gave Satan in the wilderness when tempted to turn stones into bread? (Matthew 4:4)

   b. Where did Jesus look for direction on what He should do in His life? (John 5:19)

c. What was the basis for the judgments Jesus spoke during His ministry? (John 5:30a)

d. Who did Jesus seek to please in everything He did while on earth? (John 5:30b)

e. Why did Jesus come down from heaven? (John 6:38)

f. What was the source of the teachings with which Jesus amazed the crowds in Israel? (John 8:28)

g. Whose idea was it for Jesus to come to earth? (John 8:42)

h. Besides "what" to say, what else did Jesus learn from the Father? (John 12:49; check other translations of this verse besides the NKJV if possible for a different rendering.)

i. To whom did Jesus give credit for all the words He spoke and the works He accomplished? (John 14:10)

j. How do these verses help in your understanding of Jesus' unwillingness to deviate from the Father's will when tempted in the wilderness?

2. Read John 16:13-15.

a. What did Jesus say the role of the Spirit would be? (verse 13)

b. Where would the Spirit get the words that He gave to the disciples after Jesus' departure? (verse 13)

c. How would Jesus be glorified by the Spirit limiting Himself to speaking only what He was given? (verse 14)

d. The Father conveyed His will to_____, and Jesus gave it to the_____, and the Spirit conveyed it to the_____. (verses 14-15)

e. How does this divine "chain of command" raise the importance of being obedient to the Father's will in your life?

f. How is disobeying the will of God by yielding to temptation ultimately dishonoring to the Father, Son, and Spirit?

DID YOU KNOW?

The small sword mentioned by Paul is the *maxaira*, mentioned 29 times in the New Testament. The other Greek word for sword, *romphaia*—the large broadsword—occurs only seven times in the New Testament, all symbolic uses. Simeon uses it as a symbol of the anguish Mary would experience over the suffering her newborn son, Jesus, would one day endure (Luke 2:35). The rest of the uses of *romphaia* are all in Revelation as a symbol of judgment. Four of those times it refers to the sword that proceeds out of the mouth of Christ in His role as judge of the Church (Revelation 2:12, 16) or as judge of the nations (Revelation 19:15).

PRAYING ALWAYS WITH ALL PRAYER

Ephesians 6:18

In this lesson we discover how to empower the wearing of the whole armor of God.

OUTLINE

It's possible for a soldier to be fully dressed in armor and weapons for battle, but lack courage and conviction and power—the will to engage the enemy. In the spiritual life, the power to engage and be victorious over the enemy comes through prayer—for ourself and for "all the saints."

   I. **The Persistence of the Warrior's Prayer**

  II. **The Possibilities of the Warrior's Prayer**
- A. We Are to Pray on All Occasions
- B. We Are to Pray in All Places
- C. We Are to Pray in Prosperity and Adversity
- D. We Are to Pray for All Things

 III. **The Petition of the Warrior's Prayer**

 IV. **The Power of the Warrior's Prayer**

  V. **The Precision of the Warrior's Prayer**

 VI. **The Perseverance of the Warrior's Prayer**

VII. **The Purpose of the Warrior's Prayer**

The Bible, especially the Old Testament, is clear: Battles fought in the strength of the warrior are doomed to defeat, while battles fought in the strength of the Lord are destined for victory.

With only 318 men, Abraham conquered a coalition of kings that made war against the kings of Sodom and Gomorrah (Genesis 14). Gideon's army was reduced from 32,000 soldiers to 300, yet he still delivered Israel from the Midianites (Judges 7). Joshua defeated the city of Jericho without "firing a shot" by marching around the city, blowing the trumpets, and shouting (Joshua 6). King Hezekiah defeated the Assyrians and explained the victory this way: "With [Assyria] is an arm of flesh; but with us is the Lord our God, to help us and to fight our battles" (2 Chronicles 32:8a).

Because of these amazing victories, I believe Paul's final words in the passage about spiritual warfare—his exhortation to pray—should be included in the believer's armor. No, we don't "wear" prayer like one wears armor. But I believe Paul mentions prayer here because it is the key to spiritual victory. Soldiers need to stay continually in touch with headquarters—and that is the purpose of prayer.

The subject of prayer is immediately convicting to both preacher and congregation, for all realize we don't pray as we should. But rather than labor under guilt about what we don't do, in this final lesson on spiritual armor, we will allow the living Word of God to motivate us more toward Christlike dependence on God—and that means "praying always with all prayer and supplication in the Spirit" (Ephesians 6:18). After all, Jesus' ministry in heaven is to intercede for the saints at the right hand of the Father (Romans 8:34; Hebrews 4:15-16; 7:25; 8:1-2; 9:24; 1 John 2:1). Philip Yancey made the observation, "In three years of active ministry, Jesus changed the moral landscape of the entire planet. And for nearly two thousand years since, He's been using another tactic: He's been using prayer."[1]

If Jesus considers it important to have been praying for us nonstop for the last 2,000 years, perhaps we need to reconsider our own perspective on the power and value of prayer. Ephesians 6:18 is the core text for prayer in spiritual warfare.

THE PERSISTENCE OF THE WARRIOR'S PRAYER

Please note in verse 18 the four-fold use of "all" and "always" —Paul is talking about a subject that is comprehensive! We should always pray, never giving up, for all the saints— including ourselves. That is certainly consistent with what Jesus taught: ". . . men always ought to pray and not lose heart" (Luke 18:1), a theme echoed by Paul in 1 Thessalonians 5:17: "Pray without ceasing."

Neither Jesus nor Paul meant for there to be a constant stream of audible words coming from our mouth. Rather, as someone has said, the line to heaven should always be open, the receiver always left off the hook (to use the picture of the telephones I grew up with!). It is a constant attitude of prayer, punctuated by moments, times, and seasons of literal prayer. We are always available to God and He is always available to us. We don't move in and out of God's presence; rather, we *live* in God's presence.

Thomas Kelly put it this way:

> There is a way of ordering our mental life on more than one level at once. On one level we may be thinking, or discussing, or seeing, or calculating, or meeting all the demands of the external affairs of our life; while deep within, behind the scenes, at a profounder level, we may also be in prayer and adoration, and song and worship, and a gentle receptiveness to divine breathings.[2]

Satan has no desire to see us living in that kind of continual communion with God and will do whatever he can to disrupt it. As we have noted throughout this study guide, Satan will deny, deceive, disrupt, derail, discourage, depress—anything to keep us from active prayer and active, open communication with God (both speaking and listening). In fact, the times when we feel least like praying, in spite of knowing we need to, are the times we definitely should pray. The thought that we should put off or cancel our need to pray is evidence of Satan working to disabuse us of the notion altogether.

C. S. Lewis wrote,

> I have a notion that what seems our worst prayers may really be, in God's eyes, our very best. Those, I mean, which are least supported by devotional feeling and contend with the greatest disinclination. For those, perhaps, being nearly all, will come from a deeper level than feeling.[3]

And Richard Foster concurs:

We must never wait until we feel like praying before we pray for others. Prayer is like any other work. We may not feel like working, but once we have been at it for a while, we begin to feel like working. We may not feel like practicing the piano, but once we play for a while, we like doing it. In the same way, he wrote, our prayer muscles need to be limbered up a bit once the blood-flow of intercession begins, we will find that we feel like praying.[4]

Prayer is less about getting what we want than it is about becoming who God wants us to be. And He wants us to be persistent people who never give up (Luke 11:5-8).

THE POSSIBILITIES OF THE WARRIOR'S PRAYER

Paul's next phrase—praying with "all prayer"—begs an explanation.

We Are to Pray on All Occasions

First, I think Paul is suggesting praying on all occasions. Think about it: Is there any occasion or situation in which it would be inappropriate to invoke God's presence? (If there is, it's a place we should not be.)

We Are to Pray in All Places

Second, there is no place where prayer is excluded. Public and private dining tables, church meetings, hospital rooms, our own prayer closets, when in nature—too many people think prayer is to be confined to church alone. Scripture teaches that God "does not dwell in temples made with hands" (Acts 7:48; 17:24); that "the world is [His], and all its fullness" (Psalm 50:12). God dwells throughout the earth and can hear our prayers in any place.

We Are to Pray in Prosperity and Adversity

And prayer is appropriate in every condition in life—in prosperity and in adversity; in sickness and in health; morning, noon, and night. If you have a pulse and are drawing breath, it's a good time to pray. Not necessarily formal prayers at every moment, but every moment filled with the awareness of God's presence and closeness to you.

We Are to Pray for All Things

Finally—and the one that is perhaps most needful to understand —we are to pray for all "things." Sometimes Christians are not sure what is acceptable to bring to God in prayer. I believe *everything* is acceptable to talk to God about, much as a child would sense the freedom to ask a loving father about any matter in his life, be it large or small.

Peter's prayer to Jesus, "Lord, save me!" (Matthew 14:30) is a good example of "all prayer." Peter was out on the Sea of Galilee in the midst of a stormy sea, and fearing for his life as he stepped out of the boat to meet Jesus, he began to sink in the waves. He didn't really stop to analyze the situation—he just prayed! And that is what we should do as well: Pray without ceasing and without limits; pray with "all prayer."

A word of balance is in order: We should not trivialize prayer. There are many choices in life in which God expects us to exercise the wisdom and maturity we have gained as followers of Christ. "Lord, should I have an apple or a banana?" is a choice God is happy to leave to us, along with many others. Part of growing in maturity as a Christian is understanding the boundaries God has established for our lives, and then learning to exercise our freedoms within those boundaries with choices that glorify Him. No doubt those choices are different for every Christian as we make progress in being conformed to the image of Christ. As in human maturity, when we are babes, we have many more questions and need more help in finding answers than when we are adults. God is always there for us, but He also expects us to take on the responsibility of "growing in wisdom and stature" in our walk with Him (Luke 2:52).

When we are not sure whether or how to pray, we can always follow the advice of the Norwegian pastor Ole Hallesby:

> If it is difficult for you to pray, and this is all like a foreign language to you, and you're a Christian, then just offer this little prayer: Lord, teach me to pray. There's nothing that He, the Spirit of prayer, would rather do.[5]

Jesus answered that prayer for the disciples (Luke 11:1) and He will answer it for us.

THE PETITION OF THE WARRIOR'S PRAYER

What is "supplication"—the term Paul uses along with "all prayer" in verse 18? Very simply, supplication means to ask, or in this case, to ask God for something, to present a request to Him. It's the asking Jesus referred to in Matthew 7:7-8 ("Ask, and it will be given to you") and in James 4:2 ("Yet you do not have because you do not ask").

God already knows what we need before we ask (Matthew 6:8) and could give us whatever we need without our asking, yet He has ordained prayer (asking) as the way we are to relate to Him. So if there is something we need and we have not asked for it, the ball remains in our court, as they say. It is our job to ask.

There has never been a time when we have more needs in our world than today, which means there should be more prayer than ever. Yet I wonder if that is happening; if some of our needs go unmet, personally and as a society, because we don't ask God to meet them. We don't hesitate to call on friends and commiserate with them when we have a need, or ask them to help us. We should be depending on God, our heavenly Father, with even greater consistency.

The story Jesus told in Luke 11:5-8—about the man who needed food for an unexpected guest and would not stop asking his neighbor for bread until he received it—was to picture how we are to pray. We are to keep on asking, shamelessly and persistently, until we get what we need.

THE POWER OF THE WARRIOR'S PRAYER

Paul addresses the need for power in prayer by exhorting us to pray "in the Spirit." Power in prayer comes when we pray in concert with the will of God. And it is the Spirit of God, who knows the mind of God and wrote the Word of God (which reflects the will of God) who lives and works within us to shape our character and the content of our prayer to be pleasing to God. There is great power and confidence in prayer when we pray according to the will of God.

Romans 8:26-27 is the classic text on how the Spirit helps us to pray: ". . . but the Spirit Himself makes intercession for us with groanings which cannot be uttered. Now He [the Father] who searches the hearts knows what the mind of the Spirit is, because He [the Spirit] makes intercession for the saints according to the will of God." When we don't know how to pray and ask the Lord for guidance, the Spirit steps in between us and the Father and "makes intercession" for us "according to the will of God." That is power in prayer.

THE PRECISION OF THE WARRIOR'S PRAYER

Next, Paul says we are to be "watchful to this end." What end? While there are many exhortations in Scripture to be alert and watchful in a general sense, (1 Corinthians 16:22; Revelation 22:20), I think Paul's words in this instance are more specific. I believe the watchfulness here is being careful about our prayer life; guarding against anything that might disrupt or hinder our prayers.

There are three times in Scripture where watchfulness is urged in the context of prayer. Regarding the end of days, Jesus told the disciples to "watch and pray" since no one knows the day or the hour of the end (Mark 13:32-33). In the Garden of Gethsemane, Jesus exhorted the disciples to "watch and pray" (Matthew 26:41; Mark 14:38). And in Nehemiah 4:9, Nehemiah describes how they defeated their enemies who were trying to disrupt the rebuilding of the wall around Jerusalem by setting a watch and praying.

So there is watching and praying so as not to be overcome by the *world* at the end of days, not to be overcome by the *flesh* by being weary and sleepy, and not to be overcome by the agents of the *devil* who were allied against God's plans in Jerusalem. In every case, "watch" means to be awake and vigilant, to be on guard against powers and temptations that would lead us away from what God wants to accomplish through our prayer.

Personally, I have fought the temptation of my flesh to fall asleep during extended, private prayer times by using my walking-for-exercise times as an occasion to pour out my heart to the Lord. I believe the Lord would rather hear my walking prayers than not hear the prayers disrupted by sleep. Colossians 4:2 says to be "vigilant in [prayer]," and we do that by being watchful.

THE PERSEVERANCE OF THE WARRIOR'S PRAYER

I love this last description of Paul's regarding prayer: "with all perseverance." Perseverance in prayer certainly characterized the early church: They "continued . . . in prayer and supplication" (Acts 1:14); they "continued steadfastly . . . in prayers" (Acts 2:42); the apostles gave themselves "continually to prayer" (Acts 6:4). And Paul exhorts all believers to follow that same pattern: "not lagging in diligence [but] . . . continuing steadfastly in prayer" (Romans 12:11-12).

This idea is one of holding on and holding out in prayer. Don't quit, faint, yield, or be distracted or deterred or detoured when it comes to prayer. In my experience, when I go through a season of consistency in prayer, Satan will suggest to me that I've got it licked, that it will always be that way. Then, I'll immediately begin to fail in my consistency in prayer, and he will accuse me of unfaithfulness which makes me not want to start praying again. Avoid this trap with this simple guideline: Anytime you stop praying, start again regardless of how you feel. Prayer is not about feeling like praying, feeling successful. It is about perseverance.

God knows we are not perfect. He knows we will have weak moments in our life. But the key is not to let weak moments discourage us from praying. I have books on prayer that I have read multiple times—like the books on prayer by Andrew Murray—because they strengthen me in the shallow seasons of prayer to begin again. I encourage you to "prime the prayer pump" in your life by doing the same.

THE PURPOSE OF THE WARRIOR'S PRAYER

Finally, Paul touches the purpose of prayer—actually, the purpose of spiritual armor as believers undertake God's ultimate purpose for the church on earth. We are to pray for "all the saints" (Ephesians 6:18), "and for me," Paul says (verse 19), that he might have boldness to proclaim "the mystery of the gospel" (verse 20).

Prayer is mostly intercession, and mostly for others as they accomplish God's purpose in their life. Paul's purpose was to be the apostle to the Gentiles, and he asked for prayer that he might be bold in proclaiming the Gospel. But "all the saints" have a calling and a purpose, and we are to be faithful in praying for them. If every Christian is praying for "all the saints," then we don't need to worry about praying for ourselves as others are praying for us. The more we focus on the needs of others, the less serious our own needs seem to become.

Put on the whole armor of God to be victorious in the spiritual life. And make sure the wearing of it is bathed in prayer for "all the saints."

Notes:

1. Philip Yancey, *Prayer* (Grand Rapids, MI: Zondervan Publishers, 2006), 88.

2. Thomas Kelly, *A Testament of Devotion* (NY: HarperCollins Publishers, 1996), 9.

3. Yancey, *Prayer*, 197.

4. Richard J. Foster, *The Celebration of Discipline* (San Francisco, CA: HarperCollins Publishers, 1998), 45.

5. Ole Hallesby, *Prayer* (Minneapolis, MN: Augsburg Fortress, 1994), 175.

1. Read Romans 8:33-34.

   a. What is Paul's subject in this context? (See verse 31.)

   b. How do Job 1:9-11 and 2:4-5 illustrate verse 33?

   c. What was Job's regular practice for his household so as not to be subject to charges of sin? (Job 1:4-5)

   d. How is the Christian today able to stand before God without condemnation? Christ_____for us and is now _____ for us at the_____ of God. (Romans 8:34)

e. Toward whom is intercession directed: self or others?

f. If Christ is interceding for us, what is He asking of the Father in our behalf?

g. Why is Satan unable to bring charges against us when we sin? (Romans 8:33)

h. What rights does Satan have to bring charges against non-Christians?

i. Hypothetically speaking, what would happen to Christians if Christ ceased His ministry of intercession at the right hand of the Father?

j. How does Christ's ministry of intercession serve as a positive example of "praying always" and persevering in prayer?

2. Read Hebrews 4:15-16.

   a. Why is Christ qualified to intercede for us before the Father? (verse 15)

   b. How does your experience as a sinner saved by grace qualify you to intercede in prayer effectively for others?

   c. Since "all have sinned" (Romans 3:23), why is intercession a better response to others' failures than judgment or criticism? (See also Matthew 7:3-5.)

   d. How does 2 Corinthians 1:3-5 serve as a foundation for interceding for others the way Christ intercedes for us?

e. Who are the people in your life that you feel most qualified to intercede for, based on your experience and theirs?

3. What do the words "uttermost" and "always" suggest to you about the faithfulness of Christ's intercession for you? (Hebrews 7:25)

   a. We are saved by grace through faith. (Ephesians 2:8-9) What does Christ bring to us through His sacrifice? (Ephesians 2:14-16)

   b. How might your intercession for others—especially those going through serious struggles—impact their being "saved"?

4. What idea from this lesson on prayer has the greatest potential for changing your prayer life?

DID YOU KNOW?

The phrase "practicing the presence of God," often used to refer to the practice of continual and prayerful communion with God, can be traced back to *The Practice of the Presence of God*, a book written by Brother Lawrence of the Resurrection (born Nicolas Herman, 1614-1691), a Carmelite monk in a Parisian monastery. He entered the monastery after fighting as a soldier and spent the rest of his life there, working in the kitchen and repairing sandals. Brother Lawrence's peaceful and close relationship with God drew other monks, as well as visitors, to him for counsel. The wisdom he shared, through conversations and correspondence, became the basis for the book, which was compiled after his death.

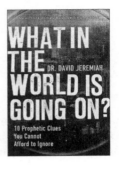

What in the World Is Going On?

The Bible has much to say about the End Times, yet it is hard to piece together all the information. That is why Dr. David Jeremiah has written a unique book identifying the ten most essential clues to Bible prophecy.

What to Do When You Don't Know What to Do

In his study on the book of James, David Jeremiah shows readers that a life lived with focused devotion to God should make a genuine difference in the way a person lives. This book will help you tap into God's supernatural strength to meet the challenges of your life.

God in You:
Releasing the Power of the Holy Spirit

As stunning as Jesus' miracles were, the disciples were astonished to hear Him announce that another would do even greater works – the Holy Spirit. This book reveals God's Spirit in concrete terms, shaping a fresh, clear image of how He places God not only with us, but in us.

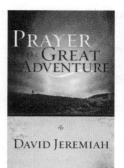

Prayer – The Great Adventure

Prayer can be the believer's greatest adventure. In this book, Dr. David Jeremiah invites you to look into his own personal prayer journal as he teaches the scriptural map for discovering your own prayer adventure.

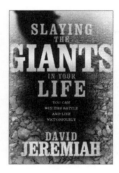

Slaying the Giants in Your Life

Whether you're battling fear, anger, temptation, jealousy, loneliness, resentment, worry, or discouragement, this book will motivate you to stand up to the daunting foes you face. Dr. Jeremiah will help you discover the eternal promises that will help you face and slay the spiritual giants in your life.

For pricing information and ordering, contact us at

with Dr. David Jeremiah

P.O. Box 3838
San Diego, CA 92163
(800) 947-1993
WWW.DAVIDJEREMIAH.ORG

Who is the King in America?

And Who are the Counselors to the King?

An Overview of
6,000 Years of History
& Why America is Unique

William J. Federer

Who is the King in America?
And Who are the Counselors to the King?
—An Overview of 6,000 Years of History & Why America is Unique
by William J. Federer

Cover design by
DustinMyersDesign.com 573-308-6060
Library of Congress
WORLD HISTORY / UNITED STATES HISTORY
ISBN-13: 978-0-9896491-2-4

Sincere appreciation for valuable editorial insight is given to my wife, Susan M. Federer.

ebook

For a limited time, as owner of this book, you may receive it as an **ebook.** Email wjfederer@gmail.com with subject line "Who is the King." A pdf file will be sent by reply email.

Amerisearch, Inc.
1-888-USA-WORD, 314-502-8924
wjfederer@gmail.com
www.AmericanMinute.com

To
David & Cindy Lane,
Founders of the American Renewal Project.

This book
is a synthesis of lessons
from the author's previous books,
assembled specifically for
a series of national lectures
given on behalf the
American Renewal Project.

"The farther back you can look,
the farther forward you are likely to see."
– Winston Churchill
∽

"I know of no way of judging the future
but by the past."
– Patrick Henry
∽

"Those who cannot remember the past
are condemned to repeat it."
– George Santayana, 1905
∽

"When the past no longer illuminates the future, the
spirit walks in darkness."
– Alexis de Tocqueville
∽

"Live both in the future and the past.
Who does not live in the past
does not live in the future."
– Lord Acton
∽

"When a nation goes down ... one condition may
always be found;
they forgot where they came from."
– Carl Sandburg
∽

CONTENTS

HAS AMERICA LOST ITS MEMORY?

John F. Kennedy wrote in the *Introduction to The American Heritage New Illustrated History of the United States* (Dell Publishing Co., 1960):

> History, after all, is the memory of a nation.

Pulitzer Prize winning historian Arthur M. Schlesinger, Jr., wrote in an op-ed titled "Folly's Antidote" (*The New York Times,* January 1, 2007):

> History is to the nation as memory is to the individual.

Have you ever met an individual who has lost their memory? Maybe they have Alzheimer's? They cannot remember who you are, or who they are. Someone could easily take things away from them.

In a sense, America has had national Alzheimer's. We have lost our collective memory.

Here we are the most prosperous and independent nation in world history, with more individual liberty and opportunity than any previous people, and yet we forgot how we got here.

As a result, our freedoms are being taken right out of our hands.

Is this by accident or on purpose?

There is actually a socialist–communist tactic called "deconstruction," where you separate a people from their past, get them into a neutral position where they do not remember where they came from, then you can easily brainwash them into whatever future you have planned for them. It is like cultural gene-therapy.

This actually mirrors a sales technique.

If I were a toothpaste salesman, the first thing I would do is say negative things about the toothpaste you are currently using – "You are using that old stuff – it will dry out your gums and eat the enamel off your teeth!"

"Yikes" – you are repulsed by it. Now I have you in a neutral position, where you are open-minded – "What are all the toothpastes out there nowadays?"

Then I can give you my pitch for this new tartar-control, breath-freshener toothpaste.

This technique is applied nationally.

First, students are taught negative things about the country's founders – "They took land from Indians, sold people into slavery, and were chauvinists."

"Yikes" – students are repelled by them. Now, students are in a neutral position where they are open-minded to other belief systems.

Then students can be given the pitch for socialism, the LGBT agenda or Islam, being peer-pressured, intimidated or ridiculed into accepting it through white privilege indoctrination and common core curriculum.

Just as a car has to go from drive into neutral before it can go into reverse, this process has taken place in Western Civilization.

Let us look at Europe. It has gone:

• from a Judeo–Christian PAST –

• into a Secular–Free–Sex PRESENT –

• now Europe it entering an Islamic FUTURE.

For centuries, Europe was Catholic, with many cities having Jewish neighborhoods. In 1517, the Protestant Reformation began.

Then Europe had a secular French Revolution.

As head France's Committee of Public Safety – their "Department of Homeland Security," Robespierre began the Reign of Terror in 1793. He put a prostitute in Notre Dame Cathedral, covered her with a sheet and declared her the goddess of reason.

Paris sent its military to the Vendée, a rural, Catholic area. Soldiers killed over 300,000 men, women and children, forcing them to comply. Napoleon spread this new French secularism across Europe, effectively cutting cultural ties with the Judeo–Christian PAST.

Europe then drifted into a secular PRESENT, with its non-religious atheistic, free sex, and LGBT agenda.

Now, Europe is entering an Islamic FUTURE, with: "Mohammed" as the number one name given to newborns in London, Brussels & Milan; Paris surrounded by 5 million Muslims in over 700 neighborhoods; women raped on streets in Germany, Sweden & Denmark; trucks being driven into crowds.

African Archbishop Robert Sarah of Guinea told the Synod of Bishops in Rome, October 12, 2015:

> Like two "apocalyptic beasts" ... on the one hand ... atheistic secularism ... on the other, Islamic fundamentalism ... We find ourselves between "gender ideology and ISIS" ...

> Two major threats ... Disintegration in the secularized West through quick and easy divorce, abortion, homosexual unions, euthanasia etc. (cf. the LGBT lobby ...)

> On the other hand ... Islam which legitimizes polygamy, female subservience, sexual slavery, child marriage etc. (cf. Al Qaeda, ISIS, Boko Haram.)

Italian Archbishop Carlo Liberati stated (*Breitbart,* January 14, 2017):

> We have a weak Christian faith ... Seminaries are empty ... Italy and Europe live in a pagan and atheist way, they make laws that go against

God and they have traditions that are proper of paganism.... All this paves the way to Islam ... Europe will soon be Muslim.

This drive–neutral–reverse process has been successful in fundamentally transforming Europe, and it is advancing to the point of no return in America.

Consistent with this is the practice of fundamentalist Muslims, who upon entering an "infidel" country, destroy museums, libraries, statues, artwork, and artifacts linking the conquered people to their past.

In the article "ISIS Burns Books at Mosul Libraries," (*Breitbart News,* February 5, 2015), it was reported:

> The Islamic State continues to purge anything they deem to defy Islam ... They raided the Central Library of Mosul to destroy all non-Islamic books.
>
> "These books promote infidelity and call for disobeying Allah," announced a militant to the residents. "So they will be burned."
>
> Militants targeted the library at the University of Mosul. They burned science and culture textbooks in front of the students...
>
> Extremists started wrecking the collections of other public libraries ... particularly heavy damage to ... the Mosul Museum Library with works dating back 5,000 years.

This is similar to the first emperor of China, Qin Shi Huangdi, who conquered kingdoms to unify China in 221 BC, then destroyed all books linking them to the past. *The Basic Annals of the First Emperor of Qin* reported Chancellor Li Si told the Emperor in 213 BC:

> I, your servant, propose that all historians' records other than those of Qin's be burned...
>
> If anyone under heaven has copies of the Classics of History [Shu Jing] ... they shall deliver them to the governor ... for burning.

Anyone who dares to discuss the Classics of History shall be publicly executed.

Anyone who uses history to criticize the present shall have his family executed ...

Anyone who has failed to burn the books after thirty days of this announcement shall be subjected to tattooing and be sent to build the Great Wall.

In 1933, the Nazi leader Adolf Hitler burned books by Jewish authors, including Einstein. Jewish poet Heinrich Heine prophetically penned in 1822:

Where they burn books, they will, in the end, burn human beings too.

Any hope of preserving America's freedoms is dependent upon Americans learning their history – regaining their corporate memory – and rediscovering how truly rare their liberties are.

LESSONS FROM 6,000 YEARS OF HISTORY

To appreciate how unique America is, one must answer the question – what is the most common form of government in world history?

If you study the past, you will discover that there are approximately 6,000 years of recorded human history?

Writing was invented around 3,300 BC, with Sumerian cuneiform on clay tablets in the Mesopotamian Valley. This is the beginning of human beings writing down human records. Astrophysicist Neil deGrasse Tyson stated in the *Cosmos* TV series (2014, natgeotv. com, episode 10, "The Immortals"):

Around 5,000 years ago ... Mesopotamia–the land between the Tigris and Euphrates Rivers ... It was here that we learned how to write.

Following this, were Egyptian hieroglyphs on papyrus and stone around 3,000 BC. Around 2,600 BC the China's Yellow Emperor oversaw the invention of Chinese characters in bamboo annals.

Added together, 3,000 or 4,000 years BC plus around 2,000 years AD equals around 5,000 or 6,000 thousand years of written records.

Franklin D. Roosevelt stated in 1940:

> Five thousand years of recorded history have proven that mankind has always believed in God in spite of many abortive attempts to exile God.

Richard Overy, editor of *The Times Complete History of the World,* stated in "The 50 Key Dates of World History" (October 19, 2007):

> No date appears before the start of human civilizations about 5,500 years ago and the beginning of a written or pictorial history.

Secretary of State William Jennings Bryan wrote in "Prince of Peace" (*New York Times,* September 7, 1913):

> Six thousand years of recorded history and yet we know no more about the secret of life than they knew in the beginning.

Astronomer Johannes Kepler wrote in *The Harmonies of the World* (1619):

> The book is written, to be read either now or by posterity ... It may be well to wait a century for a reader, as God has waited 6,000 years for an observer.

James Wilson was a signer of the Declaration of Independence and the U.S. Constitution, and was appointed a Supreme Court Justice by President George Washington. Wilson remarked at Pennsylvania's Ratifying Convention, November 26, 1787:

> After a period of 6,000 years has elapsed since the creation, the United States exhibit to the world the first instance ... of a nation ... assembling voluntarily ... and deciding calmly

concerning that system of government under which they would wish that they and their posterity should live.

Daniel Webster stated in 1802:

Miracles do not cluster, and what has happened once in 6,000 years, may not happen again. Hold on to the Constitution, for if the American Constitution should fail, there will be anarchy throughout the world.

These leaders thought something unique happened in America.

In a sense, 6,000 years is not that long. It is only 60 people living 100 years each, back-to-back. Everyone has met someone who has lived 100 years, or close to it – maybe a grandmother. 6,000 years is just 60 grandmothers living 100 years each back-to-back.

What is the most common form of government revealed by these 6,000 years of written history?

Consensus is that the first civilizations emerged in the Mesopotamian Valley, called the Fertile Crescent.

Neil deGrasse Tyson added in his *Cosmos* TV series:

They call this place Uruk. We call it Iraq ...
The "city" was invented here.

Around 2,500 BC, Uruk's king was Gilgamesh. *The Epic of Gilgamesh,* written in the Sumerian language of Akkadian, is considered the oldest story ever recorded in any language.

It tells the story of Gilgamesh going on a quest to meet Utnapishtim, an old man who survived a Great Deluge by building a large boat, covering it with tar, and putting his family on it, along with many animals.

When the ship rested on a mountain, he opened the hatch and sent out a dove, which returned. He then sent out a raven, which did not return. He released the animals to replenish the earth, and his family reintroduced farming and animal domestication into the Mesopotamian Valley.

Interestingly, hundreds of ancient civilizations have accounts of an immense flood, including: Babylon, India, China, Sumatra, Wales, Scandinavia, Russia, Peru, Australia, Hawaii and Polynesia.

This area is also the location of the Biblical account of the first government – Nimrod building the Tower of Babel. Jewish commentaries state that Nimrod wanted to build the Tower so high that if God destroyed the world again with a flood, he could survive on top. It expressed a defiant, in-your-face, attitude toward God.

In response, God confused the languages and the people were scattered, migrating as far as Egypt, Indus Valley, and China. This is the beginning of a recurring theme – fallen man's desire to concentrate power without God, and God's plan of separated power.

It is as if each generation has its own version of a "Nimrod" who wants to concentrate power and rebuild the Tower Babel.

An allegory can be seen in a popular sci-fi movie, *Terminator 3: Rise of the Machines* (2003), where a killer robot T-X is sent from the future to assassinate the character John Connor.

In one scene, T-X is destroyed, but to the dismay of the audience, the scattered metal pieces melt into little shiny droplets, which roll together into a molten pool, out of which the hand of the T-X begins to rise, then the entire T-X robot re-emerges and begins chasing John Connor again.

In like manner, people were scattered from the Tower of Babel, but each generation has a "Nimrod" trying to rebuild it, conquering ever larger areas, with an ultimate goal of a global one world government.

Though the succeeding centuries of pharaohs, emperors, caesars, czars, sultans, kaisers and khans, dictators, tyrants, kings – POWER inevitably concentrated into the hands of one person.

Sargon of Akkad, c.2250 BC, conquered from the Persian Gulf to the Mediterranean;

From c.2500 to 30 BC, Egypt was ruled by 33 major dynasties, with pharaohs owning the land, the cattle and the people.

From c.2700 BC to 1900 AD, China was ruled by emperors of 18 major dynasties.

Kingdoms, dynasties, and empires grew larger and larger, any of which, if circumstances would have permitted, would have ultimately culminated in global, one-world control. Some notable empires include:
• Pharaoh Ramesses the Great, 19th Dynasty, 1279–1213 BC
• Ashurbanipal, Assyrian Empire, 669–627 BC
• Nebuchadnezzar II, Babylonian Empire, 634–562 BC
• Cyrus the Great, Achaemenid Persian Empire, 559–530 BC
• Darius the Great, Medo–Persian Empire, 522–486 BC
• Alexander the Great, Macedonian Empire, 336–323 BC
• Chandragupta, India Mauryan Empire, 324–297 BC
• Emperor Qin Shi Huang, China's Qin Dynasty, 247–210 BC
• Queen Candace of Meroe, Africa Nubian Empire, 170–150 BC
• Augustus Caesar, Roman Empire, 27 BC–14 AD
• Attila the Hun, Hunnic Empire, 434–453
• Emperor Justinian, Byzantine Empire, 527–565
• Genghis Khan, Mongolian Empire – largest contiguous land empire ever – Korea to Hungary, 1206–1227
• Montezuma II, Aztec Mexican Empire, 1460–1520
• Charles V, Holy Roman Empire, 1519–1556
• Suleiman the Magnificent, Ottoman Empire, 1520–1566
• Louis XIV, the "Sun King," French Empire, 1643–1715
• Shah Jahan, India Mughal Empire, 1628–1658
• Catherine the Great, Russian Empire, 1762–1796
• King Kamehameha, Hawaiian Empire, 1782–1819
• Napoleon Bonaparte, French Empire, 1804–1814

- Franz Joseph I of Austro-Hungarian Empire, 1848–1916
- Czar Nicholas II of Russia, 1894–1917
- Kaiser Wilhelm II, German Empire, 1888–1918
- Emperor Hirohito of Japan, 1926–1989
- King George V, British Empire, 1910–1936.

Global maritime empires existed under the kings of Portugal, Spain, Sweden, Japan and France.

The most common form of government in world history is kings, ruling their kingdoms by claiming a "divine right" to control people. How did this develop?

Initially, humans were hunter-gatherers. The Bible described Adam and Eve as being in the Garden picking fruit off of trees. Mankind then transitioned to agriculture. Again, the Bible described that after Adam sinned he had to "till the ground," and "Cain was a tiller of the soil."

As mankind learned to cultivate agriculture, it necessitated knowing when to plant and harvest crops. This gave rise to a preoccupation with observing the stars in order to predict the change of seasons. Large, immovable structures were erected to observe the sky.

Someone would then ascend these structures to observe the heavens, and descend with special knowledge of when to plant and harvest. Gradually, this person would gain importance and claim to be an intermediary between "heaven" and "the people."

Ancient civilizations exhibit three common features:

1) a fascination with stars and heavens;

2) buildings to observe stars and heavens;

3) a king who ascended the building and claimed to be the divinely-appointed political intermediary between the heavens and the people, thus legitimizing his totalitarian rule and justifying his condemnation of those who disagreed with him as being guilty of treason, even demanding they be sacrificed for the state.

Kings claiming to be "divinely appointed" included:

- King Gilgamesh of Uruk – claimed to be a "demigod" of superhuman strength able to lift huge stones to build a wall around his city.
- Mesopotamia Kings – were considered "god-kings" or deities upon their deaths.
- Babylonia and Assyrian Kings – claimed to be "king – priests."
- Egyptian Pharaohs – claimed to be son of the god Osiris.
- Tyre Kings – claimed to be a bridge between temporal & celestial world.
- Persian Kings – had a privileged relationship with the divine to maintain his creation.
- South Asian Kings – were "agents of God" protecting the world like God did.
- Chinese Emperors – ruled by claiming they had a mandate from heaven.
- Roman Emperors – had a cult of deified Caesars. "August" meant "sacred" or "divine."
- India Rajas – considered semi-divine caste of rulers, as post-Brahminism in Tamilakam.

A temple inscription at Thiruvalangadu, India, referred to Arulmozhi–Emperor Raja Raja Chola I:

> Having noticed by the marks (on his body) that Arulmozhi was the very Vishnu (Hindu deity).

- Inca Emperors – claimed to be delegates of the Sun god.
- Japanese Emperors – claimed to be descendants of the Shinto god Amaterasu.
- Caliphs – successors of the Messenger of Allah.
- Sultans – who maintained they ruled in the "shadow of Allah."

Sultan Balban of Delhi, India (1266–1286) declared:

FEAR of the GOVERNING POWER ... is the BASIS of all good government.

- Europe's Monarchs christianized this claim to power, calling it the "divine right of kings."

England's King James I stated:

KINGS are ... God's lieutenants ... upon earth ... sit upon God's throne ... The KING is overlord of the whole land ... MASTER over every person ... having POWER over the life and death of every one.

France's Louis XIV was called "The Sun King" as his subjects revolved around him like planets. He claimed absolute power over an empire stretching from Canada, Louisiana, Haiti, French Guiana, to the Indian Ocean and Far East.

Having the longest reign of any European monarch, he ruled from his Palace of Versailles, exclaiming:

L'État, c'est moi [I am the state].

After the Seven Years War, the British Empire grew to became the largest empire in history, as the saying went: "The sun never set on the British Empire." Its global domain ruled a half-billion people, stretching 13 million square miles, including India, which alone contained a quarter of the world's population.

Franklin D. Roosevelt stated June 27, 1936:

In 1776 we sought freedom from the tyranny of a political autocracy – from the 18th century royalists who held special privileges from the crown ... They governed without the consent of the governed ... They denied the right of free assembly and free speech ... They restricted the worship of God ...

They put the average man's property and the average man's life in pawn to the mercenaries of dynastic power ... They regimented the people ...

A small group had concentrated into their own hands an almost complete control over other people's property, other people's money, other people's labor – other people's lives.

%

DEFAULT SETTING FOR GOVERNMENT

The most common form of government in recorded history is that of a king. This is the default-setting.

Yale President Ezra Stiles stated May 8, 1783:

Almost all the polities [governments] may be reduced to hereditary dominion, in either a monarchy or aristocracy, and these supported by a standing army.

People today may think that kings no longer exist in the modern world, yet in Muslim countries, like Saudi Arabia, kings and royal families rule.

Communist and socialist countries operate effectively as a monarchies. That statement may seem strange until one considers that Hitler was the head of the National *Socialist* Workers Party and Stalin was the head of the United Soviet *Socialist* Republics.

Franklin Roosevelt stated February 10, 1940:

The Soviet Union ... is run by a dictatorship as absolute as any other dictatorship in the world.

Franklin Roosevelt described Hitler, who led the National Socialist Workers Party, December 15, 1941:

Government to him is not the servant ... of the people but their absolute master and the dictator of their every act.

To the annoyance of liberal academia, in practice, socialist and communist country end up being run by dictators, such as Mao Zedong, Stalin, Pol Pot, Ho Chi Min, Kim Jong-il, Castro, Ceausescu, and Tito.

Though proclaiming the high ideal of a classless

society, "communist Party members" effectively become "the new royalty," living in special neighborhoods with special shops, and getting special treatment before the law. They exist to enforce the dictator's will. If they are suspected of opposing the dictator, they disappear.

"Citizens" in communist countries are equivalent to subjects, peasants and serfs, with their fate dictated by the dictator and his enforcers. Controlled media and rigged elections insure that dictators stays in power.

Naive students are taught that in socialist and communist countries, everybody owns everything equally – "From each according to his ability, to each according to his needs" (Karl Marx, *Critique of the Gotha Program,* 1875).

But does this ever happen in practice? Only one question needs to be asked: "Who gets to live in the nice house and who lives in the dumpy house?"

The answer is: "Someone in the government dictates those things." Well, whoever ultimately dictates those things is the dictator.

Despite its rhetoric, in application, communism is nothing more than a monarchy makeover – a top-down system of government where one supreme leader forces his will on others. In oligarchies and aristocracies, too, the strongest personality dominates.

Ben Franklin stated at the Constitutional Convention, 1787, in his address, Dangers of a Salaried Bureaucracy:

> There is a natural inclination in mankind to kingly government ... They would rather have one tyrant than five hundred. It gives more of the appearance of equality among citizens; and that they like.

POWER WANTS TO CONCENTRATE

History bears out that POWER wants to concentrate.

It is like the law of gravity or the pull of a magnet. It is like a pecking order observable in animals species.

In J.R.R. Tolken's *The Lord of the Rings,* Gandalf said:

> Always remember, Frodo, the Ring is trying to get back to its master. It wants to be found.

This tendency was spliced into the human DNA at the fall in the garden, followed by Cain killing Abel, and centuries of kings attacking kings. Selfishness had infected human nature. St. Augustine called it "libido dominandi"– lust for domination.

British Prime Minister William Gladstone wrote:

> Selfishness is the greatest curse of the human race.

Sir Alexander Fraser Tytler wrote:

> Man is a being instigated by the love of power – a passion visible in an infant.

Human nature can be observed:

> • If you put some babies in a playpen, one will take the rattle from the others:
>
> • If you put some kids on a playground, one will be the bully hogging the ball;
>
> • If you put some junior high girls in a clique, one will be the diva;
>
> • If you put some people in the woods, one will be the Indian chief;
>
> • If you put some people in an inner-city, one will be the gang leader.

A king, in a sense, is just a glorified gang leader. It is hierarchical patronage system, where:

> • if you are friends with the king, you are more equal;
>
> • if you are not friends with the king you are less equal; and

• if you are an enemy of the king, you are dead – it is called treason, or you are a slave.

The dilemma is this. Each one of us has "the dictator" gene in our DNA. Alexander Solzhenitsyn wrote in *The Gulag Archipelago* (1973):

> If only there were evil people somewhere insidiously committing evil deeds, and it were necessary only to separate them from the rest of us and destroy them.

> But the line dividing good and evil cuts through the heart of every human being. And who is willing to destroy a piece of his own heart?

Matthew 15:19

> For out of the heart proceed evil thoughts, murders, adulteries, fornications, thefts, false witness, blasphemies.

The popular sci-fi movie, *The Matrix* (1999), starring Keanu Reeves, is set in a futuristic, virtual reality computer-generated world.

In a chase scene, the hero is pursued by an evil computer-generated Mr. Anderson, but shockingly, any person the hero runs passed can be transformed into Mr. Anderson. In like fashion, every human being could potentially be transformed into a corrupt dictator.

Think not?

It is hard to visualize corruption, but another word with a similar meaning is "favoritism."

You may say, "If I were king, I would be fair."

But what if you had a dear sister with a teenage son who drank at a party with the wrong friends, and driving home, hit someone with his car and killed him.

As the teenager sits in a jail cell facing manslaughter charges and possibly decades in prison, your sister comes begging to you, saying:

"You are not going to let my little Johnny be locked away for half his life, are you? It was not his fault. Those other kids talked him into it, etc., etc., etc."

What are you going to say to your sister?

"OK, I will let little Johnnie off the hook this time, but don't let it happen again."

Guess what – as soon as you said that, you became the corrupt dictator. You just sent ripples through your kingdom that if someone is family or friends of the king, they get "favored" treatment, being "more equal."

George Orwell wrote in *Animal Farm* (1945):

All animals are equal but some animals are
more equal than others.

If a person is not family or friend, they do not get that special treatment. And if they are an enemy, pointing out your favoritism and corruption, you will be tempted to use your power to shut them up.

Aristotle (384–322 BC) wrote nearly 23 centuries ago:

This is why we do not permit a man to rule
... because a man rules in his own interest, and
becomes a tyrant.

When power concentrates, it is inevitable that it will be accompanied with favoritism and corruption.

British Parliament Member Lord Acton wrote:

Power tends to corrupt and absolute power
corrupts absolutely.

Since this trend is inevitable, death is a blessing.

Death is blessing? Yes, especially when one considers the horrible death tolls which occur under dictators.

Imagine if dictators never died? By now, some tyrant would have the whole world under his thumb. A person's life would only have value if it benefited the king, as under Ramesses, Nero, Ivan the Terrible, Sultan

Moulay Ismail, Idi Amin, Leopold II, or Hirohito.

Either directly or through their policies, dictators are responsible for enormous death tolls:

• 100,000 killed in Peru by Abimael Guzmán's "Shining Path" Revolution, 1960–1992;

• 1.1 million in Nigeria by Yakubu Gowon, 1966–1975;

• 1.6 million in North Korea by Kim Il Sung, 1948–1994;

• 1.7 million in North Vietnam by Ho Chi Minh, 1945–1969;

• 2 million in Ethiopia by Mengistu Haile Mariam, 1977–1991;

• 2.4 million in Cambodia by Pol Pot, 1963–1997;

• 2.5 million in Turkey by Enver Pasha, 1908–1918;

• 4 million in U.S.S.R., by Vladimir Lenin, 1917–1924;

• 4 million in Asia by Tojo Hideki, 1941–1948;

• 6 million across Europe by Napoleon, 1804–1814;

• 12 million Pakistan/Bangladesh by Yahya Khan, 1969–1971;

• 17 million across Central Asia by Tamerlane, 1370–1405;

• 17 million across Europe by Adolf Hitler, 1933–1945;

• 30 million in Central Asia by Genghis Khan, 1206–1227;

• 60 million in U.S.S.R. by Joseph Stalin, 1922–1953;

• 80 million in China by Mao Zedong, 1949–1976;

• 240 million worldwide by Muslim Sultans & Caliphs, 622 AD–present, plus an estimated 180 million enslaved.

When dictators die, the people get a brief reprieve, until the next dictator begins to re-accumulate power.

Though some kings genuinely sought to do good, they were often followed by their heirs who ruled selfishly, as illustrated by Solomon's son Rehoboam,

In either case, whether a good king or bad king, wherever there is a king, his will is the law.

France's King Louis XIV – the Sun King – declared:

It is legal because I wish it.

Thomas Paine wrote (*Common Sense,* January 1776):

> In absolute governments the king is the law.

Fundamental Muslims who desire a caliphate ruled by a "caliph," include Anjem Choudary of Islam4UK who stated (*London Daily Express,* October 15, 2009):

> We have had enough of democracy and man-made law ... We will call for a complete upheaval of the British ruling system ... and demand full implementation of Sharia in Britain.

If took centuries before America was given the chance to break away from the "top-down" government of a king, and set up a "bottom-up" form a government – "of the people, by the people, and for the people."

At the time of the Revolutionary War, the King of Great Britain controlled the largest empire the world had ever seen. Americans, with a courageous volunteer army, miraculously won its independence. The Founding Fathers proceeded to set up a government that was as far away from a king as possible.

U.S. Supreme Court Justice John Jay, serving as Chief Justice of the State of New York, gave a charge to the Grand Jury of Ulster County, September 8, 1777:

> This glorious revolution ... is distinguished by so many marks of the Divine favor and interposition, that no doubt can remain of its being ... supported in a manner so singular, and I may say miraculous, that when future ages shall read its history they will be tempted to consider a great part of it as fabulous ...
>
> Will it not appear extraordinary that thirteen colonies ... should immediately become one people, and though without funds, without magazines, without disciplined troops, in the face of their enemies, unanimously determine to be free, and, undaunted by the power of Britain, refer their cause to the justice of the

Almighty, and resolve to repel force by force, thereby presenting to the world an illustrious example of magnanimity and virtue scarcely to be paralleled.

George Washington wrote to General Nathanael Greene, February 6, 1783:

It will not be believed that such a force as Great Britain has employed for eight years in this country could be baffled in their plan of subjugating it by numbers infinitely less, composed of men oftentimes half starved; always in rags, without pay, and experiencing, at times, every species of distress which human nature is capable of undergoing.

Washington wrote November 2, 1783:

The singular interpositions of Providence in our feeble condition were such, as could scarcely escape the attention of the most unobserving; while the unparalleled perseverance of the Armies of the United States, through almost every possible suffering and discouragement for the space of eight long years, was little short of a standing miracle.

At a time when kings killed to keep power, Washington gave up power. Jaws dropped around the world when he stepped down.

In 1783, the American-born painter Benjamin West was in England painting the portrait of King George III. When the King asked what General Washington intended to do now that he had won the war.

West replied: "They say he will return to his farm."

King George exclaimed: "If he does that, he will be the greatest man in the world."

Later, Washington set the example of stepping down after two terms. Poet Robert Frost wrote:

I often say of George Washington that he

was one of the few men in the whole history of the world who was not carried away by power.

A study of concentrated power is in the book *Change to Chains: The 6000 Year Quest for Global Control.*

∽

SETTING THE HISTORICAL STAGE

To understand how unique it was for America to break from a king, it is necessary to review momentous events of preceding centuries which set the stage.

Starting with the spread of Christianity around 33 AD, Roman Emperors carried out ten major persecutions of Christians in the next three centuries.

Then in 313 AD, Emperor Constantine ended the persecution of Christians. Though Christianity was now legal, Rome was still ruled by emperors who gradually began to enforce religious uniformity.

In the next several centuries, the Christian Roman Empire experienced internal conflicts, such as divisive heresies and ruthless responses to them, and external conflicts, such as attacks from Persia, Visigoth and Ostrogoth hordes, and the scourge of Attila the Hun.

The greatest attack upon Greco–Roman, Judeo–Christian Western Civilization came from Islam.

In 610 AD, Mohammed became "the prophet" of Islam. Initially, he was just a religious leader in Mecca, making only 70 converts in 12 years.

When he became confrontational, the pagans of Mecca considered him a disturber of the peace and drove him out. He attempted to go to the city of al-Taif, but they pelted him with rocks and chased him out.

With no where to go, Mohammed was, in effect, the first Muslim refugee.

In 622 AD, he fled 210 miles north to Medina, a city controlled by three Jewish tribes. The Jews were tolerant and let Mohammed in as a Muslim immigrant.

Mohammed went into Medina's minority pagan neighborhood and began to organize the community. He built up a following among those who had grievances against the Jewish controlled government.

When his new following was sufficiently large, he pressured the Jews to accommodate him and his followers politically. The Jews made a treaty with Mohammed, recognizing him as a political leader, in addition to him being a religious leader.

Back in Mecca, Mohammed's followers became confrontational, argumentative, and threatening. They, too, were considered disturbers of the peace and chased out, becoming Muslim refugees.

Traveling to Medina, the tolerant Jews let them in as Muslim immigrants.

✦

TRANSITION WHICH ALTERED THE WORLD

Mohammed began to allow his followers to rob the trade caravans headed to Mecca in retaliation for the Meccans driving them out. This was a departure from the teachings of Jesus, who admonished: love your enemies; bless them that curse you; do good to those hate you; if they take your coat give them your shirt.

Mohammed's instruction were, in essence, if someone takes your house – retaliate and take their caravan.

Mohammed had 300 warriors who robbed caravans. He received a whole chapter of the Qur'an – Sura 8 – on how to distribute spoils and booty from robbing caravans. His portion was a fifth of the booty.

In 624 AD, the pagans of Mecca sent a thousand soldiers to escort and protect their caravans. Mohammed, with only 300 warriors, defeated them at the Battle of Badr. This amazing victory, having been outnumbered

3 to 1, convinced Mohammed to be a military leader.

He proceeded to fight in 66 battles and raids in the next 8 years before he died, killing an estimated 3,000.

U.S. Minister to Spain, Washington Irving, wrote *Lives Of Mahomet And His Successors* (NY: George P. Putnam, 1850), naming chapter 16 "The Sword Announced as the Instrument of Faith – First Foray Against the Koreishites – Surprisal of a Caravan":

> We come now to an important era in the career of Mohammed. Hitherto he had relied on argument and persuasion to make proselytes ...
>
> His exhortations to them to bear with patience and long-suffering the violence of their enemies, almost emulated the meek precept of our Saviour, "if they smite thee on the one cheek, turn to them the other also."
>
> He now arrived at a point where he completely diverged from the celestial spirit of the Christian doctrines ...
>
> The means of retaliation unexpectedly sprung up within his reach. He had come to Medina a fugitive seeking an asylum ...
>
> In a little while, and probably to his own surprise, he found an army at his command ...
>
> The fugitives flocking to him from Mecca ... were men of resolute spirit, skilled in the use of arms, and fond of partisan warfare ...
>
> He endeavored to persuade himself ... that the power thus placed within his reach was intended as a means of effecting his great purpose, and that he was called upon by divine command to use it."

Mohammed proved to be an extremely effective military leader, primarily because he was creative, unpredictable, and unconventional – not playing by the rules of traditional Arab warfare.

He used the catapult when attacking the city of al-Taif. When told the hurling stones were killing innocent women and children, Mohammed's response was "they are among them."

Today's suicide bombers, ISIS fighters, San Bernadino shooters, Orlando killers, Paris bombers, Nice and Berlin truck driving attackers, etc., approve of killing non-Muslims to advance Islam because Mohammed did.

Since Mohammed is considered the perfect Muslim, those who want to be "better" Muslims strive to follow his example: religiously, politically and militarily.

The West is faced with the dilemma of granting freedom for all religions, but in a sense, Islam is not just a religion, because Mohammed was not just a religious leader. He was also a political and military leader.

A mosque, therefore, may be a religious building, but also a political and military building. Bowing to Mecca is a religious bowing, also a political and military pledging of allegiance to another capital. The effort to split the religious side of Islam away from the political–military side is essentially an attempt to split Mohammed.

Alexis de Tocqueville acknowledged in *Democracy in America* (1840), that Islam is not just a religion:

> Mohammed ... put into the Koran not RELIGIOUS doctrines only, but POLITICAL maxims, CRIMINAL and CIVIL laws.

Pagans in Arabia had one month off a year where they agreed not to fight – it was their pilgrimage month. They would set aside their differences and go to Mecca to worship the 360 gods kept in the square building called a Kaaba.

Mohammed received verses instructing him to attack the caravans during this month, catching them by surprise and carrying away much booty.

In 627 AD, the pagans of Mecca sent 10,000 soldiers to Medina to stop Mohammed's warriors from robbing their caravans. Mohammed's version of roadside bombs was to dig trenches and potholes all around the city of Medina, thus rendering the superior cavalry of the Meccans useless, as they could not charge their horses and camels across such an uneven field.

This threw off the Meccan battle strategy. Mohammed then went out at night and bribed some Meccans to slip away from the battle. He later went to others and threatened them, and they slipped away – a type of bribe or the bullet.

When the weather turned freezing cold, the rest of the Meccans lost heart and retreated.

This left a power vacuum, similar to August 31, 2010, when President Obama declared that the war in Iraq and Afghanistan was over, "mission complete," and ordered all American troops to be brought home.

Did fundamental Muslims become more peaceful after Americans retreated? No, they began committing what Secretary of State John Kerry labeled "a genocide."

Similarly, when Mohammed saw that the Meccan soldiers had retreated, he was emboldened that his enemies were cowards and unable to subdue him. This began a concept in Islam: when your enemy is strong, retreat; when your enemy is weak, attack. An enemy's weakness is a sign that is Allah giving them to you.

∽

FATE OF JEWISH TRIBES

What happened to the three Jewish tribes who let Mohammed immigrate into Medina?

The first Jewish tribe, Banu Qurayza, did something that offended Mohammed. He accused his hosts of being intolerant – a tactic called psychological projection or blame-shifting, where the attacker blames the victim. He stirred up his followers into a sudden outbreak, they attacked that tribe, and drove them out.

The second Jewish tribe, Banu Nadir did something Mohammed considered offensive. He again stirred his followers into an outbreak of violence. They attacked that tribe, confiscated their property and drove them out.

This set a precedent in Islam called "hudna," which means, when you are weak make treaties until you are strong enough to disregard them.

This tactic is cited by Frederick Leiner in *The End of the Barbary Terror–America's 1815 War Against the Pirates of North Africa* (Oxford Univ. Press, 2006):

> Commodore Stephen Decatur ... withdrew to consult in private ... Algerians were believed to be masters of duplicity, willing to make agreements and break them as they found convenient.

Medina's third Jewish tribe, Banu Qurayza, was bottled in their neighborhood for 25 days. When they surrendered, Mohammed took them into the market and beheaded an estimated 700 men. He sold the women and children into slavery, though he did keep one of the Jewish women, Rayhana, for his personal harem.

Within five years of Mohammed immigrating into the tolerant Jewish city of Medina there was not a Jew left in the city. They were driven out, killed or enslaved.

Within five years of Mohammed's death, every preexisting culture in Arabia was driven out.

It was a three step process. Like Caesar's "veni, vidi, vici" – "I came, I saw, I conquered" – Mohammed's three steps were immigrate, increase, eliminate:

• immigrate as a religious refugee into the host country;

• increase the number of followers among disadvantaged minorities and demand political accommodation, insisting the host community not offend them;

• then eliminate the previous community & civilization with sudden outbreaks of militant violence.

Islam is a religion of peace, but the Islamic definition of the word "peace" is different than the Western definition. In the West, peace is achieved when different groups get along. In Islam, peace is achieved when the world submits to the will of Allah. To a fundamental Muslim, world peace means world Islam.

This is like Abraham Lincoln's statement at the Sanitary Fair in Baltimore, MD, April 18, 1864:

> We all declare for liberty, but in using the same word, we do not all mean the same thing.

✥

ARAB SPRING

The first Arab Spring lasted from 622 AD to 1071 AD, where Mohammed and those called "rightly-guided" Caliphs conquered Yemen, Persia, Pakistan, Afghanistan, and northern India.

Areas they conquered were previously strongholds of Christianity, namely, the Middle East, Egypt, Syria, North Africa, and Spain. Jerusalem had been Christian for three centuries since Emperor Constantine, until Caliph Umar conquered it in 638 AD.

Syria was the first country that was completely Christian, evangelized by the Apostle Paul. The name "Christian" was first used in Syria. In fact, there is more ancient Christian literature in the Syriac language than any other language, other than Greek and Latin.

Syrians Christians had evangelized into Persia, India, Mongolia and even China during the Tang Dynasty around 600 AD. Caliph Umar began to conquer Syria in 641 AD.

Egypt was Christian, having been evangelized by Mark, who wrote the Gospel of Mark, until Muslim Commander Amir ibn Alas invaded in 639 AD.

Pyramid treasures were looted, notably beginning in 832 AD by Caliph al-Ma'mun.

There used to be 250 Catholic dioceses along North Africa in the 6th century, until the Umayyad Muslims conquered them.

The Islamic expansion happened so fast that it devastated Mediterranean trade and the Roman economy. Rome previously traded across the Mediterranean from Italy and Constantinople to North Africa, Egypt and the Middle East.

Suddenly, all trade was halted.

Today's equivalent would be if China and other foreign suppliers held back their ships for a few months. Department store shelves would soon be empty and America's retail economy would grind to a halt.

One of the commodities becoming scarce after Islamic conquests interrupted trade was papyrus.

Papyrus reeds grew along the Nile River delta. They were dried out and used for paper. When Muslims cut off Mediterranean trade, there was a paper shortage in Europe. This led to fewer books being written, a decline in literacy, and the beginning of Europe's Dark Ages.

Muslims warriors were also credited with destroying the oldest library in the world at Alexandria, Egypt, similar to current news reports of ISIS fighters destroying libraries in Iraq.

In the year 711 AD, 80,000 Muslims invaded Spain, riding Arabian horses with stirrups, and fighting with scimitar swords. Europeans were still fighting on foot with heavy swords which took two hands to wield.

In just ten years, all of Spain was conquered.

Over a million Europeans were carried into slavery. Catholic Orders, such as the Trinitarians and Mathurins, were founded to raise money from churches across Europe to ransom back those captured from the coasts of Italy, Spain, France, and the Greek Islands.

Muslim crusaders crossed the Pyrenees Mountains and conquered into Southern France. Pope Gregory put out a plea that anyone who could fight should join Charles Martel, the grandfather of Charlemagne.

Charles Martel assembled 30,000 volunteers, all on foot, and miraculously stopped the Muslim calvary at the Battle of Tours in 732 AD, just 100 years after the death of Mohammed in 632 AD.

This was the first "Arab Spring" – a military campaign conquering from the Arabian desert to near Paris. Had Martel not stopped them, we would be speaking Arabic right now, as German, French, English, and Spanish would have never developed as languages. It would be like Egypt, where the Coptic language became almost extinct.

Theodore Roosevelt addressed the American Sociological Congress in 1916:

> The civilization of Europe, America and Australia exists today ... because of victories stretching through the centuries from Charles Martel ...

> The Christians of Asia and Africa proved unable to wage successful war with the Moslem conquerors; and in consequence Christianity practically vanished from the two continents.

Since these Islamic crusades were carried out by Mohammed and the Rightly Guided Caliphs, Muslims today who want to be more devout strive to follow their example religiously–politically–militarily.

They strive to follow the example of Islam's first century just as devout Christians strive to follow the first century example of Jesus and the Apostles.

∽

TURKISH SPRING

The Turkish Spring began in 1071, when fundamental Muslims, led by Seljuk Sultans, conquered into the Byzantine Christian Empire. All seven churches mentioned in the Book of Revelations were wiped out.

Cities and provinces mentioned in New Testament letters, such as Ephesus, Colossae, Corinth, Galatia, Thessolonica, Philipi, and Antioch, were destroyed.

Sultans conquered lands bordering the Mediterranean sea. Untold thousands were carried away into slavery and harems, and boys were forced into the Muslim pederasty – the sodomy of the Turks.

Persecuted Greek Christians begged the Catholic west for help. This was very humbling for the Eastern Church, as they considered themselves the true Christians. They spoke Greek, the language of the New Testament, and their land was where John and Paul spoke. The Eastern and Western Churches had only recently split in the Great Schism of 1054.

Western Europeans sent help, it was called the Crusades. There were nine major European crusades over the next two centuries.

Richard the Lionheart led the Third Crusade. He had left his brother, King John, in charge of England.

This is the same King John of the Robinhood legends, who was surrounded in 1215 by 25 barons on the fields of Runnymede and forced to sign the Magna Carta, limiting the arbitrary power of a king.

Saint Louis led the Seventh and Eighth Crusades When the Crusades ended, Muslim warriors picked back up where they left off and resumed invading Europe.

While the Europeans had two centuries of crusades to try to reclaim Christian lands, Islam has had fourteen centuries of crusades, which are still continuing.

By 1300, Muslims controlled Spain, Turkey, the Holy Land, North Africa, the Zanzibar Coast, Madagascar, Northern India, Indonesia, and Central Asia.

Christianity was largely wiped out of Central Asia. Muslim leader Tamerlane, or Timur, killed an estimated 17 million. His descendants, Babur and the Mughals, conquered Sikhs, Northern India, and into Indonesia.

Ottomans crossed the Bosporus, where the Black Sea enters into the Mediterranean Sea, and surrounded Constantinople, the ancient capital of the Christian Roman Empire – the gateway to Western Europe.

In the next centuries, they invaded Eastern Europe, conquering Greece, Romania, Bulgaria, Albania, Serbia, Kosovo, Moldova, Transylvania, Walachia, and into Austria, Hungary, Poland, and Russia.

When Sultan Mehmet II conquered Constantinople in 1453, it effectively ended the land routes from Europe to India and China. Prior to Islam's conquests, trade existed between Europe and Asia.

In 1271, Marco Polo had traveled from Venice to China, where he worked for Kublai Khan for years. Polo brought back to Europe tales of Chinese innovations, such as spaghetti noodles, gunpowder, wheelbarrow, piñata, compass, pony express, "China" porcelain plates, and thread from worms – silk worms.

The Chinese had invented paper from tree pulp rather than papyrus reeds. What did the Chinese print with this paper? Currency! The first paper currency in the world was from China, famous during Kublai Khan's Yuan Dynasty.

China was technologically superior to Europe, and India had teas, dyes and spices.

After Tamerlane conquered Central Asia, 1370–1405, and Ottoman Sultans conquered Eastern Europe, culminating with the fall of Constantinople in 1453, the land routes from Europe to India and China were cut off. This inspired Columbus to proposed a sea route.

In 1492, Genoa born Columbus wrote to the King and Queen of Spain in his *Journal of the First Voyage (El Libro de la Primera Navegacion,* recounted in the abstract of Bartolome' de Las Casas, translated by Samuel Eliot Morison, *Journals & Other Documents on the Life & Voyages of Christopher Columbus,* NY: Heritage Press, 1963):

> In this present year 1492, after Your Highnesses had made an end to the war with the Moors who ruled in Europe, and had concluded the war in the very great City of Granada, where in the present year, on the 2nd day of the month of January,
>
> I saw the Royal Standards of Your Highnesses placed by force of arms on the towers of the Alhambra (which is the citadel of the said city),
>
> And I saw the Moorish King come forth to the gates of the city and kiss the Royal Hands of Your Highnesses ...
>
> Soon after in that same month, through information that I had given to Your Highnesses concerning the lands of India, and of a Prince who is called Gran Can [Khan], which is to say in our vernacular "King of Kings," how many times he and his predecessors had sent to Rome to seek doctors in our Holy Faith to instruct him therein, and that never had the Holy Father provided them, and thus so many people were lost through lapsing into idolatries and receiving doctrines of perdition;
>
> And Your Highnesses, as Catholic -Christians and Princes devoted to the Holy Christian Faith and the propagators thereof, and enemies of the sect of Mahomet and of all idolatries and heresies,

WHO IS THE KING IN AMERICA?

resolved to send me, Christopher Columbus, to the said regions of India, to see the said princes and peoples and lands and the dispositions of them and of all, and the manner in which may be undertaken their conversion to our Holy Faith,

And ordained that I should not go by land (the usual way) to the Orient, but by the route of the Occident, by which no one to this day knows for sure that anyone has gone.

Columbus wrote in his Journal, October 10, 1492:

He had come to the Indies, and so had to continue until he found them, with the help of Our Lord.

Columbus thought he had reached India, so he named inhabitants "Indians." In a sense, European impact on Native Americans was collateral damage from the Islamic jihad conquering the trade routes from Europe to India and China.

Politically correct individuals who hate Columbus should turn one chapter back in the pages of history and realize they should actually blame Islamic conquest of the east for motivating Columbus to set sail west.

∽

THE RENAISSANCE

As Muslims invaded Constantinople, Byzantium, and Greece, they destroyed churches, libraries, schools, museums, graves and artwork. Mohammed had stated:

Do not leave an image without obliterating it, or a high grave without leveling it. (Hadith Sahih Muslim, 2115)

Greeks scholars fled west to Florence, Italy, reintroducing their Greek art, architecture and philosophy to western Europe.

This is called "The Renaissance."

President Obama referred to this while giving a speech in Egypt, June 4, 2009:

> It was Islam ... paving the way for Europe's Renaissance.

Jean-Jacques Rousseau (1712–1778), considered the Father of the French Revolution, owned a dog named "Sultan." He wrote in *Discourse on the Arts and Sciences* (1750, translated by Ian Johnston):

> Europe had fallen back into the barbarity ... A revolution was necessary to bring men back to common sense, and it finally came from a quarter where one would least expect it. It was the stupid Muslim, the eternal blight on learning, who brought about its rebirth among us.

> The collapse of the throne of Constantine carried into Italy the debris of ancient Greece. France, in its turn, was enriched by these precious remnants.

> The sciences soon followed letters. To the art of writing was joined the art of thinking.

In retrospect, Islam was responsible for bringing about "The Dark Ages" when it conquered Egypt, cut off trade across the Mediterranean and held back ships of papyrus; and Islam was instrumental in "The Renaissance" when it invaded Greece, destroyed Greek culture, and caused scholars to flee to Italy.

In fact, the very concepts of "Europe" and "Christendom" took shape in response to the Islamic invasion, as previously Europe viewed itself as innumerable independent kingdoms. This was similar to the 13 American colonies having to work together against the King of England, giving birth to the concept of the "united" states.

As the Greek culture was devastated, scholars also carried to the west their Greek New Testaments and ancient Biblical manuscripts. Soon, western European scholars, like Erasmus – a friend of Martin Luther – translated the Bible not just from Latin, but from Greek.

This renewed interest in the original language and meaning of words in Greek New Testament laid the foundation for "The Reformation."

In 1517, Martin Luther began the Reformation by posting Ninety-Five Theses, or debate questions, on the Wittenberg Church door in Saxony, Germany.

Different German kings became Lutheran or "Reformed Christian" and broke away from the Catholic Holy Roman Empire.

In 1529, a hundred thousand Ottoman Muslim warriors surrounded Vienna, Austria, under the command of Sultan Suleiman the Magnificent. He sent suicide bombers at the gates and had miners tunnel under the walls.

Miraculously, Vienna was saved by torrential freezing rain which fell for weeks, resulting in sickness among Suleiman's troops. He abandoned the attack and left, but not before beheading 4,000 Christian hostages.

Suleiman attempted to attack Vienna again in 1532, but was turned back. In 1534, Suleiman led his Ottoman Turkish Sunni Muslims to conquer the Shi'a Muslims of Persia (Iran). He annexed most of the Middle East and huge areas of North Africa, including the Barbary States of Tripoli, Tunisia, Algeria, and Morocco.

Catholic Spain used the gold from the New World to finance the defense of Europe against the Ottoman invasion. Holy Roman Emperor Charles V of Spain, fought Suleiman's ships which attacked the southern coasts of Europe.

In 1535, Charles won a victory against the Muslims at Tunis. Unfortunately, like the West's political disunity prior to the fall of the Byzantine Empire,

France decided in 1536 to begin allying itself with Muslim Sultan Suleiman against Spain's Charles V.

As a result, Charles V was forced to sign a humiliating treaty with the Ottomans, allowing them to gain naval dominance on the Mediterranean Sea.

Later notable battles against the Ottomans include:

- Siege of Malta, September 11, 1565;
- Battle of Lepanto, October 7, 1571;
- Battle of Vienna, September 11, 1683;
- Battle of Zenta, September 11, 1697.

An in depth look at the 1,400 year Islamic conquest is in the book *What Every American Needs to Know about the Qur'an – A History of Islam & the United States.*

❧

EUROPE THREATENED

To understand how seriously Europe felt threatened, it is insightful to read quotes from notable leaders. As recorded in *Luther's Works – American Edition,* 55 volumes (Philadelphia: Fortress; St. Louis: Concordia, 1955–1986, vol. 46:170–171), Martin Luther stated:

> The Turk is the rod of the wrath of the Lord our God ... If the Turk's god, the devil, is not beaten first, there is reason to fear that the Turk will not be so easy to beat ... Christian weapons and power must do it ...

> [The fight against the Turks] must begin with repentance, and we must reform our lives, or we shall fight in vain.

> [The Church should] drive men to repentance by showing our great and numberless sins and our ingratitude, by which we have earned God's wrath and disfavor, so that He justly gives us into the hands of the devil and the Turk.

Luther wrote in *Preface to Book of Revelation* (1530):

2nd woe ... the 6th [evil] angel, the shameful
Mohammed with his companions, the Saracens,
who inflicted great plagues on Christendom,
with his doctrine and with the sword.

In *On War Against the Turk* (1529), Luther wrote:

The Turk is the very devil incarnate ... The
Turk fills heaven with Christians by murdering
their bodies.

In *Luther's Works* (3:121–122), Luther wrote:

Yet it is more in accordance with the truth
to say that the Turk is the Beast, because he is
outside the church and openly persecutes Christ.

Luther wrote (*Tischreden,* 1532, Weimer, ed., 1, 330):

The Turk is the flesh of Antichrist ...
[which] slaughters bodily by the sword.

John Calvin wrote to Philip Melanchthon in 1543
(*Selected Works of John Calvin: Tracts & Letters,* I:373):

I hear of the sad condition of your Germany!
... The Turk again prepares to wage war with a
larger force. Who will stand up to oppose his
marching throughout the length and breadth of
the land, at his mere will and pleasure?

Calvin wrote in *Commentary of 2nd Thessalonians:*

Since Mohammed was an apostate, he
turned his followers, the Turks, from Christ...

The sect of Mohammed was like a raging
overflow, which in its violence tore away about
half of the Church.

John Calvin wrote in *Commentary on Daniel:*

Turks have spread far and wide, and the
world is filled with impious despisers of God.

John Calvin wrote in *Sermons on Timothy & Titus:*

The Turks at this day, can allege and say
for themselves: "We serve God from our
ancestors!" – It is a good while since Mahomet

gave them the cup of his devilish dreams to drink, and they got drunk with them. It is about a thousand years since cursed hellhounds were made drunk with their follies –

Let us be wise and discreet! – For otherwise, we shall be like the Turks and Heathen.

John Calvin wrote in *Institutes of the Christian Religion* (Book II, Chapter VI):

For even if many men once boasted that they worshiped ... the Maker of heaven and earth, yet because they had no Mediator it was not possible for them truly to taste God's mercy, and thus be persuaded that he was their Father ...

So today the Muslim Turks, although they proclaim at the top of their lungs that the Creator of heaven and earth is God, still, while repudiating Christ, substitute an idol in place of the true God.

Methodist founder John Wesley wrote in *The Doctrine of Original Sin* (1817, p. 35; *Works,* 1841, ix. 205):

Let us now calmly and impartially consider what manner of men the Mahometans in general are ...

Men who have but a moderate share of reason, cannot but observe in his Koran ... the most gross and impious absurdities ... Who can swallow such absurdities as divinely revealed.

Mahometans not only condemn all who cannot swallow them to everlasting fire; not only appropriate to themselves the title of ... true believers: but even anathematise ... all their brethren ... who contend for a figurative interpretation ...

That these men then have no knowledge or love of God is undeniably manifest, not only from their gross, horrible notions of him, but from their not loving their brethren...

Mahometans will butcher each other by thousands ... Why is it that such numbers of Turks and Persians have stabbed one another in cool blood?

Truly, because they differ in the manner of dressing their head. The Ottoman vehemently maintains ... that a Mussulman should wear a round turban ... whereas the Persian insists upon his liberty of conscience, and will wear it picked before.

So, for this wonderful reason ... they beat out each other's brains from generation to generation.

Wesley concluded:

Ever since the religion of Mahomet appeared in the world, the espousers of it, particularly those under the Turkish emperor, have been as wolves and tigers to all other nations; rending and tearing all that fell into their merciless paws, and grinding them with their iron teeth ...

Numberless cities are razed from the foundation, and only their name remaining ... Many countries which were once as the garden of God, are now a desolate wilderness... Such was, and is at this day, the rage, the fury, the revenge, of these destroyers of humankind!

Jonathan Edwards, first President of Princeton, wrote in *A History of the Work of Redemption* (1739):

Those mighty kingdoms of Antichrist and Mohammed ... trampled the world under foot ... Great works of the devil ... swallowed up the Ancient Roman Empire ... Satan's Mohometan kingdom [swallowed] the Eastern Empire.

Jonathan Edwards stated in *The Fall of Antichrist* (1829, NY: S. Converse pub., part vii, p. 395):

By the false prophet ... here an eye seems to be had to Mahomet, whom his followers call the great prophet of God. [Revelation 16:13]

In 1258, two centuries before the Reformation, Thomas Aquinas wrote *Summa contra Gentiles* (translated by Anton C. Pegis, University of Notre Dame Press, 1975). He wrote in Book 1, Chapter 6:

> Mohammed ... seduced the people by promises of carnal pleasure to which the concupiscence of the flesh goads us ... and he gave free reign to carnal pleasure. In all this, as is not unexpected, he was obeyed by carnal men.

> As for proofs of the truth of his doctrine, he brought forward only such as could be grasped by the natural ability of anyone with a very modest wisdom.

> Indeed, the truths that he taught he mingled with many fables and doctrines of the greatest falsity. He did not bring forth any signs produced in a supernatural way, which alone fittingly gives witness to divine inspiration ...

> On the contrary, Mohammed said that he was sent in the power of his arms – which are signs not lacking even to robbers and tyrants ...

> Those who believed in him were brutal men and desert wanderers, utterly ignorant of all divine teaching, through whose numbers Mohammed forced others to become his followers by the violence of his arms ...

> He perverts almost all the testimonies of the Old and New Testaments by making them into fabrications of his own, as can be seen by anyone who examines his law.

> It was, therefore, a shrewd decision on his part to forbid his followers to read the Old and New Testaments, lest these books convict him of falsity ... Those who place any faith in his words believe foolishly.

Voltaire (1694–1778) wrote to Pope Benedict XIV of his play *Fanaticism, or Mahomet,* August 17, 1745:

> Your holiness will pardon the liberty taken by ... this performance written in opposition to the founder of a false and barbarous sect. To whom could I with more propriety inscribe a satire on the cruelty and errors of a false prophet.

Voltaire wrote to Frederick II of Prussia, December 1740, referring to Muhammad:

> But that a camel-merchant should stir up insurrection in his village; that in league with some miserable followers he persuades them that he talks with the angel Gabriel;
>
> that he boasts of having been carried to heaven, where he received in part this unintelligible book, each page of which makes common sense shudder;
>
> that, to pay homage to this book, he delivers his country to iron and flame; that he cuts the throats of fathers and kidnaps daughters;
>
> that he gives to the defeated the choice of his religion or death:
>
> this is assuredly nothing any man can excuse, at least if he was not born a Turk, or if superstition has not extinguished all natural light in him.

Montesquieu wrote in *The Spirit of the Laws* (1748):

> Moderate government is most agreeable to the Christian Religion, and a despotic government to the Mahometan ...
>
> While the Mahommedan princes incessantly give or receive death, the religion of the Christians renders their prince ... less cruel. The Christian religion ... has hindered despotic power ...
>
> From the characters of the Christian and Mahometan religions, we ought, without any

further examination, to embrace the one and reject the other:

The Mahometan Religion, which speaks only by the sword, acts still upon men with that destructive spirit with which it was founded.

Scottish philosopher David Hume (1711–1776) wrote in *Of the Standard of Taste* (1760):

Followers of the Alcoran [Qur'an] insist on the excellent moral precepts interspersed through that wild and absurd performance.

It is to be supposed, that the Arabic words, which correspond to the English, equity, justice, temperance, meekness, charity ... must always be taken in a good sense ... But would we know, whether the pretended prophet had really attained a just sentiment of morals?

Let us attend to his narration; and we shall soon find, that he bestows praise on such instances of treachery, inhumanity, cruelty, revenge, bigotry, as are utterly incompatible with civilized society.

No steady rule of right seems there to be attended to; and every action is blamed or praised, so far only as it is beneficial or hurtful to the true believers.

∾

PEACE OF AUGSBURG

The most powerful man in the Western World was Charles V of Spain. Being the Catholic Holy Roman Emperor, he exercised controlled over most of Europe, as well as areas in the Americas and the Philippines.

Charles V was faced with a double dilemma:

1) Protestant Reformation on one hand;

2) Muslim invasion on the other hand.

As the Turks rapidly advanced up the Danube River, Charles V of Spain decided to strike a deal with the

Protestants. In 1532, an initial truce was negotiated in Nuremburg. Then in 1555, Charles V negotiated the monumental Peace of Augsburg.

Eric W. Gritisch wrote in *Martin – God's Court Jester: Luther in Retrospect* (Philadelphia: Fortress, 1983, p. 69–70):

> Afraid of losing the much-needed support of the German princes for the struggle against the Turkish threat from the south, Emperor Charles V agreed to a truce between Protestant and Catholic territories ...

> Thus the Lutheran movement was, for the first time, officially tolerated and could enjoy a place in the political sun of the Holy Roman Empire.

The Peace of Augsburg in 1555, which was the first treaty to recognize Protestants, contained a little Latin phrase that had enormous repercussions across Europe: "curios regio eius religio," which meant "whose is the reign his is the religion."

In other words, the Treaty allowed each king to decide what would be believed in his kingdom if they agreed to work together to stop the Islamic invasion.

❧

EUROPE'S ESTABLISHED CHURCHES

The Peace of Augsburg started a ripple effect across Europe, where, in the succeeding years, different kings chose different denominations of Christianity for their kingdoms. A partial list includes:

- ITALY, SPAIN, PORTUGAL, AUSTRIA, POLAND, LIECHTENSTEIN, LITHUANIA, LUXEMBOURG, MALTA, MONACO were Roman Catholic.

- HUNGARY was a majority Catholic with Calvinist, Lutheran and Hungarian Byzantine–Catholic minorities.

• FRANCE established the Roman Catholic Church. Dissenters were Protestant Huguenots.

• IRELAND established the Church of Ireland (Anglican) till 1871. Dissenting Catholics, made up a majority of the population, especially in south.

• SWITZERLAND established Calvinist Church in the eastern cantons and the Roman Catholic Church in the western cantons.

• GERMANY was numerous kingdoms (Prussia, Saxony, Bavaria, etc.) The Lutheran Church was established in northern kingdoms. Dissenters included Anabaptists, called Mennonites & Amish.

• THE NETHERLANDS (Holland) established the Dutch Reformed Church, with liberal toleration of dissenters, in the north and the Roman Catholic Church in the south.

• BELGIUM established the Roman Catholic Church. Dissenters in the north were Anglicans and Protestants.

• SWEDEN established the Church of Sweden (Evangelical Lutheran).

• DENMARK established the Church of Denmark (Evangelical Lutheran).

• FINLAND established the Church of Finland (Evangelical Lutheran).

• NORWAY established the Church of Norway (Evangelical Lutheran).

• ICELAND established the Church of Iceland (Evangelical Lutheran).

• ROMANIA established the Romanian Orthodox Church.

• SERBIA established the Serbian Orthodox Church.

• CROATIA was mostly Roman Catholic and Croatian Greek Catholic.

• GREECE established the Greek Orthodox Church.

- RUSSIA established the Russian Orthodox Church.
- BULGARIA established the Bulgarian Orthodox Church.
- ARMENIA established the Armenian Apostolic Church.
- CYPRESS was mostly Cypriot Orthodox, with a Sunni Muslim minority.
- SCOTLAND established the Church of Scotland (Presbyterian)
- ENGLAND established the Church of England (Anglican). Dissenters were Puritans, Separatists and Quakers.

In Europe during the 1500–1800s, only one denomination was allowed or preferred in each country. It was whatever a king believed – his kingdom had to believe. If someone believed differently than their king, they were considered guilty of treason.

England's King James I enforced religious uniformity or he would "harry them out of the land."

This resulted, in the following centuries, wars, displaced peoples, and mass migrations across Europe, simply for conscience sake.

A typical "established" church was supported by:

1) Mandatory attendance;

2) Mandatory tithes; and

3) One could not hold public office unless they were a faithful member of the established denomination.

In most cases, church leaders were selected or approved by government leaders, being paid salaries by the government. Dissenters, nonconformists, and Jews, suffered disadvantages, were taxed, penalized, punished, persecuted, banished or killed.

For example, the English Corporation Act of 1661, which was not repealed until 1828, required all members of corporations to receive the Lord's Supper according to the rites of the Church of England. The Test Acts of 1673 and 1678 allowed only faithful members of the Church of England to hold civil or military office.

In the Supreme Court case *Pollock v. Farmers' Loan & Trust Co.* (1895), Justice Stephen J. Field concurred that income tax was unconstitutional, being:

> ... the same in essential character as that of the English income statute of 1691, which taxed Protestants at a certain rate, Catholics, as a class, at double the rate of Protestants, and Jews at another and separate rate.

Queen Anne's Test Act of 1703 did not allow Nonconformists, particularly Catholics, to vote, or be members of the Bar, or jurors, or parish vestrymen, or own a weapon. Catholics could not own a horse worth more than £5, nor buy, inherit or receive land as a gift, and their children were denied education.

The Act even permitted sheriffs to ransack their homes upon suspicion of owning a weapon, and if found, they were fined, whipped or imprisoned.

After the Peace of Westphalia in 1648, most countries of Europe had established, or officially gave preference, to a particular denomination. Eventually, some of these displaced Christian refugees spilled over and founded colonies in America.

America had been claimed by Spain since the time of Columbus' discovery, calling it New Spain.

Following the massive victory over the Ottoman Turks at the Battle of Lepanto, Spain and the other European powers began to bicker, and the "Holy League" dissolved. Spain's opportunity to capitalize on the victory and free the rest of the Mediterranean from Muslim domination was squandered.

Now Spain turned its attention to stop the spread of the Protestant Reformation by committing the "Spanish Furies" in the Netherlands, and sending its invincible Armada to capture England and Holland in 1588.

Spain sent 130 ships to the English Channel, carrying 18,000 soldiers, 7,000 sailors, 1,500 brass guns and 1,000 iron guns. They planned to pick up an additional 30,000 Spanish soldiers from the Netherlands on their way to invade Queen Elizabeth's England.

The English and Dutch had smaller, more maneuverable vessels which proved difficult for the Spanish to catch. English and Dutch ships lured Spanish ships to chase them into shallow waters where they became stuck on sand bars.

Sir Francis Drake dispersed the Spanish fleet by waiting till night and floating burning ships downwind toward where they were anchored. In the confusion, the Armada was scattered. A timely hurricane destroyed two dozen more Spanish ships.

With Spain's Armada gone, its dominance of the seas declined and its monopoly on colonizing the New World ended. Soon England, Holland, Sweden, and France began colonies in America.

Adam Smith wrote in *The Wealth of Nations* (1776):

> The Spaniards, by virtue of the first discovery, claimed all America as their own, and ... such was ... the terror of their name, that the greater part of the other nations of Europe were afraid to establish themselves in any other part of that great continent ...

> But ... the defeat ... of their Invincible Armada ... put it out of their power to obstruct any longer the settlements of the other European nations. In the course of the 17th century ... English, French, Dutch, Danes, and Swedes ... attempted to make some settlements in the new world.

A CLOSER LOOK AT ENGLAND

England's Reformation began with Henry VIII in the 1530s, not because he had a spiritual experience like Martin Luther, but because he wanted another wife.

He was married to Catherine of Aragon, daughter of King Ferdinand and Queen Isabella of Spain, who sent Columbus to America. After eighteen years, Catherine did not produce a male heir, so Henry decided to divorce her.

The Pope refused to recognize the divorce on scriptural grounds, though some speculate it may have been, at least in part, influenced by the fact she was the daughter of the most powerful man in the world at the time – the King of Spain, whose soldiers that same year, 1527, had ransacked Rome and imprisoned the Pope for six months.

Henry VIII declared himself the head of the Church of England and granted himself permission to divorce. He eventually had six wives, and their fates were: divorced, beheaded, died, divorced, beheaded, survived.

Henry's advisors, such as Thomas Cromwell, suggested that to finalize his break with Rome, England should stop using the Latin Bible, and instead use an English Bible – so people would look to England for their spiritual heritage instead of Rome. Henry liked the idea and circulated the English *Matthew–Coverdale Bible,* which relied heavily on William Tyndale's work.

But something unexpected happened – people began to read it, and compare the actions of King Henry to what was in the Book. A movement arose to "purify" the Church of England, being nicknamed "Puritans."

The King obviously did not think he needed "purifying," so he persecuted them.

Years later, King Charles I's Anglican Archbishop, William Laud, had an obsession for uniformity.

Laud published a new *Book of Common Prayer* to standardize worship in England, derogatorily referred to as "Laud's liturgy." Like modern-day threats of the IRS, he sent spies into churches to enforce its observance.

Laud purged academia of all Puritans and in 1625 compiled a list of churchmen, placing an "O" for Orthodox beside the names of those to be promoted, and a "P" for Puritan of those not to be.

The Test Act of 1673 effectively barred non Anglicans from office by requiring public office holders to receive the sacraments in the Church of England.

Voltaire wrote in his *Letters Concerning the English Nation* (1733):

> No one can hold office in England or in Ireland unless he is a faithful Anglican.

Another group gave up hope of trying to "purify" the Church of England. They were called "Separatists" because they met in secret, at night, by candlelight, in barns and basements, similar to illegal house churches in China or North Korea. These Separatists were punished by being put in stocks, whipped, imprisoned or even branded as heretics.

In 1607, the Separatists, who came to be called "Pilgrims," fled to Holland, where they lived for twelve years. Seeing their children assimilating into the Dutch culture, they realized they would be a short-lived movement unless they did something – so they sailed to America in 1620.

Governor William Bradford wrote in his *History of the Plymouth Settlement* (1650):

> They shook off this yoke of anti-christian bondage, and as the Lord's free people, joined

themselves by a covenant of the Lord into a church estate in the fellowship of the gospel, to walk in all His ways, made known unto them, according to their best endeavors, whatsoever it should cost them, the Lord assisting them.

Ronald Reagan spoke of the Pilgrims in his National Day of Prayer Proclamation, March 19, 1981:

The earliest settlers of this land came in search of religious freedom. Landing on a desolate shoreline, they established a spiritual foundation that has served us ever since.

It was the hard work of our people, the freedom they enjoyed and their faith in God that built this country and made it the envy of the world.

These Pilgrims, through much hardship, built a successful colony in America, which encouraged the Puritans back in England, who were experiencing increased persecution, to come to America's shores.

Though not as severe as Islamic Sharia Law, it is difficult for modern society to imagine the abuse of power with the king as the head of the Anglican Church and religious leaders under his control. This, though, was the only frame of reference for America's settlers.

When this background is properly understood, certain quotations of founders which appear critical of faith were actually critical of the corruptions resulting from church leaders being regulated by the government.

On September 16, 1620, according to the Gregorian Calendar, 102 passengers set sail on the Pilgrims' ship, *Mayflower,* with the blessings of their separatist pastor, John Robinson. Their 66–day journey of 2,750 miles encountered storms so rough the beam supporting the main mast cracked and was propped back in place with "a great iron screw."

One youth, John Howland, was swept overboard by

a freezing wave and rescued. His descendants include Ralph Waldo Emerson, Humphrey Bogart, Franklin D. Roosevelt and George W. Bush. During the Pilgrims' voyage, a man died and a mother gave birth.

The Pilgrims intended to land in Virginia and submit its king-appointed government, but a storm blew them off-course to Massachusetts. As the weather was too dangerous, the captain insisted they disembark.

This caused a dilemma, as there was no "king-appointed" person on board to take charge. To solve this, the Pilgrims did something unprecedented – they gave themselves the authority and created their own government – The Mayflower Compact.

Where did the Pilgrims get this idea? From their separatist Pastor John Robinson, who is considered one of the founders of the Congregational Church.

The word "compact" or "commonwealth" refers to a group of people in "covenant" with each other, a concept studied by Reformation scholars John Calvin, Huldrych Zwingli, Thomas Cromwell, John Knox, Scottish Covenanters, and translators of the Geneva Bible.

Jesus stated in Matthew 16:18, "… upon this rock I will build My church (ekklesia); and the gates of Hades will not overpower it."

In another place, Jesus stated "If he refuses to listen to them, tell it to the church (ekklesia); and if he refuses to listen even to the church (ekklesia), let him be to you as a gentile and a tax collector." (Matthew 18:17.)

Ekklesia was a Greek word meaning: a called-out assembly; a gathering of citizens called out from their homes into some public place; an assembly of the people convened at the public place of the council for the purpose of deliberating; assembly of the Israelites.

King James reportedly insisted the word "ekklesia" be translated "church" rather than "assembly" or "congregation," so as to back his claim of being its head.

๛

PILGRIM PASTOR JOHN ROBINSON

Pastor Robinson is prominently depicted kneeling in prayer in a painting hanging in the U.S. Capitol Rotunda – *The Embarkation of the Pilgrims.*

Of the Pilgrims' landing at Plymouth, Massachusetts, Governor William Bradford wrote:

> Being thus arrived in a good harbor, and brought safe to land, they fell upon their knees and blessed the God of Heaven who had brought them over the vast and furious ocean, and delivered them from all the perils and miseries thereof, again to set their feet on the firm and stable earth, their proper element.

Though half died that first bitter winter, Governor William Bradford wrote:

> Last and not least, they cherished a great hope and inward zeal of laying good foundations ... for the propagation and advance of the gospel of the kingdom of Christ in the remote parts of the world.

"Covenant" theology was held by colonial leaders. John D. Eusden wrote in "Natural Law and Covenant Theology in New England, 1620–1670" (Notre Dame Law School, *Natural Law Forum.* 1960, Paper 47):

> The idea of the covenant – that central, permeating idea of Puritanism ... Covenanted men actually constructed political communities – the emerging "American character" in the realm of governmental theory and jurisprudence...

> Names dominate the dramatis personae: John Cotton, influential minister of the First Church in Boston ... John Winthrop, long-time governor of the Massachusetts Bay Colony

... Nathaniel Ward, chief framer of the 1641 Body of Liberties for the Bay Colony; William Bradford, governor of Plymouth Plantation; Thomas Hooker, preacher and potentate of Hartford; John Norton, official apologist for New England Congregationalism; John Eliot, evangelist and occasional political writer; and John Davenport, founder of New Haven ...

Political and social thought of early American Puritanism was drawn from four sources: the Bible, the covenant tradition in Reformation theology, the common law of England, and the long Western tradition of natural law."

Puritans back in England attempted to have a covenant government, called "Commonwealth," in 1649, led by Lord Protector Oliver Cromwell. After a decade, though, King Charles II was restored to the throne. Os Guinness stated in an interview on "Thinking in Public" with Dr. Albert Mohler, June 5, 2017:

The covenantal ideas in England were the lost cause, sadly. They failed. The king came back. But the lost cause became the winning cause in New England. And covenant shaped constitutionalism ...

The American Constitution is a nationalized, secularized form of covenant ... Covenant lies behind constitution.

To the Protestant Reformers of the 16th century, the perfect example of a nation with a "covenant"form of government was Ancient Israel– a group of people in agreement with each other under God. Their rights came from God and they were accountable to God.

In the 17th century, during the Age of Enlightenment, "covenant" evolved into "social contract"–a group of people in agreement with each other, with or without God.

In the 18th century, the French Revolution morphed

"social contract" into intentionally excluding God. Rights came from the group and people are accountable to the group. This culminated in a bloody Reign of Terror, 1789–1794, against those who resisted the group.

Ironically, the group never really decides, but rather those who control the information and propaganda the group receives:

- the country is controlled by laws;
- laws are controlled by politicians;
- politicians are controlled by voters;
- voters are controlled by public opinion;
- public opinion is controlled by media & education;
- therefore, whoever controls media & education controls the country.

The flaw of the social contract was displayed at the Nuremburg Trials of 1945–1946, where the Nazi officials who killed 6 million Jews in the Holocaust defended their actions by explaining they were only following laws agreed upon by the people of Germany.

To remedy this, an appeal was made to a "higher law," namely, rules agreed upon by all the nations of the world. Eleanor Roosevelt proudly helped compose the U.N. Declaration of Human Rights in 1948. It listed rights all nations agreed on, such as freedom of religion and that women are equal to men, but nowhere did the document reference the Creator as the source of rights.

The naiveté of this effort was revealed when a U.N. subgroup of 57 Muslim countries formed the OIC–Organization of Islamic Cooperation. On June 30, 2000, the OIC rejected the U.N. Declaration of Human Rights to embrace their own "superior" Cairo Declaration on Human Rights in Islam, which allowed for beating of women and killing of apostates.

If laws are simply what a group agrees upon, what

is wrong with them agreeing upon sharia law?

Secretary of State Daniel Webster defended the Judeo–Christian concept of "covenant" at the Bicentennial Celebration of the Pilgrims' Landing at Plymouth Rock, December 22, 1820:

> There is a ... sort of genius of the place, which ... awes us. We feel that we are on the spot where the first scene of our history was laid; where the hearths and altars of New England were first placed; where Christianity, and civilization ... made their first lodgement, in a vast extent of country ...

> "If God prosper us," might have been the ... language of our fathers, when they landed upon this Rock, "... we shall here begin a work which shall last for ages ... We shall fill this region of the great continent ... with civilization and Christianity."

Webster continued:

> The morning that beamed ... saw the Pilgrims already at home ... a government and a country were to commence, with the very first foundations laid under the divine light of the Christian religion ...

> Our ancestors established their system of government on morality and religious sentiment ... Whatever makes men good Christians, makes them good citizens.

> Our fathers came here to enjoy their religion free and unmolested; and, at the end of two centuries, there is nothing upon which we can pronounce more confidently ... than of the inestimable importance of that religion to man.

In regards to America's founding, Franklin D. Roosevelt stated October 28, 1936:

> Rulers ... increase their power over the common men. The seamen they sent to find

gold found instead the way of escape for the common man from those rulers ...

What they found over the Western horizon was not the silk and jewels of Cathay but MANKIND'S SECOND CHANCE – a chance to create a new world after he had almost spoiled an old one ...

The Almighty seems purposefully to have withheld that SECOND CHANCE until the time when men would most need and appreciate liberty ... Those who came ... had courage ... to abandon language and relatives ... to start ... without influence, without money ...

Perhaps Providence did prepare this American continent to be a place of the SECOND CHANCE.

Daniel Webster concluded his 1820 address:

Whoever shall hereafter write this part of our history ... will be able to record no ... lawless and despotic acts, or any successful usurpation. His page will contain no exhibition of ... civil authority habitually trampled down by military power, or of a community crushed by the burden of taxation ...

He will speak ... of that happy condition, in which the restraint and coercion of government are almost invisible and imperceptible ...

Let us not forget the religious character of our origin. Our fathers were brought hither by their high veneration for the Christian religion. They journeyed by its light, and labored in its hope.

They sought to incorporate its principles with the elements of their society, and to diffuse its influence through all their institutions, civil, political, or literary.

The Plymouth Rock Foundation was founded in 1970 with the mission:

To make more widely known and understood the Pilgrim principles and characteristics – their devotion to God and the Bible, to freedom and to tolerance, and their embodiment of courage, brotherhood, and individual moral character.

Dr. Paul Jehle, Executive Director of the Plymouth Rock Foundation, whose ancestors were on the Mayflower, wrote "Mayflower Compact Day" (*Plymouth Rock Foundation's E–News,* November, 2011):

We remember when the Mayflower Compact was signed on board the *Mayflower,* while it lay anchored in what is now Provincetown Harbor, November 11, 1620 ...

A compact is a covenant ... Since the Pilgrims were children of the Reformation, their view of covenant came from the Bible.

It was God that initiated the concept of covenant, first with Adam and Eve (Genesis 2:15–17 and 2:24).God also made a covenant with Noah in Genesis 9 and of course the process of "cutting" covenant was depicted in visual form for Abraham in Genesis 15.

Throughout the Bible covenants were used both vertically (with God directly) and horizontally (with humans) to depict God's process of bringing people into unity with Him and one another.

Unity of purpose and harmony with God set the highest ideals for good behavior.

Dr. Jehle continued:

No wonder when Pastor John Robinson sent his farewell letter to the Pilgrims upon their departure in 1620, knowing that they would need to form their own civil government, he gave this sound advice:

"Whereas you are become a body politic, using amongst yourselves civil government, and are not furnished with any persons of special eminency above the rest, to be chosen by you into office of government; let your wisdom and godliness appear, not only in choosing such persons as do entirely love and will promote the common good ... not being like the foolish multitude who more honor the gay coat than either the virtuous mind of the man, or glorious ordinance of the Lord."

The question the founders wrestled with was does POWER flow from:

> the Creator > to the King > to the People;

or does POWER flow from:

> the Creator > to the People > to their Representatives?

Dr. Marshall Foster of the World History Institute), co-produced Kirk Cameron's 2012 film *Monumental: In Search of America's National Treasure.* Dr. Foster wrote in "A Shining City on a Hill" (Feb. 27, 2013):

> 400 years ago the conflict between tyranny and liberty was red hot ... When King James died in 1625, his son Charles I ascended to the throne with the arrogance of a Roman emperor.
>
> He was the quintessential "divine right" monarch. He declared martial law and suspended the rights of the individual ... The king's inquisitors at his "Star Chamber" in the tower of London used torture techniques to "discover the taxpayer's assets" ...
>
> A turning point in public opinion took place on January 30, 1637. Three prisoners were locked down in the pillory in London before a huge crowd ... These men included a Puritan minister, a Christian writer and Dr. John Bastwick, a physician.
>
> What was their crime? They had written pamphlets disagreeing with the king's religious views. The sheriff began by branding the men

with red hot irons on the forehead with an SL for seditious libel.

Dr. Foster continued:

> The tyranny of the king ... finally aroused the Christian sensibilities of the people. They would no longer tolerate burnings or mutilations for matters of conscience on religious views ...

> The persecutions drove tens of thousands of liberty loving believers to follow the Pilgrims to New England where they laid the foundation for the world's most biblically based nation.

Ten years after the Pilgrims arrived in America, Puritans fled the persecutions in England and began arriving in New England in 1630. In the following 16 year period, called the Great Migration, 20,000 Puritans settled in Massachusetts, being led by John Winthrop.

John Winthrop authored his work, *A Model of Christian Charity*, June 11, 1630, which became a guideline for colonial constitutional "covenants":

> It is of the nature and essence of every society to be knit together by some covenant, either expressed or implied ... We are a Company, professing ourselves fellow members of Christ, we ought to account ourselves knit together by this bond of love ...

> It is by a mutual consent through a special overruling Providence ... to seek out a place of Cohabitation ... under a due form of Government both civil and ecclesiastical ...

> Thus stands the cause between God and us: we are entered into covenant with Him for this work. We have taken out a Commission; the Lord hath given us leave to draw our own articles ...

> For this end, we must be knit together in this work as one man ... We must delight in each other, make one another's condition our

own, rejoice together, mourn together, labor and suffer together, always having before our eyes our Commission and Community in this work, as members of the same body. So shall we keep the unity of the Spirit in the bond of peace ...

We shall find that the God of Israel is among us, when ten of us shall be able to resist a thousand of our enemies, when He shall make us a praise and glory, that men of succeeding plantations shall say, "The Lord make it like that of New England." For we must Consider that we shall be as a City upon a Hill, the eyes of all people are upon us ...

John Winthrop ended with a warning:

If we shall deal falsely with our God in this work we have undertaken and so cause him to withdraw his present help from us, we shall be made a story and a by-word through the world, we shall open the mouths of enemies to speak evil of the ways of God and all professors for God's sake; we shall shame the faces of many of God's worthy servants, and cause their prayers to be turned into curses upon us till we be consumed out of the good land whether we are going.

In 1702, Puritan leader Cotton Mather published a history of New England's first 50 years, *Magnalia Christi Americana* (*Great Achievement of Christ in America*):

From the beginning of the Reformation in the English nation, there had always been a generation of godly men, desirous to pursue the reformation of religion, according to the Word of God ... (though resisted by individuals with) power in their hands ... not only to stop the progress of the desired reformation but also, with innumerable vexation, to persecute those that heartily wish well unto it ...

The Puritans were driven to seek a place for the exercise of the Protestant religion, according to the light of conscience, in the deserts of America.

Puritan John Higginson (1616–1708) gave an *Election Sermon – The Cause of God & His People in New England* (1663):

> My Fathers and Brethren, this is never to be forgotten – that New England is originally a plantation of religion, not a plantation of trade.

Henry Wilson (1812–1875), was Vice-President under Ulysses Grant. He told the Young Men's Christian Association, Natick, Massachusetts, December 23, 1866:

> God has given us an existence in this Christian republic, founded by men who proclaim as their living faith, amid persecution and exile:
>
> "We give ourselves to the Lord Jesus Christ and the Word of His Grace, for the teaching, ruling and sanctifying of us in matters of worship and conversation."
>
> Privileged to live in an age when the selectest influences of the religion of our fathers seem to be visibly descending upon our land, we too often hear the Providence of God, the religion of our Lord and Saviour Jesus Christ, the inspiration of the Holy Bible doubted, questioned, denied with an air of gracious condescension.
>
> Remember ever, and always, that your country was founded, not by the "most superficial, the lightest, the most irreflective of all European races," but by the stern old Puritans who made the deck of the *Mayflower* an altar of the living God, and whose first act on touching the soil of the new world was to offer on bended knees thanksgiving to Almighty God.

George Bancroft (1800–1891), was Secretary of Navy under President Polk. He established the U.S. Naval Academy at Annapolis and the Naval

Observatory in Washington, D.C. Bancroft wrote in *History of the United States* (1834–1876):

> Puritanism had exalted the laity ... For him the wonderful counsels of the Almighty had appointed a Saviour; for him the laws of nature had been compelled and consulted, the heavens had opened, the earth had quaked, the sun had veiled his face, and Christ had died and risen again.

Harvard Professor James Russell Lowell (1819–1891), was U.S. Minister to Spain and editor of the *Atlantic Monthly* and *North American Review*. In *Literary Essays* (1810–1890), Lowell wrote "New England Two Centuries Ago":

> Puritanism, believing itself quick with the seed of religious liberty, laid, without knowing it, the egg of democracy.

∽

PURITAN RELIGIOUS UNIFORMITY LED TO OTHER SETTLEMENTS

After Puritans settled Massachusetts, they extended religious toleration only to Puritans. Their fear was that if other denominations were tolerated, they might gain ascendancy and persecute Puritans again – a memory still fresh in their minds from England. Puritans had a kind of "us–versus–them" mentality.

Though Puritans did not like the government controlling their churches in England, they favored it in America, as they were in charge of the government.

Justice Hugo Black wrote in *Engel v. Vitale* (1962):

> When some of the very groups which had most strenuously opposed the established Church of England found themselves sufficiently in control of colonial governments ... they passed laws making their own religion the official religion of their respective colonies.

In his Election Sermon, 1672, Rev. Thomas Shepherd described tolerance as "having its origin with the devil."

Harvard President Urian Oakes described tolerance in his Election Sermon, 1673, as "The first of all abominations."

When Boston's Puritan leader, Rev. John Cotton, enforced religious conformity, dissenting pastors and their churches fled, founding new communities.

A generation before Europe's "Age of Enlightenment" and John Locke's *Two Treatise on Government* (1680–1690), Scotland's Presbyterian "Covenanters" championed the Old Testament model of Israel's covenant with God. This idea came to New England with pastors who founded communities:

> • Rev. John Wheelwright founded Exeter, New Hampshire in 1638;
>
> • Rev. John Lothropp founded Barnstable, Massachusetts in 1639;
>
> • Rev. Roger Williams founded Providence, Rhode Island in 1636;
>
> • Rev. Thomas Hooker founded Hartford, Connecticut in 1636.

❧

REV. JOHN WHEELWRIGHT (1592–1679)

Rev. John Wheelwright was banished from Boston in 1637 for his religious opinions. He fled with some adherents and founded Exeter, New Hampshire, in 1638. When the Puritans assumed control over New Hampshire, he fled again to Maine.

❧

REV. JOHN LOTHROPP (1584–1653)

Rev. John Lothropp and his followers, called "Independents," were arrested in England in 1632, being prosecuted for not taking the oath of loyalty to the established Anglican church. His wife died while he was in prison and his children had to beg.

Released in 1634, he sailed to America, where according to John Winthrop's journal, he was glad to find a "church without a bishop ... and a state without a king." Lothropp asked Governor Thomas Prence for a "place for the transplanting of us, to the end that God might have more glory and we more comfort."

In 1639, Lothropp and his church members founded Barnstable, Massachusetts. His descendants include six U.S. Presidents.

◌

REV. ROGER WILLIAMS (1603–1683)

Rev. Roger Williams had "notorious disagreements" with the Puritan leader Rev. John Cotton over whether the government should control the church. As a result, Williams was banished in 1636. He fled and founded Providence, Rhode Island, writing in 1641:

> The Government ... in this island ... is a Popular Government; that is to say, it is in the Power of the Body of Freemen orderly assembled.

Williams, with Dr. John Clarke, founded the first Baptist Church in America. One of the founders of the Baptist faith in England was Thomas Helwys, who died in the notorious Newgate Prison. Helwys wrote in 1612:

> The King is a mortal man, and not God, therefore he hath no power over the mortal soul of his subjects to make laws and ordinances for them and to set spiritual Lords over them ...

> If the King's people obey all humane laws made by the King, our lord the King can require no more ... For men's religion to God is betwixt God and themselves; the King shall not answer for it, neither may the King be judge between God and man.

A later Baptist preacher, John Leland, wrote in *Rights of Conscience Inalienable,* 1791:

> Every man must give account of himself to God, and therefore every man ought to be at liberty to serve God in a way that he can best reconcile to his conscience.

> If government can answer for individuals at the day of judgment, let men be controlled by it in religious matters; otherwise, let men be free.

Roger Williams wrote *The Bloody Tenet [Practice] of Persecution for Conscience Sake* in 1644, stating:

> Mr. Cotton ... hath not duly considered these following particulars ... That the Church of the Jews under the Old Testament in the type and the Church of the Christians under the New Testament in the anti-type, were both SEPARATE from the world;

> and that when they have opened a gap in the hedge, or WALL OF SEPARATION, between the garden of the Church and the wilderness of the world, God hath ever broken down the wall itself, removed the candlestick ... and made his garden a wilderness, as at this day.

> And that therefore if He will ever please to restore His garden and paradise again, it must of necessity be walled in peculiarly unto Himself from the world, and that all that shall be saved out of the world are to be transplanted out of the wilderness of the world and added unto His Church or garden ... a SEPARATION of Holy from unHoly, penitent from impenitent, Godly from unGodly.

Rev. Roger Williams was alluding to Isaiah 5:1–7, that when God's people sin, He judges them by allowing his vineyard to be trampled by an ungodly government:

> My well-beloved hath a vineyard ... And he fenced it ... and planted it with the choicest

vine ... and he looked that it should bring forth grapes, and it brought forth wild grapes.

And now, O inhabitants of Jerusalem ... judge, I pray you, betwixt me and my vineyard ... When I looked that it should bring forth grapes, brought it forth wild grapes? ...

I will tell you what I will do to my vineyard: I will take away THE HEDGE thereof, and it shall be eaten up; and break down THE WALL thereof, and it shall be trodden down ...

For the vineyard ... is house of Israel ... He looked for judgment but found oppression.

Williams wrote in *Plea for Religious Liberty* (1644):

The doctrine of persecution for cause of conscience is most contrary to the doctrine of Christ Jesus the Prince of Peace ...

God requireth not a uniformity of religion to be enacted and enforced in any civil state ... Enforced uniformity (sooner or later) is the greatest occasion of civil war, ravishing of conscience, persecution of Christ Jesus in his servants, and of the hypocrisy and destruction of millions of souls.

Quaker founder of Pennsylvania William Penn wrote in *England's Present Interest Considered,* 1675:

Force makes hypocrites, 'tis persuasion only that makes converts.

Roger William's metaphor of a "wall of separation" was referred to by Thomas Jefferson. Connecticut had established the Congregational denomination. Baptists were allowed in, but felt disadvantaged. The Danbury Baptist Association wrote to Jefferson, October 7, 1801:

Sir ... Our sentiments are uniformly on the side of religious liberty

– that religion is at all times and places a matter between God and individuals

– that no man ought to suffer in name, person or effects on account of his religious Opinions

– that the legitimate power of civil government extends no further than to punish the man who works ill to his neighbor.

Jefferson replied with his famous letter, January 1, 1802, agreeing with the Danbury's Baptists, repeating sections of their letter almost verbatim:

Gentlemen ... Believing WITH YOU

– that religion is a matter which lies solely between man and his God,

– that he owes account to none other for faith or his worship,

– that the legislative powers of government reach actions only, and not opinions,

I contemplate with solemn reverence that act of the whole American people which declared that their legislature should "make no law respecting an establishment of religion, or prohibiting the free exercise thereof," thus building a wall of separation between church and state.

Jefferson concluded:

Adhering to this expression of the supreme will of the nation in behalf of the rights of conscience,

I shall see with sincere satisfaction the progress of those sentiments which tend to restore man to all his natural rights, convinced he has no natural right in opposition to his social duties.

I reciprocate your kind prayers for the protection and blessing of the common Father and Creator of man, and tender you for yourselves and your religious association, assurances of my high respect and esteem.

REV. THOMAS HOOKER (1586–1647)

Puritan Rev. John Cotton insisted that only Puritans could vote in Massachusetts. Rev. Thomas Hooker believed anyone who was a Christian should be allowed to vote. This disagreement led Rev. Hooker and his church to flee in 1636. They traveled through the wilderness to found the city of Hartford, Connecticut, and the first Congregationalist Church in America.

Once there, his church members inquired of him how they should set up their government. In reply, Rev. Hooker preached a sermon, May 31, 1638, explaining:

> Deuteronomy 1:13 "Choose you wise men and understanding and known among your tribes and I will make them heads over you captains over thousands, captains over hundreds, fifties, tens" ...

> The choice of public magistrates belongs unto the people by Gods own allowance ... The privilege of election ... belongs to the people ... according to the blessed will and law of God ...

> They who have power to appoint officers and magistrates it is in their power also to set the bounds and limits of the power and places unto which they call them ...

> The foundation of authority is laid firstly in the free consent of the people.

The ideas proposed in Hooker's sermon were revolutionary, as for most of the world, the foundation of authority was the will of a divinely-appointed king.

Rev. Hooker's sermon became the basis for The Fundamental Orders of Connecticut, 1639. Nowhere in The Fundamental Orders is there an acknowledgment made to the king, as in other charters, ie.: "our dread Sovereign"; "our gracious Lord the King."

Instead of the top-down government of a "divinely-appointed" king, Rev. Hooker's government was bottom-up, like the roots of a tree drawing nourishment from every citizen's involvement.

The Fundamental Orders of Connecticut, 1639, stated:

> Where a people are gathered together the word of God requires that to maintain the peace and union ... there should be an orderly and decent government established according to God ...
>
> The people ... conjoin ourselves to be as one public state or commonwealth ... to maintain and preserve the liberty and purity of the Gospel of our Lord Jesus which we now profess ...
>
> According to the truth of the said Gospel ... our civil affairs to be guided and governed according to such laws, rules, orders and decrees as shall be made ...
>
> The Governor ... shall have the power to administer justice according to the laws here established, and for want thereof, according to the rule of the Word of God.

The Fundamental Orders were used in Connecticut till 1818. They served as a blueprint for other New England colonial governments and even influenced the Declaration of Independence, "... that to secure these rights, governments are instituted among men, deriving their just powers from the consent of the governed," and the U.S. Constitution, "We the people ... in order to form a more perfect union ... and secure the blessings of liberty to ourselves and our posterity."

George Washington even suggested this form of government in a dictated "talk," August 29, 1796:

> Beloved Cherokees, The wise men of the United States meet together once a year, to consider what will be for the good of all their people ... I have thought that a meeting of your wise men once or twice a year would be alike useful to you.

The Fundamental Orders of Connecticut were described by Historian John Fiske (*Beginnings of New England,* Cambridge, 1889) as:

> The first written constitution known to history that created a government.

> It marked the beginnings of American democracy, of which Thomas Hooker deserves more than any other man to be called the father.

> The government of the United States today is in lineal descent more nearly related to that of Connecticut than to that of any of the other thirteen colonies.

Connecticut was designated "The Constitution State" in 1959. A statue of Rev. Thomas Hooker holding a Bible stands prominently at the Connecticut State Capitol, with the inscription on the base:

> Leading his people through the wilderness, he founded Hartford in June of 1636. On this site he preached the sermon which inspired The Fundamental Orders. It was the first written constitution that created a government.

A plaque erected in Hartford by the Daughters of the American Revolution reads:

> In 1636, The Church in Newtown, Massachusetts, Thomas Hooker, Minister, was transplanted to this locality, called Meeting House Yard, Old State House Square, City Hall Square.

> Near this site on May 31, 1638, Thomas Hooker preached his Famous Sermon: "The Foundation of Authority is Laid In the Free Consent of the People."

> Near this site on January 14, 1639, representatives of the three river towns adopted The Fundamental Orders Of Connecticut, "The first written constitution known to history that created a government."

WHO IS THE KING IN AMERICA?

Hartford's Traveller's Square has a bronze statue of Connecticut's first settlers and a plaque which reads:

> In June of 1635, about one hundred members of Thomas Hooker's congregation arrived safely in this vicinity with one hundred and sixty cattle. They followed old Indian trails from Massachusetts Bay Colony to the Connecticut River to build a community.
>
> Here they established the form of government upon which the present Constitution of the United States is modeled.

A historical marker in England reads:

> Thomas Hooker 1586–1647, Curate of St. Mary's Church, Chelmsford and Town Lecturer 1626–1629, Founder of the State of Connecticut 1636, "Father of American Democracy."

Another marker reads:

> Hinckley & Bosworth Borough Council, Thomas Hooker, (1586–1647), Puritan Clergyman, Pupil of this School, Reputed Father of "American Democracy."

A plaque in Cambridge, Massachusetts, reads:

> Here Stood The Original Meeting House of the First Church in Cambridge. Built in 1632 and the center of the Civic and Religious Life of the Town. Here Ministered 1633–1636 Thomas Hooker – A Peerless Leader of Thought and Life in both Church and State.

Dr. Charles Hull Wolfe was a Marxist till his views were changed after conducting an independent study of American economics. He helped found and was the first executive director of The Plymouth Rock Foundation.

Dr. Wolfe and Dr. D. James Kennedy wrote "Restoring the Real Meaning of Thanksgiving" (1989), stating:

> When the brilliant Rev. Thomas Hooker left

Boston and settled in Hartford, he promptly called for three Connecticut towns to join together in forming a colony.

Hooker followed the Pilgrim pattern and led the people of Connecticut in framing a written compact for civil self-government rooted in Mosaic tradition.

He used as his text, "Take you wise men, and understanding, and known among your tribes, and I will make them rulers over you." (Deuteronomy 1:13).

Hooker preached a scholarly sermon that guided the men of Connecticut in framing the Fundamental Orders of Connecticut in 1639, commonly called "the world's first complete written constitution," though, in fact, Plymouth had framed a complete constitutional charter, the Pilgrim Code of Law, three years before.

In New England, instead of separation of church and state, it was pastors and churches that created the state.

This was a significant advancement over the European tradition of Thomistic "subsidiarity," namely, that whenever possible, civic problems should be solved at the most local level, allowing parishes and communities a limited degree of autonomy.

Calvin Coolidge stated at the 150th Anniversary of the Declaration of Independence, July 5, 1926:

The principles ... which went into the Declaration of Independence ... are found in ... the sermons ... of the early colonial clergy who were earnestly undertaking to instruct their congregations in the great mystery of how to live.

They preached equality because they believed in the fatherhood of God and the brotherhood of man. They justified freedom by the text that we are all created in the divine image ...

WHO IS THE KING IN AMERICA?

Placing every man on a plane where he acknowledged no superiors, where no one possessed any right to rule over him, he must inevitably choose his own rulers through a system of self-government ...

In order that they might have freedom to express these thoughts and opportunity to put them into action, whole congregations with their pastors migrated to the colonies.

Instances of church government affecting civil government also followed the First Great Awakening Revival, 1730–1755, and the Second Great Awakening Revival, 1790–1840. Baptists, Presbyterians and Methodists held revival meetings in Thomas Jefferson's county of Albemarle, with even Jefferson's daughter, Mary, attending one preached by Baptist Lorenzo Dow.

An account was published in the *Christian Watchman* (Boston, MA, July 4, 1826):

ANDREW TRIBBLE was the pastor of a small Baptist Church, which held its monthly meetings at a short distance from Mr. JEFFERSON'S house, eight or ten years before the American Revolution.

Mr. JEFFERSON attended the meetings of the church for several months in succession, and after one of them, asked Elder TRIBBLE to go home and dine with him, with which he complied.

Mr. TRIBBLE asked Mr. JEFFERSON how he was pleased with their church government?

Mr. JEFFERSON replied, that it had struck him with great force, and had interested him much; that he considered it the only form of pure democracy that then existed in the world, and had concluded that it would be the best plan of government for the American colonies.

Thomas F. Curtis wrote in *The Progress of Baptist*

Principles in the Last Hundred Years (Charleston, S.C.: Southern Baptist Publication Society, 1856):

> A gentleman ... in North Carolina ... knowing that the venerable Mrs. Dolley Madison had some recollections on the subject, asked her in regard to them. She expressed a distinct remembrance of Mr. Jefferson speaking on the subject, and always declaring that it was a Baptist church from which these views were gathered.

Calvin Coolidge stated at the 150th anniversary of the Declaration of Independence, July 4, 1926:

> This preaching reached the neighborhood of Thomas Jefferson, who acknowledged that his "best ideas of democracy" had been secured at church meetings.

∽

COLONIAL CHARTERS & ESTABLISHED DENOMINATIONS

Following the example of Europe, each American colony initially favored only one denomination, often providing them tax support, special privileges, and requiring mandatory church membership of its citizens.

This caused rival denominations to flee and start new settlements favoring their own denominations.

Virginia had established the Anglican or Church of England. The House of Burgesses passed in 1624:

> There shall be an uniformity in our Church as near as may be to the Canons in England.

Establishment meant:

> 1) Mandatory membership in the Anglican church;
>
> 2) Mandatory taxes to support the Anglican church;
>
> 3) One could not hold office unless they took the oath of supremacy, acknowledging the king as the head of the church.

England's Oath of Supremacy, 1535, stated:

> I declare ... that the King's Highness is the ONLY Supreme Governor of this Realm ... in all Spiritual or Ecclesiastical things.

The Second Charter of Virginia, 1609, stated:

> None be permitted to pass in any voyage ... into the said country, but such as first shall have taken the Oath of Supremacy.

Another Virginia ordinance stated, March 5, 1624:

> Whosoever shall absent himself from Divine service any Sunday without an allowable excuse shall forfeit a pound of tobacco.

The original denominations in the Colonies were:

NEW ENGLAND COLONIES:

- Massachusetts 1630 – Puritan;
- Rhode Island 1636 – Baptist;
- Connecticut 1636 – Congregational;
- New Hampshire 1638 – Congregational

MIDDLE COLONIES:

- New York 1626 – Dutch Reformed;
- Delaware 1638 – Lutheran & Dutch Reformed;
- Pennsylvania 1682 – Quaker & Lutheran;
- New Jersey 1664 – Lutheran & Dutch Reformed

SOUTHERN COLONIES:

- Virginia 1607 – Anglican;
- Maryland 1633 – Catholic;
- North Carolina 1653 – Anglican;
- South Carolina 1663 – Anglican;
- Georgia 1732 – Protestant

Though not part of America's founding colonies:

- Spanish Florida 1565 – Catholic
- French Canada & Louisiana Territory 1604 – Catholic

The colonial settlers mostly followed the European model of one Christian denomination per colony, and if a person did not believe the way their colony's government did, they were persecuted and fled.

Their attitude was generally, "if you do not like our denomination, fine, start your own colony!"

Over time, due to the country's sparse population, settlers found that by working together with those of other churches they would all mutually benefit. They bonded during times of financial distress, as well as in famines, smallpox epidemics, Indian attacks, and wars.

When the Revolutionary War started, they all had to work together to be free from the king. After the Revolution, their attitude changed to "we may not always agree on religion, but you were willing to fight and die for my freedom, I need to let you practice yours."

Christians gradually convinced themselves to tolerate those they did not agree with because of:

1) Jesus' teaching to "do unto others as you would have them do unto you";

2) Jesus' example of never forcing anyone to follow Him;

3) Jesus' command to share the Gospel, which encouraged permitting non-Christians to enter the colonies in hopes of evangelizing them.

Rather than viewing the many denominations negatively, as the Body of Christ being divided, it was viewed positively, as a free market competition for converts, insuring that no one denomination would become so large as to become the official denomination of the state, as was the case in European countries.

Charles Carroll, the only Catholic to sign the Declaration, wrote to Rev. John Stanford, October, 9, 1827:

> Observing the Christian religion divided into many sects, I founded the hope that no one would be so predominant as to become

the religion of the state. That hope was thus early entertained because all of them joined in the same cause.

Colonies eventually ended mandatory tax support and special privileges for state-sanctioned denominations. America gave birth to a new kind of liberty which would benefit all immigrants and citizens.

This era in history is examined further in the book *THE ORIGINAL 13 – A Documentary History of Religion in America's First Thirteen States.*

∽

PASTORS HELD TWO VIEWS

Before the Revolution, pastors held two distinct views:

1) Calvinist Puritan

2) Pietism

The Calvinist Puritan view was, that God had a plan for your life, your marriage, your family, your church and your government. The pastor's job was to search the Scriptures to find out what God's plan is, and teach people to put it into effect.

Pietism was different. When Martin Luther had the revelation that "the just shall live by faith," it was very personal to him. Later, kings who wanted to break away from Rome told their kingdoms – you must all now be Lutheran – if you do not like it, leave.

Subjects in these kingdoms answered – OK. We are Lutheran, but what do we believe?

For people in these kingdoms, it was not necessarily the same personal experience that Luther had. For many, it was just mental assent to state approved doctrine.

Then a revival movement started among Germany's Lutherans called "Pietism," which held that being a Christian was not just agreeing with doctrine, as good as it might be – a person needed to have a personal experience with Jesus, and when they did, their life should change. They would no longer hang around "worldly" people in bars, brothels, theaters, and government.

Wait! What was that last thing?

Yes – government! Since it is filled with worldly people, if someone really becomes a Christian they will not get involved in "worldly" government.

These conflicting views are illustrated by two brothers who were Lutheran pastors:

• Rev. John Peter Muhlenberg, Pastor of Emanuel Lutheran Church, Woodstock, Virginia;

• Rev. Frederick Augustus Muhlenberg, Pastor of Christ Lutheran Church, New York City.

Their father, Rev. Henry Muhlenberg, was the founder of the Lutheran Church in America.

John Peter Muhlenberg heard Patrick Henry give his famous "Give me liberty or give me death" speech and afterwards approached General Washington offering to help. Washington appointed him colonel and told him to go get his men.

John Peter preached a sermon at his church from the Book of Ecclesiastes 3:1:

For everything there is a season, and a time for every matter under heaven.

He closed by saying:

In the language of the Holy Writ, there is a time for all things. There is a time to preach and a time to fight. And now is the time to fight.

He then led 300 men of his church and surrounding churches off to formed the 8th Virginia Regiment. They fought courageously in many battles, and John Peter was promoted to Major–General. After the war, John Peter was elected to the first session of the U.S.

Congress, where he helped pass the First Amendment.

Meanwhile, his brother, Rev. Frederick Muhlenberg, wrote to John Peter:

> You have become too involved in matters which, as a preacher, you have nothing whatsoever to do.

John Peter wrote back, accusing Frederick of being a Tory British sympathizer. Frederick wrote back saying he could not serve two masters.

Then the British bombarded New York City and Frederick's church was burned. His wife and children were forced to flee the city. Changing his mind, he became active in the Revolution.

Afterwards, Frederick was elected to Congress and chosen to be the first Speaker of the U.S. House of Representatives, overseeing the first session which passed the Bill of Rights, with the First Amendment.

There are two signatures on the Bill of Rights which were sent to the states for ratification: Vice-President John Adams – in his role as President of the Senate; and Speaker Frederick Augustus Muhlenberg.

Does anyone honestly think that these two Pastor–Congressmen, Rev. John Peter Muhlenberg and Rev. Frederick Muhlenberg, would vote to outlaw themselves? Would they pass an amendment to prohibit people of faith from involvement in government when they were people of faith and they were involved in government?

∽

RELIGION UNDER
EACH STATE'S JURISDICTION

U.S. Supreme Court Justice Joseph Story wrote in *Commentaries on the Constitution,* 1833:

> The whole power over the subject of religion is left exclusively to the state governments, to

be acted upon according to their own sense of justice and the state constitutions.

James Madison introduced the First Amendment in the first session of Congress. As the fourth President, Madison appointed Joseph Story to the Supreme Court in 1811. Story served on the Court 34 years and almost single-handedly founded Harvard Law School.

The Constitution of the United States of America – Analysis and Interpretation, prepared by the Legislative Reference Service of the Library of Congress (Edward S. Corwin, editor, U.S. Government Printing Office, Washington, 1953, p. 758), stated:

> In his *Commentaries on the Constitution,* 1833, Justice Joseph Story asserted that the purpose of the First Amendment was not to discredit the then existing state establishments of religion, but rather "to exclude from the national government all power to act on the subject."

> Justice Story continued: "In some of the states, Episcopalians constituted the predominant sect; in other, Presbyterians; in others, Congregationalists; in others, Quakers; and in others again, there was a close numerical rivalry among contending sects.

> It was impossible that there should not arise perpetual strife and perpetual jealousy on the subject of ecclesiastical ascendancy, if the national government were left free to create a religious establishment.

> The only security was in the abolishing the power. But this alone would have been an imperfect security, if it had not been followed up by a declaration of the right of the free exercise of religion ...

> Thus, the whole power over the subject of religion is left exclusively to the state governments, to be acted upon according

to their own sense of justice and the state constitutions."

Like a race track with 13 lanes, some states expanded religious freedom quickly and others slowly. This is similar to the present-day where:

- some states limit underage drinking & others do not;
- some states have smoking bans & others do not;
- some states legalized marijuana & others do not;
- some states allow gambling & others do not;
- some states allow prostitution (Nevada and formerly Rhode Island) & others do not;

When the Constitution and Bill of Rights were ratified:

- some states allowed more religious freedom (ie. Pennsylvania, Maryland, and Rhode Island) & others did not (ie. Massachusetts, New Hampshire, and Connecticut).

Before the 1947 *Everson* case, religious freedom was under each individual state's jurisdiction. Where some states chose to expand it generously, other states had strict "blue laws" which required all stores and businesses to be closed on Sundays – but it was up to the people in each state to decide.

In summary, when colonial settlers came over from England, it was as if America was a lifeboat amidst the sea of persecution. Over time, settlers put into effect the principle from the Sermon on the Mount, "whatever you wish that others would do to you, do also to them."

The lifeboat rescued:

- the Pilgrims and Puritans;
- then Congregationalists, Presbyterians, Quakers, Dutch Reformed, Baptists, Lutherans, Reformed, Mennonite, French Huguenot, Methodist, Evangelical, Calvinist Reformed, Moravian, Seventh Day Baptist, Amish, Dunker, & Brethren;

- then all Protestants;
- then Catholics;
- then Spanish–Portuguese Sephardic Jews;
- then new Christian denominations & pseudo–christian sects (Unitarian, Universalists, etc.);
- then German Ashkenazic Jews:
- then monotheists;
- then groups bordering on cults;
- then polytheists (Chinese Buddhists, Indian Hindus);
- then finally atheists and Muslims.

Ironically, it seems the last ones in the boat consider it too crowded and are endeavoring to throw the first ones out – being intolerant of the same beliefs of those who founded the country.

This progression is examined in the book, *Backfired – A Nation Born for Religious Tolerance No Longer Tolerates the Religion of Its Founders.*

STATES EXPAND RELIGIOUS LIBERTY

At the time the Declaration of Independence and Constitution were written, Americans were:

- approximately 98 percent Protestant;
- a little less than 2 percent were Catholics;
- just a tenth of one percent were Jewish.

Patricia U. Bonomi, Professor Emeritus of New York University, wrote in "The Middle Colonies as the Birthplace of American Religious Pluralism":

The colonists were about 98 percent Protestant.

Catholics were initially allowed in Maryland, Pennsylvania, and to a lesser extent in New York. Bishop John Carroll wrote to Rome in 1790:

The thirteen provinces of North America

rejected the yoke of England, they proclaimed, at the same time, freedom of conscience ...

Before this great event, the Catholic faith had penetrated two provinces only, Maryland and Pennsylvania. In all the others the laws against Catholics were in force.

In was not until 1795 that the first Catholic Church was built in Virginia, as the Colony's 1609 Charter decreed:

We should be loath that any Person should be permitted to pass that we suspected to affect the Superstitions of the Church of Rome.

Nine of the original thirteen state constitutions required office-holders be Protestant.

SOUTH CAROLINA, the 8th state to ratify the U.S. Constitution, stated in its 1778 State Constitution:

No person shall be eligible to a seat ... unless he be of the PROTESTANT religion ... The CHRISTIAN PROTESTANT religion shall be deemed ... the established religion of this state.

MASSACHUSETTS, the 6th state to ratify the U.S. Constitution, stated in its 1780 State Constitution, written by John Adams:

Any person ... before he ... execute the duties of his ... office ... [shall] subscribe ... "I ... declare, that I believe the CHRISTIAN religion, and have a firm persuasion of its truth" ...

The legislature shall ... authorize the support and maintenance of public PROTESTANT teachers of piety, religion and morality.

GEORGIA, the 4th state to ratify the U.S. Constitution, stated in its 1777 State Constitution:

Representatives shall be chosen out of the residents in each county ... and they shall be of the PROTESTANT religion.

NEW JERSEY, the 3rd state to ratify the U.S.

Constitution, stated in its 1776 State Constitution:

> All persons, professing a belief in the faith
> of any PROTESTANT sect, who shall demean
> themselves peaceably under the government ...
> shall be capable of being elected.

NEW HAMPSHIRE, the 9th state to ratify the U.S. Constitution, stated in its 1784 State Constitution:

> No person shall be capable of being elected ...
> who is not of the PROTESTANT religion (till 1877)

Some states were more liberal. Instead of requiring office holders to be Protestant, all that was necessary was to be a generic Christian or believe in the Bible.

DELAWARE, the first state to ratify the U.S. Constitution, stated in its 1776 State Constitution:

> Every person ... appointed to any office ...
> shall ... subscribe ... "I ... profess faith in GOD
> THE FATHER, and in JESUS CHRIST His
> only Son, and in the HOLY GHOST, one God,
> blessed for evermore; and I do acknowledge
> the Holy Scriptures of the Old and New
> Testament to be given by Divine inspiration."

PENNSYLVANIA, the 2nd state to ratify the U.S. Constitution, stated in its 1776 State Constitution, signed by Ben Franklin:

> Each member, before he takes his seat, shall
> ... subscribe ... "I do believe in one GOD, the
> Creator and Governor of the Universe, the
> Rewarder of the good and the Punisher of the
> wicked. And I do acknowledge the Scriptures
> of the Old and New Testament to be given by
> Divine Inspiration."

RHODE ISLAND, the 13th state to ratify the U.S. Constitution, retained its 1663 Colonial Constitution, which had no religious requirement – the attitude being that if it was required, an unbeliever might hypocritically say they were a Christian just to get elected:

WHO IS THE KING IN AMERICA?

By the blessing of God ... a full liberty in religious concernements ... rightly grounded upon GOSPEL principles, will give the best and greatest security ... in the true CHRISTIAN faith and worship of God ... They may ... defend themselves, in their just rights and liberties against all the enemies of the CHRISTIAN faith. (1843 Constitution added to oath "So help you God.")

VIRGINIA, the 10th state to ratify the U.S. Constitution, stated in its 1776 State Constitution, Bill of Rights, written mainly by James Madison and George Mason:

It is the mutual duty of all to practice CHRISTIAN forbearance, love, and charity towards each other.

When the Irish Potato Famine occurred in the early 1800s, millions of Irish Catholic immigrants flooded into the United States. The Catholic percentage of the population exploded from 2 percent to 20 percent.

There was an intense backlash. Many states passed laws prohibiting tax dollars from going to Catholic schools. These were called "Blaine Amendments," named for Senator James G. Blaine from Maine.

Eventually, states accommodated Catholics by changing the requirement to hold office from Protestant to Christian. For example, North Carolina, in 1776, required all office holders to be Protestant, but in 1835, just Christian. This was in effect until 1868 when all that was necessary to hold office was to believe in God.

NORTH CAROLINA, the 12th state to ratify the U.S. Constitution, stated in its 1776 State Constitution:

No person, who shall deny the being of GOD or the truth of the PROTESTANT religion, or the Divine authority either of the Old or New Testaments, or who shall hold religious principles incompatible with the freedom and safety of the state, shall be capable of holding … office.

NORTH CAROLINA stated in its 1835 Constitution:

No person, who shall deny the being of God or the truth of the CHRISTIAN religion, or the Divine authority either of the Old or New Testaments … shall be capable of holding … office.

NORTH CAROLINA stated in its 1868 Constitution:

The following persons shall be disqualified for office: First, any person who shall deny the being of Almighty God.

NORTH CAROLINA stated in its 1971 Constitution:

Beneficent provision for the poor, the unfortunate, and the orphan is one of the first duties of a civilized and a Christian state.

Spanish and Portuguese Sephardic Jews had been in America since 1654, but in the early 1800s, a persecution of Ashkenazic Jews in Bavaria and Eastern Europe resulted in a quarter of a million immigrating. America's Jewish population grew from a tenth of a percent to two percent.

Various states made accommodations, such as Maryland, which went from requiring office holders to be Christian in 1776; to Christian and Jew in 1851; to Christian and believing in God in 1864; and finally to simply believing in God in 1867:

MARYLAND, the 7th state to ratify the U.S. Constitution, stated in its 1776 State Constitution:

No other test … ought to be required, on admission to any office … than such oath of support and fidelity to this state … and a declaration of a belief in the CHRISTIAN religion.

MARYLAND stated in its 1851 Constitution:

No other test … required … than … oath to this state … and a declaration of a belief in the

WHO IS THE KING IN AMERICA?

CHRISTIAN religion ... and if the party shall profess to be a JEW the declaration shall be of his belief in a future state of rewards and punishments.

MARYLAND stated in its 1864 Constitution:

No other test ... required ... than ... oath of allegiance ... to this state ... and a declaration of belief in the Christian religion; or in the existence of God, and in a future state of rewards and punishments.

MARYLAND stated in its 1867 Constitution:

No religious test ... required ... other than a declaration of belief in the existence of God.

CONNECTICUT, the 5th state to ratify the U.S. Constitution, retained its 1639 Fundamental Orders and 1662 Colonial Constitution, which established the PROTESTANT CONGREGATIONAL faith till 1818:

By the Providence of GOD ... having from their ancestors derived a free and excellent Constitution ... whereby the legislature depends on the free and annual election ... The free fruition of such liberties and privileges as humanity, civility and CHRISTIANITY call for.

CONNECTICUT'S first state Constitution was in 1818, which proclaimed:

Every ... denomination of Christians in this state shall have ... equal rights ... Enjoyment of religious profession ... shall not be so construed as to excuse acts of licentiousness [sexual immorality, carnal intercourse, crimes against nature].

NEW YORK, the 11th state to ratify the U.S. Constitution, affirmed Judeo–Christian morality by prohibiting "licentiousness" in its 1777 Constitution:

The United American States ... declare ... "Laws of nature and of NATURE'S GOD ... All men are created equal; that they are endowed by their CREATOR with certain unalienable rights ... Appealing to the SUPREME JUDGE of the world ... A firm reliance on the protection of DIVINE PROVIDENCE" ...

People of this state, ordain ... the free exercise ... of religious profession and worship, without discrimination ... Provided, That the liberty of conscience, hereby granted, shall not be so construed as to excuse acts of licentiousness [sexual immorality, carnal intercourse, crimes against nature].

In 1811, the New York Supreme Court (*People v. Ruggles),* sentenced John Ruggles to 3 months in prison and fined him $500 for taking the name of Jesus in vain.

In this sense, the United States was established as a "Christian Nation" at the state level. Justice Hugo Lafayette Black wrote in *Engel v. Vitale* (1962):

As late as the time of the Revolutionary War, there were established Churches in at least eight of the thirteen former colonies and established religions in at least four of the other five.

John K. Wilson wrote in "Religion Under the State Constitutions 1776–1800" (*Journal of Church and State,* Volume 32, Autumn 1990, Number 4, pp. 754):

An establishment of religion, in terms of direct tax aid to Churches, was the situation in nine of the thirteen colonies on the eve of the American revolution.

Congressman James Meacham (VT) gave a House Judiciary Committee report, March 27, 1854 (*Journal of the U.S. House,* 33rd Congress):

At the adoption of the Constitution, we believe every state – certainly 10 of the 13 – provided as regularly for the support of the church as for the support of the government: one, Virginia, had the system of tithes.

Down to the Revolution, every colony did

sustain religion in some form. It was deemed peculiarly proper that the religion of liberty should be upheld by a free people.

Had the people, during the Revolution, had a suspicion of any attempt to war against Christianity, that Revolution would have been strangled in its cradle.

During North Carolina's Ratifying Convention, Governor Samuel Johnston stated, July 30, 1788:

I know but two or three states where there is the least chance of establishing any particular religion. The people of Massachusetts and Connecticut are mostly Presbyterians. In every other state, the people are divided into a great number of sects.

In Rhode Island, the tenets of the Baptists, I believe, prevail. In New York, they are divided very much; the most numerous are the Episcopalians and the Baptists.

In New Jersey, they are as much divided as we are. In Pennsylvania, if any sect prevails more than others, it is that of the Quakers.

In Maryland, the Episcopalians are most numerous, though there are other sects. In Virginia, there are many sects; you all know what their religious sentiments are.

So in all the southern states they differ; as also New Hampshire.

I hope, therefore, that gentlemen will see there is no cause of fear that any one religion shall be exclusively established.

President John F. Kennedy stated February 9, 1961:

This country was dedicated to ... two propositions: First, a strong religious conviction, and secondly, a recognition that this conviction could flourish only under a system of freedom ...

The Puritans and the Pilgrims of my own section of New England, the Quakers of Pennsylvania, the Catholics of Maryland, the Presbyterians of North Carolina, the Methodists and Baptists who came later, all shared these two great traditions which, like silver threads, have run through the warp and the woof of American History.

Gustave de Beaumont, who traveled with de Tocqueville, wrote in *Marie ou L'Esclavage aux E'tas – Unis* (1835):

All of the American constitutions exhort the citizens to practice religious worship as a safeguard both to good morals and to public liberties. In the United States, the law is never atheistic ...

All of the American constitutions proclaim freedom of conscience and the liberty and equality of all the confessions.

The Constitution of Massachusetts proclaims the freedom of the various faiths in the sense that it does not wish to persecute any of them; but it recognizes within the state only Christians and protects only the Protestants.

Maryland's Constitution also declares that all of the faiths are free, and that no one is forced to contribute to the maintenance of a particular Church. However, it gives the legislature the right to establish a general tax, according to the circumstances, for the support of the Christian religion.

The Constitution of Vermont recognizes only the Christian faiths, and says specifically that every congregation of Christians should celebrate the Sabbath or the Lord's Day, and observe the religious worship which seems to it most pleasing to the will of God, manifested by revelation.

WHO IS THE KING IN AMERICA?

Sometimes the American constitutions offer religious bodies some indirect assistance: thus, Maryland Law declares that, to be admitted to public office, it is necessary to be a Christian.

The Pennsylvania Constitution requires that one believe in the existence of God and in a future life of punishment or rewards ...

I have just indicated how the law ... confirms the power of religion ... There is not a single state where public opinion and the customs of the inhabitants do not forcefully constrain an obligation to these beliefs.

Massachusetts Supreme Court stated in *Commonwealth v. Abner Kneeland* (1838):, 37 Mass., 20 Pick, 206, 216–217):

In New Hampshire, the Constitution of which state has a similar declaration of rights, the open denial of the being and existence of God or of the Supreme Being is prohibited by statute, and declared to be blasphemy.

In Vermont, with a similar declaration of rights, a statute was passed in 1797, by which it was enacted, that if any person shall publicly deny the being and existence of God or the Supreme Being, or shall contumeliously reproach his Providence and government, he shall be deemed a disturber of the peace and tranquillity of the state, and an offender against the good morals and manners of society, and shall be punishable by fine ...

The State of Maine also, having adopted the same constitutional provision with that of Massachusetts, in her declaration of rights, in respect to religious freedom, immediately after the adoption of the Constitution reenacted, the Massachusetts statue against blasphemy ...

In New York the universal toleration of all religious professions and sentiments, is secured in the most ample manner. It is declared in the Constitution ... that the free exercise and enjoyment of religious worship, without discrimination or preference, shall for ever be allowed in this state to all mankind ...

Notwithstanding this constitutional declaration carrying the doctrine of unlimited toleration as far as the peace and safety of any community will allow, the courts have decided that blasphemy was a crime at common law and was not abrogated by the Constitution [*People v. Ruggles*].

[The First Amendment] embraces all who believe in the existence of God, as well ... as Christians of every denomination ...

This provision does not extend to atheists, because they do not believe in God or religion; and therefore ... their sentiments and professions, whatever they may be, cannot be called religious sentiments and professions.

French political writer Alexis de Tocqueville wrote in *Democracy in America* (1840):

The sects that exist in the United States are innumerable ... Moreover, all the sects of the United States are comprised within the great unity of Christianity, and Christian morality is everywhere the same ...

In the United States Christian sects are infinitely diversified and perpetually modified; but Christianity itself is a fact so irresistibly established, that no one undertakes either to attack or to defend it.

The Constitution of the United States of America – Analysis and Interpretation (Library of Congress, U.S. Gov. Printing Office, Washington, 1953, p. 759), stated:

Justice Story contended, the establishment clause, while it inhibited Congress from giving preference to any denomination of the Christian faith, was not intended to withdraw the Christian religion as a whole from the protection of Congress.

Justice Joseph Story continued:

"Probably at the time of the adoption of the Constitution, and of the Amendment to it now under consideration, the general if not the universal sentiment in America was, that Christianity ought to receive encouragement from the state so far as was not incompatible with the private rights of conscience and the freedom of religious worship.

Any attempt to level all religions, and make it a matter of state policy to hold all in utter indifference, would have created universal disapprobation, if not universal indignation."

John Bouvier's Law Dictionary (Philadelphia: J.B. Lippincott Co., 1889), stated in its definition of "religion":

The Constitution of the United States provides that "Congress shall make no law respecting an establishment of religion or prohibiting the free exercise thereof."

This provision and that relating to religious tests are limitations upon the power of the Congress only ...

The Christian religion is, of course, recognized by the government, yet ... the preservation of religious liberty is left to the states.

U.S. Supreme Court Justice John Paul Stevens wrote in *Wallace v. Jaffree* (1985):

The individual's freedom to choose his own creed is the counterpart of his right to refrain from accepting the creed established by the majority. At one time it was thought that this right merely proscribed the preference of one Christian sect over another, but would not require equal respect for the conscience of the infidel, the atheist, or the adherent of a non-Christian faith.

Patricia U. Bonomi, Professor Emeritus of New York University, wrote in "The Middle Colonies as the Birthplace of American Religious Pluralism":

> Early American churchmen and churchwomen soon discovered that if they wanted to practice their beliefs unmolested in a diverse society, they had to grant the same right to others. This wisdom did not come easily.

President Calvin Coolidge stated May 3, 1925:

> Many and scattered colonial communities ... had been planted along the Atlantic seaboard ... There were well-nigh as many divergencies of religious faith as there were of origin, politics and geography ...
>
> From its beginning, the new continent had seemed destined to be the home of religious tolerance. Those who claimed the right of individual choice for themselves finally had to grant it to others.

The original states, by "successive relaxations," advanced religious tolerance at their own discretion, as Madison wrote in 1832 to Rev. Jasper Adams, President of the College of Charleston:

> In the colonial state of the country, there were four examples, Rhode Island, New Jersey, Pennsylvania and Delaware, and the greater part of New York where there were no religious establishments; the support of religion being left to the voluntary associations and contributions of individuals; and certainly the religious condition of those colonies will well bear a comparison with that where establishments existed ...
>
> The New England states have not

discontinued establishments of religion formed under very peculiar circumstances; but they have by successive relaxations advanced towards the prevailing example; and without any evidence of disadvantage either to religion or good government.

And if we turn to the southern states ... there was, previous to the Declaration of Independence, a legal provision for the support of religion ...

Since that event a surrender of it to a spontaneous support by the people, it may be said that the difference amounts ... to a contrast in the greater purity and industry of the pastors and in the greater devotion of their flocks, in the latter period than in the former.

In Virginia ... the abolition of the legal establishment of religion ... account for the change in the religious character of the community ...

Now more than 50 years since the legal support of religion was withdrawn sufficiently prove that it does not need the support of government.

The State of Virginia chose to expand religious liberty, as noted by U.S. Supreme Court Justice Hugo Lafayette Black in *Engel v. Vitale* (1962):

But the successful Revolution against English political domination was shortly followed by intense opposition to the practice of establishing religion by law.

This opposition crystallized rapidly into an effective political force in Virginia where the minority religious groups such as Presbyterians, Lutherans, Quakers and Baptists had gained such strength that the adherents to the established Episcopal Church were actually a minority themselves.

In 1785–1786, those opposed to the established Church ... obtained the enactment of the famous "Virginia Bill for Religious Liberty" by which all religious groups were placed on an equal footing.

This subject is covered in more depth in *For God and Country – A Handbook for the Statesman–Citizen.*

❧

PURPOSE OF BILL OF RIGHTS

The Constitution and the Bill of Rights are essentially a collection of hurdles to prevent power from snapping back into the hands of a king.

Thomas Paine wrote (*Common Sense,* January 1776):

> For as in absolute governments the king is law, so in free countries the law ought to be king ... Let the Crown be ... demolished, and scattered among THE PEOPLE whose right it is.

Like horizontal and vertical lines of a cross, the founders scattered the POWER of a king horizontally into three competing branches, then vertically into federal, state, and local levels.

They then tied up this Federal "Frankenstein" with ten handcuffs – the first Ten Amendments.

President Eisenhower referred to the Federal Government as "Frankenstein," June 24, 1957:

> The national government was itself ... the creature, of the states ... Yet today ... the creature, Frankenstein-like, is determined to destroy the creators.

The Preamble to the Bill of Rights explained:

> The states, having at the time of their adopting the Constitution, expressed a desire, in order to prevent misconstruction or abuse of its powers that further declaratory and restrictive clauses should be added.

George Washington warned September 19, 1796:

> A just estimate of that love of power, and proneness to abuse it, which predominates the human heart is sufficient to satisfy us of the truth of this position.

> The necessity of reciprocal checks in the exercise of political power; by dividing and distributing it into different depositories ... each the guardian ... against invasions by the others, has been evinced by experiments ancient and modern; some of them in our country and under our own eyes.

> To preserve them must be as necessary as to institute them ....

> But let there be no change by usurpation; for though this, in one instance, may be the instrument of good, it is the customary weapon by which free governments are destroyed.

> The precedent [of usurpation] must always greatly overbalance in permanent evil any partial or transient benefit which the use can at any time yield."

❧

FIRST AMENDMENT

Ten days after his Inauguration, President Washington wrote to the United Baptist Churches of Virginia, May 10, 1789:

> If I could have entertained the slightest apprehension that the Constitution framed by the Convention, where I had the honor to preside, might possibly endanger the religious rights of any ecclesiastical Society, certainly I would never have placed my signature to it.

During the debates of the Bill of Rights, Rep. Thomas Tucker of South Carolina made a motion to completely strike the establishment clause from the

First Amendment, as he thought it could be misapplied to preempt the religious clauses existing in the various state constitutions.

Rep. Roger Sherman of Connecticut thought the First Amendment was completely unnecessary, as the state delegates, when writing the U.S. Constitution, only gave the Federal Government specific powers, and authority over religion was not one of them.

Jefferson viewed the "wall" as limiting the Federal Government from "inter-meddling" in church affairs, as he wrote to Samuel Miller, January 23, 1808:

> I consider the government of the United States as interdicted [prohibited] by the Constitution from inter-meddling with religious institutions, their doctrines, discipline, or exercises.
>
> This results not only from the provision that no law shall be made respecting the establishment or free exercise of religion, but from that also which reserves to the states the powers not delegated to the United States [10th Amendment] ...
>
> Certainly no power to prescribe any religious exercise, or to assume authority in religious discipline, has been delegated to the General [Federal] Government ...
>
> I do not believe it is for the interest of religion to invite the civil magistrate to direct its exercises, its discipline, or its doctrines ...
>
> Every religious society has a right to determine for itself the times for these exercises, and the objects proper for them, according to their own particular tenets.

James Madison made a journal entry, June 12, 1788:

> There is not a shadow of right in the General [Federal] Government to inter-meddle with religion ... The subject is, for the honor of

America, perfectly free and unshackled. The government has no jurisdiction over it.

Like dealing a deck of cards in a card game, the states dealt to the Federal Government jurisdiction over a few specific things, such as providing for the common defense and regulating interstate commerce, but the rest of the cards were held by the states.

Jefferson explained in his Second Inaugural Address, March 4, 1805:

> In matters of religion I have considered that its free exercise is placed by the Constitution independent of the powers of the General [Federal] Government.
>
> I have therefore undertaken, on no occasion, to prescribe the religious exercise suited to it; but have left them, as the Constitution found them, under the direction and discipline of state and church authorities by the several religious societies.

States jealously guarded their freedom of religion, leading them to send representatives to the First Session of Congress where they passed the First Amendment.

> Congress shall make no law respecting an establishment of religion, or prohibiting the free exercise thereof.

If they could have seen into the future that judges would usurp power by making laws from the bench, or that Presidents would usurp power by making laws through executive orders and regulations, the founders most likely would have worded the First Amendment:

> Congress, the Supreme Court, and the President shall make no law respecting an establishment of religion, or prohibiting the free exercise thereof.

The First Amendment put two specific handcuffs on the wrists of the Federal Government:

1) the Federal Government could not establish one official national denomination, as this would conflict with the many states' established denominations. This is called "the establishment clause"; and

2) the Federal Government could not prohibit individuals within the states from enjoying the free exercise of their religion. This is called "the free exercise clause."

∽

WHAT CHANGED?

James H. Landman, director of community programs for the American Bar Association Division for Public Education in Chicago, wrote in "Trying Beliefs: The Law of Cultural Orthodoxy and Dissent" (*Insights on Law and Society,* American Bar Association Division for Public Education, Winter 2002, Vol. 2, No. 2):

> For most of our history, the majority of Americans have practiced some form of Christian Protestantism ... In 1925 ... public schools ... still played a significant role in inculcating Anglo–Protestant moral values.

Three events changed this.

•FIRST, the Irish Potato Famine in the early 1800s resulted in millions of Irish Catholics immigrating to America. A backlash resulted in laws being passed called "anti-sectarian" ordinances or Blaine Amendments, which prevented state tax money from going to Catholic schools, as the tax-supported public schools were thoroughly Protestant Christian.

•SECOND, in 1868, the 14th Amendment forced southern Democrat states to grant rights to freed slaves. When concerns arose during the debates whether the 14th Amendment might be reinterpreted by the Federal Government to usurp jurisdiction away from states in other areas, Rep. John Bingham of Ohio, the one who introduced the Amendment, replied:

> I repel the suggestion ... that the Amendment will take away from any state any right that belongs to it.

Yet the usurping process began nonetheless.

•THIRD, in 1859, Charles Darwin published his *Origin of Species.* His theory that species could evolve inspired a political theorist named Herbert Spencer, who coined the term "survival of the fittest." Spencer advocated applying Darwin's evolutionary theory to other areas of academia.

Beginning in 1870, Harvard Law Professor Christopher Columbus Langdell pioneered applying evolution to the legal process.

He innovated the "case precedent" method of practicing law, which made it no longer necessary to study the intent of those who wrote the Constitution, instead just look at the most recent cases and expand its reach a little at a time. No other law school in the nation at the time taught this.

Evolutionary law grew in acceptance after 1902 when Harvard graduate Oliver Wendell Holmes, Jr., was put on the Supreme Court. His biographer described in *The Justice from Beacon Hill: The Life and Times of Oliver Wendell Holmes* (1991), that Holmes' theory of "legal realism":

> ... shook the little world of lawyers and judges who had been raised on Blackstone's theory that the law, given by God Himself, was immutable and eternal and judges had only to discover its contents.
>
> It took some years for them to come around to the view that the law was flexible, responsive to changing social and economic climates ...
>
> Holmes had ... broken new intellectual trails

... demonstrating that the corpus of the law was neither ukase [an edict] from God nor derived from Nature, but ... was a constantly evolving thing, a response to the continually developing social and economic environment.

Justices began to fall into two general categories:

1) those who hold that laws should keep the meaning of those who wrote them; and

2) those who hold that laws can evolve to have new meanings at the justice's discretion.

The evolutionary "case-precedent" method provided a way for activist justices to use the 14th Amendment, together with an "expanded" interpretation of the "commerce clause," to side-step the Constitutional means of changing the Constitution through the Amendment process.

Soon Federal judges began to take jurisdiction away from the states over issues such as unions, strikes, railroads, farming, polygamy, freedom of speech, freedom of the press, and freedom of assembly.

Chief Justice William Howard Taft, 1921–1930, increased the Chief Justice's control over lower Federal Courts. He pushed for the Supreme Court to be moved out of the basement of the Capitol into its own building.

Religion remained under each state's jurisdiction until Franklin D. Roosevelt put the former KKK member Senator Hugo Black on the Supreme Court.

Like FDR, Justice Black concentrated power in the Federal Government, most notably in the case of *Everson v. Board of Education* (1947). Catholic students in New Jersey were getting bus rides to Catholic schools. A lawsuit based on "anti-sectarian," anti-Catholic Blaine Amendments attempted to stop the bus rides. It was lost on the state level, but was appealed to the Supreme Court.

Justice Black creatively applied the evolutionary "case precedent" method, together with an "expanded" view of the 14th Amendment, to remove religion from being under states' jurisdiction to put it under Federal.

Thomas Jefferson almost prophetically predicted this in a letter to Charles Hammond in 1821:

> The germ of dissolution of our Federal Government is in ... the Federal Judiciary ... working like gravity by night and by day, gaining a little today and a little tomorrow, and advancing its noiseless step like a thief, over the field of jurisdiction, until all shall be usurped from the states.

In 1957, the Washington Ethical Society wanted tax-exemption as a church. The IRS denied it, but the Supreme Court declared "ethical culture" to be a religion and granted them the tax-exemption.

In 1961, Roy Torcaso wanted to be a notary public in Maryland but did not want to say "so help me God" at the end of his oath, as he was an atheist. When the state denied him the job, the Supreme Court overruled, deciding that "secular humanism" was also a religion.

During the Vietnam War, Elliot Welsh wanted to be a draft dodger claiming religious conscientious objector status as an atheist. When the Army did not accept this, the Supreme Court stepped in, stating:

> We think it clear that the beliefs which prompted his objection occupy the same place in his life as the belief in a traditional deity holds in the lives of his friends, the Quakers.

In 2005, James Kaufman wanted to use a room while in the Jackson Correctional Prison for a non-Bible study. When the state denied him, the 7th Circuit Court of Appeals overruled, stating:

> Atheism is indeed a form of religion ... A religion need not be based on a belief in the

existence of a supreme being ... The Court has adopted a broad definition of "religion" that includes non-theistic and atheistic beliefs, as well as theistic ones ... Atheism is ... religious in nature even though it expressly rejects a belief in a supreme being.

Once Federal Courts recognized atheism as a "religion," in order to not prefer one "religion" over another, they kicked God out. Ironically, this results in the Federal Government establishing, by its own definition, the "religion of atheism."

Supreme Court Justice Potter Stewart warned in his dissent of *Abington Township v. Schempp* (1963):

The state may not establish a "religion of secularism" in the sense of affirmatively opposing or showing hostility to religion, thus "preferring those who believe in no religion over those who do believe" ...

Refusal to permit religious exercises thus is seen, not as the realization of state neutrality, but rather as the establishment of a religion of secularism.

U.S. District Court stated in *Crockett v. Sorenson,* W.D. Va,. 1983:

The First Amendment was never intended to insulate our public institutions from any mention of God, the Bible or religion.

When such insulation occurs, another religion, such as secular humanism, is effectively established.

Ronald Reagan described this on the National Day of Prayer, May 6, 1982:

Well-meaning Americans in the name of freedom have taken freedom away. For the sake of religious tolerance, they've forbidden religious practice.

Reagan added in a Q & A Session, October 13, 1983:

The First Amendment has been twisted to the point that freedom of religion is in danger

WHO IS THE KING IN AMERICA?

of becoming freedom from religion.

Reagan addressed the Alabama State Legislature, March 15, 1982:

> The First Amendment of the Constitution was not written to protect the people of this country from religious values; it was written to protect religious values from government tyranny.

This topic is examined in greater detail in the book *Endangered Speeches – How the ACLU, IRS & LBJ Threaten Extinction of Free Speech.*

∿

AMERICA'S EXPERIMENT
OF SELF–GOVERNMENT

Colonial pastors began an experiment in self-government. Secretary of State John Foster Dulles stated:

> The government of the United States ... was founded as an experiment in human liberty.

Secretary of State William Seward stated in 1836:

> I know not how long a republican government can flourish among a great people who have not the Bible, – the experiment has never been tried; but this I do know, that the existing government of this Country, never could have had existence but for the Bible.

Theodore Roosevelt stated October 24, 1903:

> In no other place and at no other time has the experiment of government of the people, by the people, for the people, been tried on so vast a scale as here in our own country.

Dwight Eisenhower stated in *TIME Magazine* (September 22, 1952):

> You can't explain free government in any other terms than religious. The founding fathers had to refer to the Creator in order to make their revolutionary experiment make

sense; it was because "all men are endowed by their Creator with certain inalienable rights" that men could dare to be free.

Beginning his term as President, George Washington stated April 30, 1789:

> The preservation of the sacred fire of liberty, and the destiny of the republican model of government, are justly considered as deeply, perhaps as finally staked, on the experiment entrusted to the hands of the American people.

Ending his service as President, George Washington stated December 7, 1796:

> I cannot omit the occasion, to congratulate you and my country, on the success of the experiment; nor to repeat my fervent supplications to the Supreme Ruler of the Universe, and Sovereign Arbiter of Nations, that his Providential care may still be extended to the United States.

Rep. Fisher Ames wrote in his article "Monitor" (*The New England Palladium of Boston*, 1804):

> We now set out with our experimental project, exactly where Rome failed with hers. We now begin, where she ended.

WHERE DID THE IDEA BEGIN?

The question the founders wrestled with was, does POWER flow from:

> the Creator > to the King > to the People;

or does POWER flow from:

> the Creator > to the People > to their Representatives?

In settling the New England colonies, pastors realized that the KINGDOM OF GOD could NEVER BE FORCED from the top-down. They had witnessed European kings burning people at the stake for not believing as they did, and yet, in searching Scriptures, pastors never saw Jesus forcing anyone to follow him.

Their attitude was, that if Jesus never forced anyone to believe in Him, we certainly cannot either!

This left them with a question: if the KINGDOM OF GOD cannot be forced from the top-down, how will it happen? The answer is simple – it must come voluntarily from the bottom-up.

If the majority of PEOPLE held godly values, and voted for REPRESENTATIVES with those same values, then LAWS would be passed reflecting those values, and the values of the KINGDOM OF GOD could come voluntarily, percolating from the bottom-up, not forcibly shoved from the top-down.

Where did America's colonial pastors and leaders get the idea that power could flow bottom-up, from the people to their representatives? Primarily from:

- ISRAEL, which had no king during their first 400 years out of Egypt;
- ATHENS, whose leader Solon invented democracy;
- ROME, which was a republic for 500 years, "SPQR" (Senatus Populus que Romanus–"Senate & People of Rome");
- ENGLAND, whose Magna Carta and Common Law limited the king.

∽

ANCIENT ISRAEL

After the Renaissance and Reformation, there was a Hebrew Revival among Protestant and Catholic scholars. For more than a century, they intensely studied: the ancient Hebrew republic; the Hebrew language; Jewish historian Josephus (37–100); the Jerusalem Talmud (2nd century AD); the Babylonian Talmud (4th century AD); Jewish philosopher Maimonides (1135–1204); and Rabbinic literature.

These scholars, sometimes referred to as Christian "Hebraists," included:

Thomas Erastus (1524–1583); Bonaventure Vulcanius (1535–1614); Joseph Scaliger (1540–1609); Johannes van den Driesche (1550–1616); Isaac Casaubon (1559–1614); Johannes Buxtorf (1564–1629); Daniel Heinsius (1580–1655); Hugo Grotius (1583–1645); John Selden (1584–1654); Thomas Hobbes (1588–1679); James Harrington (1611–1677); and Petrus Cunaeus (1586–1638), who published *The Hebrew Republic* in 1617.

Columnist Don Feder gave an address to the Friends of Israel, titled "America & Israel–Two Nations Joined At the Heart" (Grand Rapids, MI, May 15, 2014):

> More than Athens ... more than Roman Law, and English Common Law – Israel shaped America.

Dr. Pat Robertson wrote in *America's Dates with Destiny* (1986):

> What was happening in America had no real precedent, even as far back as the city-states of Greece. The only real precedent was established thousands of years before by the tribes of Israel in the covenant with God and with each other.

Dutch politician Geert Wilders stated in his address "America the Last Man Standing," delivered in New York, September 25, 2008:

> With an Islamic Europe, it would be up to America alone to preserve the heritage of ROME, ATHENS and JERUSALEM.

Jefferson stated in his Second Inaugural, March 4, 1805:

> I shall need, too, the favor of that Being in whose hands we are, who led our forefathers, as ISRAEL of old, from their native land and planted them in a country flowing with all the necessities and comforts of life.

Justice John Jay stated September 8, 1777:

> The many remarkable and unexpected means and events by which our wants have been supplied and our enemies repelled ... are such strong and striking proofs of the interposition of Heaven, that our having been ... delivered from the threatened bondage of Britain ought, like the emancipation of the JEWS from Egyptian servitude, to be forever ascribed to its true cause.

George Washington wrote to the Hebrew Congregations of the city of Savannah, Georgia, 1790:

> May the same wonder-working Deity, who long since delivering the HEBREWS from their Egyptian Oppressors planted them in the promised land whose Providential Agency has lately been conspicuous in establishing these United States as an independent Nation – still continue to water them with the dews of Heaven and to make the inhabitants of every denomination participate in the temporal and spiritual blessings of that people whose God is Jehovah.

After the Constitution was written, it needed to be ratified by nine states to go into effect. In early 1788, eight states had ratified it, and New Hampshire was in line to be the ninth, but disagreements caused its Ratifying Convention to be adjourned in February of that year.

After the annual day of fasting, set by the Governor, New Hampshire's delegates reconvened in June of 1788.

Harvard President Rev. Samuel Langdon gave an address which was instrumental in convincing the delegates to ratify the Constitution. The *Portsmouth Daily Evening Times* (January 1, 1891), acknowledged Langdon's influence:

> By his voice and example he contributed more perhaps, than any other man to the favorable action of that body.

Samuel Langdon's address, delivered June 5, 1788, was titled "The Republic of the Israelites an Example to the American States." Afterwards, New Hampshire delegates voted to ratify the U.S. Constitution, and being the ninth state to do so, put it into effect.

In his address, Samuel Langdon stated:

> Instead of the twelve tribes of ISRAEL, we may substitute the thirteen states of the American union, and see this application plainly ...

> That as God in the course of his kind providence hath given you an excellent Constitution of government, founded on the most rational, equitable, and liberal principles, by which all that liberty is secured...

> and you are impowered to make righteous laws for promoting public order and good morals; and as he has moreover given you by his Son Jesus Christ ... a complete revelation of his will ... it will be your wisdom ... to ... adhere faithfully to the doctrines and commands of the gospel, and practice every public and private virtue.

Langdon continued:

> The ISRAELITES may be considered as a pattern to the world in all ages ... Government ... on republican principles, required laws; without which it must have degenerated immediately into ... absolute monarchy ...

> How unexampled was this quick progress of the ISRAELITES, from abject slavery, ignorance, and almost total want of order, to a national establishment perfected in all its parts far beyond all other kingdoms and states!

> From a mere mob, to a well regulated nation, under a government and laws far superior to what any other nation could boast!

Langdon concluded:

WHO IS THE KING IN AMERICA?

It was a long time after the law of Moses was given before the rest of the world knew any thing of government by law ...

It was six hundred years after Moses before... Grecian republics received a very imperfect ... code of laws from Lycurgus.

It was about five hundred years from the first founding of the celebrated Roman empire ... before the first laws of that empire.

∽

THE REPUBLIC OF THE ISRAELITES

The exodus of the Children of Israel out of Egypt occurred around 1,400 BC. When they entered the Promised Land, they had no king for the first 400 years.

• ISRAEL was the first well-recorded instance of an entire nation ruled without a king.

• In ISRAEL, everyone was equal under the Law. There was no royal family to butter-up to at this time. This was the beginning of the concept of equality.

Deuteronomy 1:17

Ye shall not respect persons in judgment; but ye shall hear the small as well as the great.

• In ISRAEL, every person, male and female, was made in the image of the Creator, possessing God-given rights which no government could take away. It was the responsibility of government to guarantee individual rights.

• ISRAEL had relatively few laws, as citizens were accountable to God to treat each other fairly.

Leviticus 19:18

You shall not take vengeance or bear a grudge against your kinsfolk. Love your neighbor as yourself: I am the LORD.

• ISRAEL treated non-Israelites as equals, though

the immigrants had to abide by the Law.

Leviticus 19:34

> The stranger who resides with you shall be
> to you as one of your citizens; you shall love
> him as yourself, for you were strangers in the
> land of Egypt: I the LORD am your God.

• ISRAEL was tolerant. Though convinced they were
worshiping the only true God, they never waged war
to force other nations to accept Him, nor did they force
non-Israelites living within their borders to convert.

John Locke wrote in *A Letter Concerning Toleration*
(1689):

> Foreigners and such as were strangers to the
> commonwealth of Israel were not compelled by
> force to observe the rites of the Mosaical law...

> We find not one man forced into the Jewish
> religion and the worship of the true God ... If any
> one ... desired to be made a denizen [citizen] of
> their commonwealth ... to embrace their religion
> ... this he did willingly, on his own accord, not
> by constraint.

• ISRAEL had a system of honesty, thus providing
a basis for commerce.

Leviticus 19:36

> Just balances, just weights, a just ephah, and
> a just hin, shall ye have.

Proverbs 11:1

> A false balance is abomination to the
> LORD: but a just weight is his delight.

• In ISRAEL, land was permanently titled to the
families. This contrasted with most of the world, where
kings granted land to loyal vassals, or as in Egypt,
where the pharaohs owned the land.

Israel called it the Promised "Land" because the

people actually owned title to their land. This prevented a dictator from gathering up the land and putting the people back into slavery.

If a person owned land, they could accumulate possessions. The Bible called this being "blessed"; Karl Marx called it being a "capitalist."

• ISRAEL had a bureaucracy-free welfare system. When someone harvested their field, they left the gleanings for the poor. This way, the poor were taken care of, while maintaining their dignity, without some political leader collecting everything and doling it back out to those who could help him stay in power.

• ISRAEL had no police. Everyone was taught the Law, and everyone was personally accountable to enforce it. It was as if everyone in the nation was "deputized."

• ISRAEL had no prisons. The Law required swift justice at the "gates of the city" and a "city of refuge" where fugitives could flee to await trial.

• ISRAEL had no standing army, as every man was in the militia, armed, and ready at a moment's notice to defend his family and community.

• ISRAEL was the first nation where everyone was taught to read. At the time in history when Moses and the Children of Israel left Egypt:

> • the Hittite language had 375 cuneiform characters;

> • the Indus Valley Harappan language had 417 symbols;

> • the Luwian language of Anatolian had over 500 logographic hieroglyphs;

> • the Akkadian language in Mesopotamia had over 1,500 Sumerian cuneiform characters;

> • the Egyptian language had over 3,000

hieroglyphic characters;

- the Chinese language had nearly 10,000 pictogram and ideogram characters, invented by scribes of China's Yellow Emperor.

When Moses came down from Mount Sinai, he not only had the Ten Commandments, but he had them in a 22 character alphabet. ("aleph" is the first letter in Hebrew, and "beth" is the second). With so few characters, everyone could learn to read, even children.

Israel's priests and Levites taught the Law, and also taught people to read it for themselves. It was not just a privilege to read it, they were required to, as the law was addressed to each person who, was personally accountable to God obey it.

In most countries, reading and writing were skills only for kings, pharaohs, emperors, and their scribes, together with the ruling class and merchants.

As mentioned earlier, the first invention was the plow – "Cain was a tiller of the ground." (Genesis 4:2) Then people started hitting each other with them and they turned into weapons. People gravitated together for protection, forming the first cities.

When people get together, something happens – one person ends up being better at fighting and the people ask him to be their captain. At first, this is great, as all are better able to survive. But then this person has sons, grandsons, and great-grandsons who claim to be an elite class, and it turns into a hereditary monarchy.

Kings claimed to own everything in the city and they needed accountants and scribes to count it all. In China, scribes developed a way of counting with knots in ropes. In Sumeria, they developed rods with beads – an abacus, then they used tokens in dishes.

They began making markings in the tokens – like tallying – which turned into cuneiform. Writing evolved to keep track of a king's genealogy, decrees, astrological observations, myths, and royal propaganda.

There was no need for common people to read as they had relatively few possessions to keep track of, and obviously made no decrees. Slaves not only had no need to read, they were often forbidden to learn to read.

In Ancient Egypt, the literacy rate was less than one percent. The National Archaeological Museum in Athens, Greece, in its section on Egyptian Artifacts, has a display on "Scribes," stating:

> Only a small percentage of ancient Egypt's population was literate, namely the pharaoh, members of the royal family, officials, priests and scribes.

> Particularly popular and lucrative, the scribe's profession was mostly hereditary. Scribes had careers in the government, priesthood, and army. They began their rigorous training in their early childhood.

> Most of their training took place inside a building called the "House of Life," attached to the temple. Scribes wrote on stone or clay sherds, wooden boards, linen, papyrus, and parchment.

Writing was the scribes' secret knowledge. It is theorized they kept writing complicated as job security. They were needed to decipher cryptic hieroglyphs.

The ruling class used complicated writing to maintain control over uneducated masses. Anthropologist Claude Levi Strauss (1908–2009), wrote:

> Ancient writing's main function was to facilitate the enslavement of other human beings.

George Orwell wrote in *Nineteen Eighty-Four*:

> In the long run, a hierarchical society was only possible on a basis of poverty and ignorance.

This was similar to Europe after the fall of the Roman Empire, where only the upper class and clergy could read. Most commoners were illiterate, which allowed them to be more easily controlled.

This happened in the United States prior to the Civil War, where Southern Democrat slave-holding states had laws making it illegal to teach slaves to read, especially after Nat Turner's slave rebellion. It was easier to control illiterate, uneducated people.

Frederick Douglass, a Republican advisor to President Lincoln, was born a slave in Baltimore, Maryland. When he was about 12 years old, his master's sister-in-law, Sophia Auld, began teaching him the alphabet. When her husband found out, he adamantly forbade it, arguing that if slaves could read, they would grow discontent, forge their documents, and run away.

Douglass considered this the "first decidedly anti-slavery lecture" he had ever heard, causing him to be even more determined to learn how to read.

He wrote in his autobiography *The Life and Times of Frederick Douglass: His Early Life as a Slave, His Escape from Bondage, and His Complete History* (1881) of being caught attempting to read a newspaper. It was snatched away from him with a scolding. Frederick at last learned to read from neighborhood white children, as well as carefully observing the writings of men he worked with.

• In ISRAEL, the people chose their own leaders. Honest elections allowed for government by the consent of the governed.

Deuteronomy 1:3–13:

> Moses spoke unto the children of Israel ...
> How can I myself alone bear your ... burden
> ... TAKE YOU wise men, and understanding,
> and KNOWN AMONG YOUR TRIBES, and
> I will make them rulers over you.

Deuteronomy 16:18–19:

WHO IS THE KING IN AMERICA?

Judges and officers SHALT THOU MAKE THEE IN ALL THY GATES which the Lord thy God giveth thee throughout thy tribes.

Exodus 18:21 stated:

Moreover thou shalt provide OUT OF ALL THE PEOPLE able men, such as fear God, men of truth, hating covetousness; and place such over them, to be rulers of thousands, and rulers of hundreds, rulers of fifties, and rulers of tens.

Rather than a pyramid style, top-down form of government where the king's will was law, Israel had a bottom-up form of government, like a living tree, with each cell contributing to its growth.

Each town had their own city elders. Anyone could be raised to leadership: Jephthah was the son of a prostitute; Gideon was from an obscure family; and Deborah was an honest woman who knew the Law. Where else in the world at that time could a woman unrelated to any royalty rise to be a national leader?

Israel was truly unique. E.C. Wines wrote in *Commentaries on the Laws of the Ancient Hebrews, with an Introductory Essay on Civil Society & Government* (NY: Geo. P. Putnam & Co., 1853):

Menes in Egypt; Minos in Crete; Cadmus in Thebes; Lycurgus in Sparta; Zaleucus in Locris; and Numa in Rome.

But ... Moses differed fundamentally from ... these heathen legislators.

They employed religion in establishing their political institutions, while he made use of a civil constitution as a means of perpetuating religion ...

Moses' ... national unity ... was not that species of unity, which the world has since so often seen, in which vast multitudes of human beings are delivered up to the arbitrary will of one man.

It was a unity, effected by the abolition of

caste; a unity, founded on the principle of equal rights; a unity, in which the whole people formed the state ... contrary to the celebrated declaration of a French monarch [Louis XIV], who avowed himself to be the state.

∾

THE LAW & CONSCIENCE

Margaret Thatcher stated in 1996:

> Ten Commandments are ... the origin of ... the sanctity of the INDIVIDUAL ... It is Personal Liberty with PERSONAL RESPONSIBILITY.

President Harry Truman stated in 1950:

> The FUNDAMENTAL BASIS of this nation's laws was given to MOSES ON THE MOUNT ... If we don't have a proper fundamental MORAL background, we will finally end up with a TOTALITARIAN government which does not believe in rights for anybody except for the state.

Professors Donald S. Lutz and Charles S. Hyneman wrote "The Relative Influence of European Writers on Late 18th–Century American Political Thought" (*American Political Science Review,* 1984).

They examined nearly 15,000 writings of the 55 writers of the U.S. Constitution, including newspaper articles, pamphlets, books and monographs, and listed the sources they quoted from, ie., Montesquieu, Blackstone, Locke, Hume, Plutarch, Beccaria, etc. They discovered the most frequently quoted source was the Bible, and in particular, the book of Deuteronomy.

Calvin Coolidge stated May 3, 1925:

> A common spiritual inspiration was potent to ... mold ... together ... the many and scattered colonial communities that had been planted along the Atlantic seaboard ...

One of the factors which I think weighed heaviest on the side of unity – the Bible was the one work of literature that was common to all of them. The Scriptures were read and studied everywhere.

There are many testimonies that their teachings became the most important intellectual and spiritual force for unification...

The sturdy old divines of those days found the Bible a chief source of illumination for their arguments in support of the patriot cause. They knew the Book.

In governments, there is a continuum or spectrum of power, with NO GOVERNMENT (anarchy) on one side and TOTAL GOVERNMENT (dictatorship) on the other.

On the TOTAL government side, power is in the hands of one person who rules through favoritism and fear.

On the NO government side, there is lawless chaos, unless the people exercise self-control. To use a iPhone analogy, it would be as if everyone downloads a behavioral app, which gives GPS guidance for personal interactions.

But there is a vital question: why would someone exercise self-control? What would motivate them to resist making a wrong turn and yield to a selfish temptation? Ancient Israel introduced into the world the necessary incentive, namely, a God who:

    1) is watching everyone;

    2) wants you to be fair; and

    3) will hold you accountable in the future.

In Israel, God was king over each individual person directly and immediately, without any intermediaries.

If, for example, someone had the opportunity to steal and not get caught, they might consider it until they remembered that God was watching them, that He wanted them to be fair, and that He would hold them personally and individually accountable in the future.

This would cause them to hesitate stealing, which is called having a "conscience." If everybody in the nation believed this, there would be complete order and security, with no police.

Democrat Presidential Candidate William Jennings Bryan stated in 1908:

> A religion which teaches personal responsibility to God gives strength to morality ... There is a powerful restraining influence in the belief that an All-seeing eye scrutinizes every thought and word and act of the individual.

William Linn, the first U.S. House Chaplain, stated May 1, 1789:

> Let my neighbor ... persuade himself that there is no God, and he will ... pick my pocket, and break not only my leg but my neck ... If there be no God, there is ... no future account.

President Reagan stated in 1984:

> Without God there is no virtue because there is no prompting of the conscience.

Yale President Ezra Stiles addressed Connecticut's General Assembly, May 8, 1783:

> A discourse upon the political welfare of God's American Israel ... Our system of dominion and civil polity would be imperfect without the true religion ... From the diffusion of virtue among the people of any community would arise their greatest secular happiness.

Israel's decentralized form of government allowed for maximum individual liberty. Claude Fleury wrote in *The Manners of the Ancient Israelites* (1681):

> The Israelites were perfectly free. They

enjoyed the liberty cherished by Greece and Rome. Such was the purpose of God.

E.C. Wines wrote in *Commentaries on the Laws of the Ancient Hebrews* (NY: Geo. P. Putnam & Co., 1853):

> Another of those great ideas, which constituted the basis of the Hebrew state, was liberty ...

> The Hebrew people enjoyed as great a degree of personal liberty, as can ever be combined with an efficient and stable government.

This can only work with the God of the Bible. An Islamic Allah permits lying, stealing, and raping of infidel "kafir" non-Muslims. Only the God of the Bible states that all men and women are equal, made in the image of the Creator, and to do unto others as you would have them do unto you.

✧

WHAT FINALLY HAPPENED?

The republic of the Israelites almost fell when Abimelech, the illigetimate son of Gideon, went to the city of Shechem. As described in Judges 9:4–5, he agitated unrest by convincing his kindred to support him because they were of the same race. He took 70 pieces of silver from the temple of Baalberith, as the people had backslidden from the Lord, and hired "vain and worthless persons" to murder the sons of Gideon. Abimelech seized power as king, but reaped what he sowed when dissension spread and he was killed.

The continuation of ancient Israel's unique system was dependent upon the Levites teaching the Law.

Imagine if every computer you bought was preloaded with a software virus, and you had to immediately take it to the Geek Squad to have it cleaned and reprogrammed.

In Israel, they understood that each child was born preloaded with the virus of selfishness, and the parents would immediately take the child to the Levite computer techs, who would run an anti-virus program and recode the child, installing God's software – the Law.

When the Levites and priests neglected teaching the Law, "every man did what was right in their own eyes," immorality and domestic chaos ensued, and Israel's system of self-government collapsed.

> • Eli, the High Priest, had sons who "lay with the women that assembled at the door of the tabernacle of the congregation" (I Samuel 2:12–36)

> • A Levite with a graven image idol served as a priest for the Tribe of Dan (Judges 17:1–13)

> • A Levite had a concubine who was raped by sodomites and died (Judges 19:1–30)

Yale President Ezra Stiles wrote in 1783:

> The secular welfare of God's ancient people depended upon their VIRTUE, their religion, their observance of that holy covenant, which Israel entered into with God.

The people then begged for a king to restore order. The prophet Samuel cried, and the Lord told him:

> They have not rejected thee, but they have rejected me, that I should not reign over them. (I Samuel 8:7)

Harvard President Samuel Langdon referred to Israel in "Government Corrupted by Vice," May 31, 1775:

> The only form of government which had a proper claim to a divine establishment, was so far from including the idea of a king, that it was a high crime for ISRAEL to ask to be in this respect like other nations; and when they were thus gratified, it was rather as a just punishment..

Langdon continued:

That for the sins of a people God may suffer the best government to be corrupted, or entirely dissolved; and that nothing but a general reformation can give ground to hope that the public happiness will be restored ...

The kingdom of Israel was brought to destruction, because its iniquities were full ... because there remained no hope of reformation... Their government degenerated in proportion as their vices increased, till few faithful men were left in any public offices ...

At length, when they were delivered up for seventy years into the hands of the king of Babylon, scarcely any remains of their original excellent civil polity appeared among them ...

When a government is in its prime ... virtue prevails – every thing is managed with justice, prudence, and frugality ...

But vice will increase with the riches and glory of an empire; and this gradually tends to corrupt the constitution, and in time bring on its dissolution.

This may be considered not only as the natural effect of vice, but a righteous judgment of heaven, especially upon a nation which has been favored with the blessing of religion and liberty, and is guilty of undervaluing them; and eagerly going into the gratification of every lust.

∽

GOVERNMENT FUNDAMENTALLY TRANSFORMED

Israel got King Saul, who shortly thereafter killed many of the priests. The situation was that Saul became jealous of David and tried to kill him. David fled, stopping at the city of Nob to ask the priests for some bread and the sword of Goliath kept there.

Unaware that David had fallen out of favor with Saul, the priests helped him. Doeg the Edomite watched this.

When Saul was complaining that no one cared that his son Jonathan was friends with David, Doeg spoke up that he witnessed David being helped by the priests.

1 Samuel 22:9

> Then answered Doeg the Edomite, which was set over the servants of Saul, and said, I saw the son of Jesse coming to Nob, to Ahimelech the son of Ahitub.

Saul ordered the priests to come to his camp. When they arrived, he told his men to kill them. When they hesitated, Doeg did not hesitate.

1 Samuel 22:18

> And the king said unto the footmen that stood about him, Turn, and slay the priests ... But the servants of the king would not put forth their hand to fall upon the priests of the LORD.
>
> And the king said to Doeg, Turn thou, and fall upon the priests. And Doeg the Edomite turned, and he fell upon the priests, and slew on that day fourscore and five persons that did wear a linen ephod.

What just happened?

Israel had been a republic, where each citizen was accountable to God to keep the Law. The Law instructed there needed to be two or more witnesses. There was only one witness – Doeg.

Deuteronomy 17:6

> At the mouth of two witnesses, or three witnesses, shall he that is worthy of death be put to death; but at the mouth of one witness he shall not be put to death.

The Law also instructed that the trial was to be before "the elders of the city." Saul held no trial, but

WHO IS THE KING IN AMERICA?

just commanded the priests be executed. What Saul was telling his soldiers was to stop being individually accountable to God – stop having a conscience.

What Doeg the Edomite did was surrender his conscience to the king. If the king says kill, I will kill.

Images of the My Lai Massacre come to mind, where soldiers "following orders" killed an estimated 400 villagers in South Vietnam on March 16, 1968.

A king can demand the conscience of his subjects, pressuring them to surrender their deeply held convictions and their reason. Rather than protecting citizens' beliefs – he may be tempted to dictate them, preferring "yes men" who fear him rather than God.

Josephus wrote in *Antiquities of the Jews* (c. 94 AD):

> Nimrod ... also gradually changed the government into tyranny, seeing no other way of turning men from the fear of God, but to bring them into a constant dependence on his power.

Jesus delineated limits to a king's power:

> Render therefore unto Caesar the things which are Caesar's; and unto God the things that are God's. (Matthew 22:21)

In China, 207 BC, a corrupt political leader named Zhao Gao wanted to test who was loyal to him. He brought a deer into the court and called it a horse. Those wanting to curry his favor also called it a horse. Those insisting it was a deer were soon falsely accused by Zhao and killed.

Tyrants demand people deny their common sense and follow without questioning.

Franklin Roosevelt said of Hitler, December 15, 1941:

> The individual human being has no rights whatsoever in himself ... no right to a soul of his own, or a mind of his own, or a tongue of his own, or a trade of his own; or even to live where

he pleases or to marry the woman he loves ...
His only duty is the duty of obedience, not to his
God, not to his conscience, but to Adolf Hitler.

When Barack Obama was first campaigning for President, he promised the Christian audience at the Saddleback Church Presidential Forum, April 17, 2008:

> I believe that marriage is the union between a man and a woman. Now, for me as a Christian – for me – for me as a Christian, it is also a sacred union. God's in the mix ... I am not somebody who promotes same-sex marriage.

Yet shortly after being elected, he changed to support gay marriage and the entire LGBT agenda, and had his administration investigate and prosecute those who holding traditional Judeo–Christian beliefs – the very beliefs he professed to hold while campaigning.

Hillary Clinton caused alarm addressing the Women in The World Summit, New York City, April 23, 2015:

> Deep-seated cultural codes, religious beliefs and structural biases have to be changed.

Rev. Bill Owens of the Coalition of African American Pastors stated on *FOX Report,* January 15, 2017:

> Mrs. Clinton was not elected because of ... one great thing she said ... that we had to change our religious beliefs. – We are not going to change our religious beliefs, not for a political party, not a leader.

Louisiana Governor Bobby Jindal responded:

> Our religious beliefs are between us and God, not us and Hillary Clinton.

WHAT IS BASIS OF FREE GOVERNMENT?
Justice John Jay stated September 8, 1777:

> The Americans are the first people whom

Heaven has favored with an opportunity of ... choosing the forms of government under which they should live.

All other constitutions have derived their existence from violence or accidental circumstances ...

Your lives, your liberties, your property, will be at the disposal only of your Creator and yourselves.

You will know no power but such as you will create; no authority unless derived from your grant; no laws but such as acquire all their obligation from your consent.

Jay added:

The convention by whom that Constitution was formed were of opinion that the Gospel of Christ, like the Ark of God, would not fall, though unsupported by the arm of flesh ...

But let it be remembered that whatever marks of wisdom ... may be in your Constitution, yet like the ... forms of our first parents before their Maker breathed into them the breath of life, it is yet to be animated ... from the people it must receive its spirit ...

Vice, ignorance, and want of vigilance will be the only enemies able to destroy it ... Hence it becomes the common duty ... to unite in repressing the licentious.

The understanding was, that if the fear of God were removed, people would yield to licentious, sexually immoral behavior. Their unrestrained selfish lusts would end in lawlessness, violence and domestic chaos.

People would then beg someone to restore order, allowing them to use of whatever force was necessary, even militarized police disarming the population.

In this way, a self-governed nation would be

fundamentally transformed into being ruled by a king.

In the preface of *Webster's 1828 Dictionary,* Noah Webster wrote:

> The Christian religion is the most important and one of the first things in which all children, under a free government ought to be instructed...

> No truth is more evident to my mind than that the Christian religion must be the basis of any government intended to secure the rights and privileges of a free people.

Daniel Webster concluded his Plymouth Rock address, December 22, 1820:

> Ye future generations! We would hail you, as you rise in your long succession, to fill the places which we now fill ... We welcome you to the blessings of good government and religious liberty ...

> We welcome you to the immeasurable blessings of rational existence, the immortal hope of Christianity, and the light of everlasting truth! ...

> We are bound ... to convince the world that order and law, religion and morality, the rights of conscience, the rights of persons, and the rights of property, may all be preserved and secured, in the most perfect manner, by a government entirely and purely elective.

> If we fail in this, our disaster will be signal [momentous], and will furnish an argument ... in support of those opinions which maintain that government can rest safely on nothing but power and coercion.

∽

ATHENIAN DEMOCRACY

Where else did America's founders get the idea that THE PEOPLE are king, that they could rule themselves? Some ideas came from the Athenian Democracy.

The Greek word for city is "polis" which is the root of the word "politics."

Lord Acton wrote:

> The Laws of Plato, the Politics of Aristotle, are, if I may trust my own experience the books from which we may learn the most about the principles of politics.

Draco was the king of Athens in 622 BC. He was the first to put their laws down in writing. Unfortunately, these laws were so harsh that they gave birth to the term "draconian."

Athens got a new leader in 594 BC named Solon. As the chief magistrate, Solon instituted democracy, then left the city so the people had to live it out.

Rev. Langdon stated in "The Republic of the Israelites An Example to the American States," June 5, 1788:

> It was six hundred years after Moses before the Spartans, the most famous of the Grecian republics, received a very imperfect, and in some particulars very absurd code of laws from Lycurgus.
>
> After this feeble attempt of legislation, three hundred years more elapsed before Solon appeared and gave laws to Athens, though a city long famous for arms, arts, eloquence, and philosophy.

Montesquieu wrote in *The Spirit of the Laws* (1748):

> When the body of the people is possessed of the supreme power, this is called a democracy ...
>
> In a democracy the people are in some respects the sovereign, and in others the subject. There can be no exercise of sovereignty but by their suffrages [votes], which are their own will.

Winston Churchill addressed the House of Commons, November 11, 1947:

Many forms of government have been tried, and will be tried in this world of sin and woe.

No one pretends that democracy is perfect ... Indeed, it has been said that democracy is the worst form of government except all those other forms.

A pure democracy only ever worked on a relatively small, city-state level, as it required everyone, everyday, go the agora marketplace and talk politics. Those not keeping up with the politics were called "idiotes."

The Greek philosopher Plato (428–347 BC) stated:

Those who are too smart to engage in politics are punished by being governed by those who are dumber.

John F. Kennedy referred to Solon in his address to the American Newspaper Publishers Association at the Waldorf – Astoria Hotel, New York, April 27, 1961:

Without debate, without criticism, no Administration and no country can succeed ...

That is why the Athenian law-maker Solon decreed it a crime for any citizen to shrink from controversy.

Pericles led Athens during its Golden Age between the Persian War (478 BC) and the Peloponnesian War (404 BC). Not only did he win many battles, he succeeded in having his political enemies ostracized – forced out of the city for ten years, ending their careers.

Pericles centralized power, moved the Delian League treasury from Delos to Athens, and then raided it for ambitious building projects, such as the Parthenon.

When the governing body citizens in Athens, called "ekklesia," considered ostracizing Pericles for maladministration of funds, he began to divert public attention away from him by letting relations with Sparta to devolve into the Peloponnesian War.

War became the preferred diversionary tactic of usurping leaders as it benefited them in two ways:

> 1) public attention is diverted away from the corrupt leader and onto the crisis; and

> 2) the public always wants a strong leader in times of crisis and war.

In 346 BC, Athens finally fell. Philip II of Macedon, the father of Alexander the Great, had taken gold from the mines around the Greek city of Amphipolis and bribed some citizens of Athens to betray their city – a tactic which became known as "the fifth column."

This was like Abimelech in Judges 9:4–5, who took 70 pieces of silver from the temple of Baalberith to hire "vain and worthless persons" to murder the sons of Gideon, so that he could usurp power and be king.

Paid betrayers and bribed politicians would gather around themselves, what Vladimir Lenin later called, "useful idiots" – people who actually believed their lies.

Philip marched toward Athens to find the lying propaganda had so confused the city, that it was unable to mount a united defense, allowing him to take control.

A generation earlier, the Greek philosopher Plato predicted the fall of the Athenian Democracy.

Plato recorded dialogues of Socrates (470–399 BC) in *The Republic,* 380 BC. In chapters (books) 8 and 9, he described the 5 stages of a city government:

> • First aristocracy – rule by the capable and virtuous, who know how to successfully run farms and businesses. They are lovers of principle and truth;

> • Followed by timocracy – rule by the famous, who have no experience running anything, they just love fame and honor;

• Followed by oligarchy – rule by a clique of insiders who love money and vote themselves and their friends favors;

• Followed by democracy – rule by lovers of tolerance. The people first tolerate each other, then tolerate those a little out of the mainstream, till finally they are tolerating unrestrained selfish behavior. Abandoning virtue and self-control, this ends in chaos;

• As the chaos increases, citizens begin to seek a strong leader to restore order, transitioning back to a king – a lover of power.

Plato explained:

Democracy ... is a charming form of government, full of variety and disorder, and dispensing a sort of equality to equals and unequals alike ...

Such is democracy; – a pleasing, lawless, various sort of government, distributing equality to equals and unequals alike ...

And so the young man passes ... into the freedom and libertinism of useless and unnecessary pleasures ...

In all of us, even in good men, there is a lawless wild-beast nature ... Everyone appears to have them, but in some persons they are controlled ... while in ... others they are stronger ...

and there is no conceivable folly or crime – not excepting incest or any other unnatural union ... which ... when he has parted company with all shame and sense, a man may not be ready to commit.

Aristotle, the student of Plato, wrote:

Tolerance is the last virtue of a dying society.

Plato described the manner of the "democrat":

He was supposed from his youth upwards to

have been trained under a miserly parent, who encouraged the saving appetites in him ... and then he got into the company of a ... licentious sort of people, and taking to all their wanton ways rushed into the opposite extreme from an abhorrence of his father's meanness ...

Neither does he receive ... advice; if any one says to him that some pleasures are ... of evil desires ... he shakes his head ...

He lives from day to day indulging the appetite of the hour ... His life has neither law nor order ... He is all liberty and equality.

Plato warned further:

Can liberty have any limit? Certainly not ... By degrees the anarchy finds a way into private houses ... The son is on a level with his father, he having no respect or reverence for either of his parents; and this is his freedom ...

Citizens ... chafe impatiently at the least touch of authority... they will have no one over them ...

Such ... is the fair and glorious beginning out of which springs tyranny ... Liberty overmasters democracy ... the excessive increase of anything often causes a reaction in the opposite direction ...

The excess of liberty, whether in states or individuals, seems only to pass into excess of slavery ...

And so tyranny naturally arises out of democracy, and the most aggravated form of tyranny and slavery out of the most extreme form of liberty.

Since the people have no experience running a government, they will follow the example of preceding leaders and yield to avarice. They will vote to spread the city's wealth around till the treasury is empty.

Plato warns how they will vote to take money from the rich:

> Democracy ... of which the insatiable desire brings her to dissolution ...

> Their leaders deprive the rich of their estates and distribute them among the people; at the same time taking care to reserve the larger part for themselves ...

> And the persons whose property is taken from them are compelled to defend themselves before the people as they best can ...

> Insatiable desire ... and ... neglect ... introduces the change in democracy, which occasions a demand for tyranny ...

> Does not tyranny spring from democracy.

Plato described how unrestrained passions lead to financial irresponsibility. Without enough money to go around, bickering and fighting result, leading to chaos and anarchy. Then people will begin to look for someone to come along and fix this mess.

Plato wrote:

> Last of all comes ... the tyrant ... In the early days of his power, he is full of smiles, and he salutes every one whom he meets ... making promises in public and also in private, liberating debtors, and distributing land to the people and his followers, and wanting to be so kind and good to every one ...

> This ... is the root from which a tyrant springs; when he first appears above ground he is a protector ...

> Hinting at the abolition of debts and partition of lands ... he ... begins to make a party against the rich ... that they may be impoverished by payment of taxes, and thus compelled to devote themselves to their daily wants and therefore

less likely to conspire against him? ...

And when a man who is wealthy and is also accused of being an enemy of the people sees ... he flees ... and is not ashamed to be a coward.

Plato explained that "the protector" yields to avarice and uses his new power to target political opponents:

And the protector of the people ... having a mob entirely at his disposal, he is not restrained from shedding the blood of kinsmen;

by the favorite method of false accusation he brings them into court and murders them, making the life of man to disappear, and with unholy tongue and lips tasting the blood of his fellow citizen ...

And if any of them are suspected by him of having notions of freedom, and of resistance to his authority, he will have a good pretext for destroying them.

Plato continued:

How then does a protector begin to change into a tyrant? ...

He begins to grow unpopular ... Then comes the famous request for a bodyguard, which is the device of all those who have got thus far in their tyrannical career – "Let not the people's friend," as they say, "be lost to them" ...

The people readily assent; all their fears are for him – they have none for themselves ...

And ... the protector of whom we spoke, is to be seen ... the overthrower of many, standing up in the chariot of state with the reins in his hand, no longer protector, but tyrant absolute ...

The lion and serpent element in them disproportionately grows and gains strength.

Plato described how the tyrant would keep power:

The tyrant must be always getting up a war...

He is always stirring up some war or other,
in order that the people may require a leader.

James Madison warned of this at the Constitutional
Convention, June 29, 1787 (*Max Farrand's Records of
the Federal Convention of 1787,* Vol. I, 1911, p. 465):

In time of actual war, great discretionary
powers are constantly given to the Executive
Magistrate. Constant apprehension of War,
has the same tendency to render the head too
large for the body.

A standing military force, with an overgrown
Executive will not long be safe companions to
liberty. The means of defense against foreign
danger have been always the instruments of
tyranny at home.

Among the Romans it was a standing
maxim to excite a war, whenever a revolt was
apprehended.

Throughout all Europe, the armies kept up
under the pretext of defending, have enslaved
the people.

Madison wrote in *Federalist No. 47* (January 30, 1788):

The accumulation of all powers, Legislative,
Executive, and Judiciary, in the same hands,
whether of one, a few, or many, and whether
hereditary, self-appointed, or elective, may justly
be pronounced the very definition of tyranny.

Plato described when a tyrant loses popularity:

Then some of those who joined in setting
him up, and who are in power, speak their
minds to him and to one another, and the more
courageous of them cast in his teeth what is
being done ...

And the tyrant, if he means to rule, must
get rid of them; he cannot stop while he has a
friend or an enemy who is good for anything ...

Some he kills and others he banishes ...

Must he not either perish at the hands of his enemies, or from being a man become a wolf – that is, a tyrant? ... He who has tasted the entrails of a single human victim ... is destined to become a wolf ...

And therefore he must look about him and see who is valiant, who is high-minded, who is wise, who is wealthy; happy man, he is the enemy of them all, and must seek occasion against them whether he will or no, until he has made a purgation of the state ...

Yes, I said, not the sort of purgation which the physicians make of the body; for they take away the worse and leave the better part, but he does the reverse.

Plato continued:

And the more detestable his actions are to the citizens the more satellites and the greater devotion in them will he require? ... And who are the devoted band, and where will he procure them? ...

He will rob the citizens of their slaves; he will then set them free and enroll them in his bodyguard. To be sure ... he will be able to trust them best of all.

What a blessed creature ... must this tyrant be; he has put to death the others and has these for his trusted friends ...

These are the new citizens whom he has called into existence, who admire him and are his companions, while the good hate and avoid him ...

But they will ... attract mobs, and hire voices fair and loud and persuasive, and draw the cities over to tyrannies ...

Moreover, they are paid for this and receive

honor – the greatest honor, as might be expected, from tyrants ...

Poets ... are the eulogists of tyranny ... He also praises tyranny as godlike ...

But the higher they ascend our constitution hill, the more their reputation fails, and seems unable from shortness of breath to proceed further.

Plato added:

Let us ... inquire how the tyrant will maintain that ... ever-changing army of his. If, he said, there are sacred treasures in the city, he will confiscate and spend them ...

By heaven ... the parent will discover what a monster he has been fostering in his bosom; and, when he wants to drive him out, he will find that he is weak and his son strong. Why, you do not mean to say that the tyrant will use violence?

What! beat his father if he opposes him? Yes, he will, having first disarmed him ...

Then he is a parricide, and a cruel guardian of an aged parent; and this is real tyranny ... as the saying is, the people who would escape the smoke which is the slavery of freemen, has fallen into the fire which is the tyranny of slaves.

Thus liberty, getting out of all order and reason, passes into the harshest and bitterest form of slavery ...

May we not rightly say that we have sufficiently discussed ... the manner of the transition from democracy to tyranny? ...

A tyranny is the wretchedest form of government ...

The longer he lives the more of a tyrant he becomes.

WHO IS THE KING IN AMERICA?

Like Plato, other insightful individuals noted the correlation between virtue and self-government.

Britain's Lord Thomas MacCauley wrote to Henry S. Randall, Democrat Secretary of State for New York, May 23, 1857:

> Institutions purely democratic must, sooner or later, destroy liberty, or civilization, or both...

> France is an example ... a pure democracy was established there. During a short time there was ... a general spoliation, a national bankruptcy, a new partition of the soil, a maximum of prices, a ruinous load of taxation laid on the rich for the purpose of supporting the poor in idleness ...

> You may think that your country enjoys an exemption from these evils ... I am of a very different opinion. Your fate I believe to be certain, though it is deferred.

Lord MacCauley continued:

> The time will come when ... distress everywhere makes the laborer mutinous and discontented, and inclines him to listen with eagerness to agitators who tell him that it is a monstrous iniquity that one man should have a million while another cannot get a full meal.

> In bad years there is plenty of grumbling ... and sometimes a little rioting ... Your government will never be able to restrain a distressed and discontented majority ...

> The day will come when, in the State of New York, a multitude of people, none of whom has had more than half a breakfast, or expects to have more than half a dinner, will choose a Legislature ...

> On one side is a statesman preaching patience, respect for vested rights, strict

observance of public faith.

On the other is a demagogue ranting about the tyranny of capitalists and usurers, and asking why anybody should be permitted to drink champagne and to ride in a carriage, while thousands of honest folks are in want of necessaries.

Which of the two candidates is likely to be preferred by a working man who hears his children cry for more bread?

Lord MacCauley concluded:

I seriously apprehend that you will, in some such season of adversity ... devour all the seed-corn, and thus make the next year, a year not of scarcity, but of absolute famine ...

When a society has entered on this downward progress, either civilization or liberty must perish. Either some Caesar or Napoleon will seize the reins of government with a strong hand.

Did American leaders understand Plato's warning that democracy without virtue would end in chaos out of which a tyrant would arise?

Benjamin Franklin wrote April 17, 1787:

Only a virtuous people are capable of freedom. As nations become corrupt and vicious, they have more need of masters.

Harry S Truman stated April 3, 1951:

Without a firm moral foundation, freedom degenerates quickly into selfishness and ... anarchy. Then there will be freedom only for the rapacious and those who are stronger and more unscrupulous than the rank and file of the people.

Massachusetts Governor Samuel Adams wrote February 12, 1779:

A general dissolution of the principles

and manners will more surely overthrow the liberties of America than the whole force of the common enemy.

While the people are virtuous they cannot be subdued; but once they lose their virtue, they will be ready to surrender their liberties to the first external or internal invader.

If we would enjoy this gift of Heaven, let us become a virtuous people.

&

SELF–GOVERNMENT REQUIRES VIRTUE

An visual to help understand the relationship between prosperity and virtue is a tall construction crane: the higher it reaches, the heavier the counterweight needs to be in order to keep it from tipping over.

In other words, the more prosperity a person, or a nation, experiences, the more private virtue is needed to keep them from moral and financial bankruptcy.

Massachusetts' Constitution, 1780, drafted by John Adams, is the world's oldest functioning written constitution. It stated in PART 1, ART. 3:

> Good order and preservation of civil government, essentially depend upon piety, religion and morality ...

> The legislature shall ... require ... suitable provision ... for the institution of the public worship of God, and for the support and maintenance of public Protestant teachers of piety, religion and morality.

New Hampshire Constitution, 1784, stated (Part 1, Article 6):

> As morality and piety, rightly grounded on evangelical principles will give the best and greatest security to government ...

> The people of this state ... empower the

legislature ... to make adequate provision ... for the support & maintenance of public Protestant teachers of piety, religion and morality.

Vermont's Constitution, 1777 (ch. 2, sec. 41) stated:

Laws for the encouragement of virtue and prevention of vice and immorality, shall be made and constantly kept in force ...

All religious societies ... incorporated ... for the advancement of religion and learning, or for other pious and charitable purposes, shall be encouraged and protected in the enjoyment of the privileges.

New York's Supreme Court stated in *People v. Ruggles* (1811):

We stand equally in need, now as formerly, of all the moral discipline, and of those principles of virtue, which help to bind society together.

The people of this state, in common with the people of this country, profess the general doctrines of Christianity, as the rule of their faith and practice; and to scandalize the Author of these doctrines ... is a gross violation of decency and good order.

Nothing could be more injurious to the tender morals of the young.

New York's Legislature stated in 1838:

Our government depends for its being on the virtue of the people, – on that virtue that has its foundation in the morality of the Christian religion; and that religion is the common and prevailing faith of the people.

South Carolina's Supreme Court stated in *City of Charleston v. S.A. Benjamin* (1846):

Christianity is a part of the common law of the land, with liberty of conscience to all. It has always been so recognized ...

Christianity has reference to the principles of right and wrong ... It is the foundation of those morals and manners upon which our society is formed ... Remove this and they would fall.

Thomas Jefferson, as Virginia's Governor, November 11, 1779, proclaimed a Day for:

Prayer to Almighty God ... that He would establish the independence of these United States upon the basis of religion and virtue.

Calvin Coolidge stated October 15, 1924:

The government of a country never gets ahead of the religion of a country. There is no way by which we can substitute the authority of law for the virtue of man.

George Washington stated in his Farewell Address, September 19, 1796:

Of all the dispositions and habits which lead to political prosperity, Religion and Morality are indispensable supports.

In vain would that man claim the tribute of Patriotism, who should labor to subvert these great Pillars ...

Reason and experience both forbid us to expect that national morality can prevail in exclusion of religious principle.

Tis substantially true, that virtue or morality is a necessary spring of popular government ...

Can it be, that Providence has not connected the permanent felicity of a Nation with its virtue?

Noah Webster wrote in *A Collection of Papers on Political, Literary & Moral Subjects* (NY, 1843):

The virtue which is necessary to preserve a just administration and render a government stable, is Christian virtue, which consists in the uniform practice of moral and religious duties, in conformity with the laws of both of God and man.

U.S. Speaker of the House Robert Winthrop stated, May 28, 1849:

> Men, in a word, must be controlled either by a power within them, or a power without them; either by the word of God, or by the strong arm of man; either by the Bible or by the bayonet.

John Adams addressed the 1st Brigade, 3rd Division of Massachusetts' Militia, October 11, 1798:

> We have no government armed with power capable of contending with human passions unbridled by morality and religion.

> Avarice, ambition, revenge, or gallantry, would break the strongest cords of our Constitution as a whale goes through a net ...

> Our Constitution was made only for a moral and religious people. It is wholly inadequate to the government of any other.

British Statesman Edmund Burke told the National Assembly, 1791:

> What is liberty without virtue? It is the greatest of all possible evils ... madness without restraint. Men are qualified for civil liberty in exact proportion to their disposition to put moral chains upon their own appetites ...

> Society cannot exist, unless a controlling power upon will and appetite be placed somewhere; and the less of it there is within, the more there must be without.

∾

ROMAN REPUBLIC

America's founders drew ideas from the Roman Republic. Whereas in a pure democracy, everybody, everyday, has to go the market to talk politics, in a republic, people take care of their families and their farms, and have someone "in their place" go to the market everyday to talk politics. These are called delegates or representatives.

A pure democracy only ever worked on a city-state scale. It was prevented from getting larger because people could not travel far distances everyday. A republic, though, could grow larger, as people could send delegates or representatives in their place.

Yale President Ezra Stiles addressed Connecticut's General Assembly, May 8, 1783:

> They cannot, however, assemble from the territory of an empire, and must, therefore, if they have any share in government, represent themselves by delegation.

Samuel Langdon stated June 5, 1788:

> It was about five hundred years from the first founding of the celebrated Roman empire, and nearly three hundred years after Solon, before the first laws of that empire were imported from Greece in twelve tables, by ten ambassadors sent there for that purpose.

> But even when that empire had attained the summit of glory, and legislation was carried to great perfection, however well adapted to a government so extensive and complicated their laws might be, they were far from being worthy to be compared with the laws of Israel, as to the security of life, liberty, property, and public morals:

> and as to their religion, which was from the beginning interwoven with the state, instead of receiving any greater perfection from the increase of knowledge, wealth and power, it only became a more abundant congeries of ridiculous and detestable superstitions.

Rome had around 600 representatives, called "senators." These, however, were not elected, they were hereditary, tracing back to the original families of those who founded the Roman Republic.

Rome previously had a king named Tarquin the Proud, whose son raped a virtuous woman named Lucretia. She was so distraught that she gathered the Roman elders together and committed suicide right in front of them.

The Roman elders got so upset, that they killed King Tarquin and made a rule that if anybody in Rome ever declared themselves king, anybody could kill him without any repercussions.

As a result, for 500 years, no one in the Roman Republic wanted to come anywhere close to being called a "king." One of the popular founders of the Roman Republic was Publius. He began building a beautiful mansion, but when he heard that a rumor was spreading, claiming that he desired to be king, he destroyed his own mansion.

James Wilson stated in his *Lectures on Law* delivered at the College of Philadelphia, 1790–91:

> In the original constitution of Rome, the sovereign power, the dominium eminens, as it is called by the civilians, always resided in the collective body of the people ...

> As to the people, however, in whom the sovereign power resides ... from their authority the constitution originates: for their safety and felicity it is established: in their hands it is as clay in the hands of the potter: they have the right to mold, to preserve, to improve, to refine, and to finish it as they please.

Justice James Wilson wrote in *Chisholm v. State of Ga.* (2 U.S. 419, 1793, 453–466):

> Cicero says so sublimely, "Nothing, which is exhibited upon our globe, is more acceptable to that divinity which governs the whole universe,

WHO IS THE KING IN AMERICA?

than those communities and assemblages of men, which, lawfully associated, are denominated states" ...

By a state I mean, a complete body of free persons united together for their common benefit, to enjoy peaceably what is their own, and to do justice to others.

The Roman Republic existed until Julius Caesar found a way to usurp power. He raided the Temple of Saturn and took all the treasure accumulated since Rome's founding to buy supporters against Pompey, saying "Use money to get men and use men to get money."

This was similar to Philip II of Macedon who used gold to bribe some citizens of Athens to betray their city, or as Abimelech in Judges 9:4–5, who took 70 pieces of silver from the temple of Baalberith to hire "vain and worthless persons" to murder the sons of Gideon.

Caesar declare himself "dictator for life." Senators thought they could save the republic by stabbing Caesar to death on the Ides of March, 44 BC. Chaos ensued, allowing Augustus Caesar to usurp power as Emperor in 27 BC. The Republic was no more.

Roman poet Juvenal (circa 100 AD) described how Roman emperors controlled the masses by keeping them ignorant and obsessed with self-indulgence, so that they would be distracted and not throw them out of office, which they might do if they realized the true condition of the Empire:

Already long ago, from when we sold our vote to no man, the people have abdicated our duties; for the people who once upon a time handed out military command, high civil office, legions – everything, now restrains itself and anxiously hopes for just two things: bread and circuses.

Juvenal continued:

Tyrants would distribute largess, a bushel of wheat, a gallon of wine, and a sesterce [Roman coin]; and everyone would shamelessly cry, "Long live the king" ...

The fools did not realize that they were merely recovering a portion of their own property, and that their ruler could not have given them what they were receiving without having first taken it from them.

Marcus Tullius Cicero (106–43 BC) wrote:

The evil was not in bread and circuses, per se, but in the willingness of the people to sell their rights as free men for full bellies and the excitement of games which would serve to distract them from the other human hungers which bread and circuses can never appease.

Will and Ariel Durant wrote in *The Lessons of History* (p. 92):

The concentration of population and poverty in great cities may compel a government to choose between enfeebling the economy with a dole [a government hand-out] or running the risk of riot and revolution.

Sam Adams wrote to John Scollay, April 30, 1776:

Public liberty will not long survive the total extinction of morals. "The Roman Empire," says the historian, "must have sunk, though the Goths had not invaded it. Why? Because the Roman virtue was sunk."

John Bouvier's Law Dictionary (1856), stated:

In the state, the REPUBLIC is the proper governmental form, and VIRTUE is the mainspring [support].

Dr. Benjamin Rush, who signed the Declaration, wrote in *Thoughts Upon the Mode of Education Proper in a Republic* (1786):

The only foundation for a useful education in a REPUBLIC is to be laid on the foundation of religion. Without this there can be no VIRTUE, and without VIRTUE there can be no liberty, and liberty is the object and life of all republican governments ...

The religion I mean to recommend in this place is that of the New Testament ... All its doctrines and precepts are calculated to promote the happiness of society and the safety and well-being of civil government.

This subject is covered in more detail in the book, *Rise of the Tyrant – Volume 2 of Change to Chains: The 6,000 Year Quest for Global Power.*

∽

MAGNA CARTA & COMMON LAW

America's Founders did draw some ideas from English Common Law, which can traced back to the 5th century Irish Brehon Laws called *Senchas Már,* attributed to St. Patrick, and the Laws of England's King Alfred the Great, 893 AD.

English documents in legal development include:
- Charter of Liberties of Henry I, 1100 AD
- Magna Carta 1215
- Petition of Right 1628
- Grand Remonstrance, 1641
- English Bill of Rights 1689

The story of the Magna Carta began when England's King Richard the Lionheart was away fighting the Muslims in the Third Crusade and his brother John was left in charge of England. The legend of Robinhood dates to this time.

Richard the Lionheart returned to England in 1192, but was killed in 1199, leaving King John to rule. Through King John's negligence, the Normandy area of central France was lost to King Philip II in 1205. England's barons were frustrated by this loss, as well as by King John's absolute and arbitrary despotism.

Finally, on June 15, 1215, twenty-five barons chased King John and surrounded him on the fields of Runnymede. There they forced him to sign the Magna Carta – the Great Charter of English Liberties.

The Magna Carta limited the power of a king by delineating basic rights, and letting the king know if he abused the rights of one of the barons, the others would combine together against him.

British Judge Lord Denning said the Magna Carta was:

> ... the greatest constitutional document of all times – the foundation of the freedom of the individual against the arbitrary authority of the despot.

Winston Churchill stated in 1956:

> Here is a law which is above the king and which even he must not break.

> This reaffirmation of a supreme law and its expression in a general character is the great work of the Magna Carta; and this alone justifies the respect in which men have held it.

Sir Edwin Coke stated:

> The Magna Carta will have no sovereign.

The Magna Carta began redefining government's purpose from dominating people's lives into guaranteeing individual rights, culminating in the U.S. Constitution. Allegorically, it was a polarity switch – a flipping of the magnetic poles – where political power changed from top-down to bottom-up.

Sir Edwin Coke wrote his views on the Magna Carta in *Institutes on the Laws of England,* which was studied by John Adams, Thomas Jefferson and James Madison.

WHO IS THE KING IN AMERICA?

Sir Edwin Coke wrote in a 1610 case:

> When an act of Parliament is against common right or reason ... the common law will ... adjure [declare] such an act void.

When Britain imposed the hated Stamp Act on the American colonies, the Massachusetts Assembly responded that it:

> ... was against the Magna Carta and the natural rights of Englishmen, and therefore, according to Lord Coke, null and void.

෴

WHO IS THE KING IN AMERICA?

"King" is defined in *Webster's 1828 Dictionary,* as:

> The chief or SOVEREIGN of a nation; a man invested with supreme AUTHORITY over a nation, tribe or country; a monarch. Kings are absolute.

The Bible speaks of submitting to authorities.

Romans 13:1 states:

> Let every soul be subject unto the higher powers. For there is no power but of God: the powers that be are ordained of God. (KJV)

Other translations are:

> • Everyone must submit to governing authorities. For all authority comes from God, and those in positions of authority have been placed there by God. (NLT)

> • Every person must be subject to the governing authorities, for no authority exists except by God's permission. The existing authorities have been established by God. (ISV)

> • Let every individual be obedient to those who rule over him; for no one is a ruler except by God's permission, and our present rulers have had their rank and power assigned to them

by Him. (Weymouth New Testament)

Who is the ultimate government authority in America? In the Providence of God, America's Founders were allowed to set up government where "We the People" are the ultimate authority – the KING.

Signer of the Constitution Gouverneur Morris wrote:

This magistrate is not the king. THE PEOPLE are THE KING.

John Jay, the First Chief Justice of the Supreme Court, wrote in *Chisholm v. Georgia* (1793):

THE PEOPLE are the SOVEREIGN of this country.

Lincoln stated in a debate with Stephen Douglas (*The Political Debates Between Lincoln and Douglas*, 1897):

THE PEOPLE of these United States are the rightful MASTERS of both congresses and courts.

Justice James Wilson, who signed the Declaration and the Constitution, stated at Pennsylvania's Ratifying Convention, December 1, 1787:

SOVEREIGNTY resides in THE PEOPLE; they have not parted with it.

President Grover Cleveland stated July 13, 1887:

The SOVEREIGNTY OF SIXTY MILLIONS OF FREE PEOPLE, is, to my mind ... the working out ... of the divine right of man to govern himself and a manifestation of God's plan concerning the human race.

Thomas Jefferson wrote to William Johnson, 1823:

But the Chief Justice says, "There must be an ULTIMATE ARBITER somewhere." True, there must ... The ULTIMATE ARBITER is THE PEOPLE.

James Madison wrote in *Federalist No. 46* (*New York Packet,* January 29, 1788):

WHO IS THE KING IN AMERICA?

The ULTIMATE AUTHORITY ... resides in THE PEOPLE ALONE.

President Andrew Jackson wrote to William B. Lewis, August 19, 1841:

> THE PEOPLE are the government, administering it by their agents; they are the government, the SOVEREIGN POWER.

President James K. Polk stated December 7, 1847:

> The PEOPLE are the only SOVEREIGNS recognized by our Constitution ...

> The success of our admirable system is a conclusive refutation of the theories of those in other countries who maintain that a "favored few" are born to rule and that the mass of mankind must be governed by force.

President Gerald Ford stated at Southern Methodist University, September 13, 1975:

> Never forget that in America our SOVEREIGN is THE CITIZEN ... The state is a servant of the individual. It must never become an anonymous monstrosity that masters everyone.

President Ronald Reagan opened the John Ashbrook Center in 1983, stating of America's founders:

> The Founding Fathers understood that only by making government the servant, not the master, only by positing SOVEREIGNTY in THE PEOPLE and not the state can we hope to protect freedom.

General Omar Bradley stated in his Armistice Day Address, November 10, 1948:

> In the United States it is THE PEOPLE who are SOVEREIGN ... The government is THEIRS – to speak THEIR voice and to voice THEIR will.

President Donald J. Trump stated January 20, 2017:

> Today we are not merely transferring power from one Administration to another, or from one party to another – but we are transferring power from Washington, D.C. and giving it back to you, THE AMERICAN PEOPLE.

❧

DID FOUNDERS SEE HAND OF GOD?

George Washington opened the Constitutional Convention:

> Let us raise a standard to which the wise and the honest can repair. The event is in the hand of God.

The last line of the U.S. Constitution is:

> Done ... the seventeenth day of September, in the Year of OUR LORD one thousand seven hundred and eighty seven.

Alexander Hamilton wrote in *Letters of Caesar* (1787):

> Whether the New Constitution, if adopted, will prove adequate to such desirable ends, time, the mother of events, will show.

> For my own part, I sincerely esteem it a system, which, without the finger of God, never could have been suggested and agreed upon by such a diversity of interests.

Benjamin Franklin wrote to the Editor of the *Federal Gazette,* April 8, 1788 (*The Records of the Federal Convention of 1787, Farrand's Records,* Vol. 3):

> I beg I may not be understood to infer, that our General Convention was divinely inspired when it formed the new Federal Constitution ...

> yet I must own I have so much faith in the general government of the world by Providence, that I can hardly conceive a transaction of such momentous importance to the welfare of millions

now existing, and to exist in the posterity of a great nation, should be suffered to pass without being in some degree influenced, guided and governed by that omnipotent, omnipresent Beneficent Ruler, in whom all inferior spirits live and move and have their being.

Yale President Ezra Stiles stated May 8, 1783:

Most states of all ages ... have been founded in rapacity, usurpation and injustice ... The military history of all nations, being but a description of the wars and invasions of the mutual robbers and devastators of the human race ...

All the forms of CIVIL POLITY have been tried by mankind, EXCEPT ONE:

and that seems to have been referred in Providence to be realized in America ... in the body of the people at large ... a power, with which they are invested by the Author of their being, to wrest government out of the hands of reigning tyrants, and originate new policies, adapted to the conservation of liberty ...

A democratical polity for millions, standing upon the broad basis of the people at large, amply charged with property, has not hitherto been exhibited.

John Jay, the first Chief Justice of the U.S. Supreme Court, stated September 8, 1777:

The Americans are the first people whom Heaven has favored with an opportunity of deliberating upon, and choosing the forms of government under which they should live.

All other constitutions have derived their existence from violence or accidental circumstances ...

Your lives, your liberties, your property, will be at the disposal only of your Creator and yourselves.

John Adams wrote *on Canon & Feudal Law (*1765):

> I always consider the settlement of America with reverence ... as the opening of a grand scene and design in Providence for the illumination of the ignorant, and the emancipation of the slavish part of mankind all over the earth.

George Washington, the same week Congress passed the Bill of Rights, wrote October 3, 1789:

> Whereas both Houses of Congress have ... requested me

> "to recommend ... a Day of Public Thanksgiving and Prayer to be observed by acknowledging with grateful hearts the many signal [momentous] favors of Almighty God, especially by affording them an opportunity peaceably to establish a form of government for their safety and happiness"...

> I do recommend ... the 26th day of November ... to be devoted by the People of these United States to the service of that great and glorious Being, who is the beneficent Author of all the good that was, that is, or that will be;

> that we may then all unite in rendering unto Him our sincere and humble thanks ... for the peaceable and rational manner in which we have been enabled to establish Constitutions of Government for our safety and happiness, and particularly the national one now lately instituted, for the civil and religious liberty with which we are blessed.

Justice James Wilson stated November 26, 1787:

> Governments, in general, have been the result of force, of fraud, and accident.

> After a period of 6,000 years has elapsed since the creation, the United States exhibit to the world the first instance ... of a nation ... assembling voluntarily ... and deciding calmly

concerning that system of government under which they would wish that they and their posterity should live.

Ronald Reagan stated in 1961:

In this country of ours took place the GREATEST REVOLUTION that has ever taken place IN THE WORLD'S HISTORY ... Every other revolution simply exchanged one set of rulers for another ...

Here for the first time in all the THOUSANDS OF YEARS of man's relation to man ... the founding fathers established the idea that you and I had within ourselves the GOD-GIVEN RIGHT and ABILITY to DETERMINE OUR OWN DESTINY.

Dwight Eisenhower addressed the American Legion Back-To-God Program, February 20, 1955:

The Founding Fathers ... produced the timeless documents upon which the Nation is grounded and has grown great.

They, recognizing God as the author of individual rights, declared that the purpose of government is to secure those rights.

To you and to me this ideal of government is a self-evident truth. But in many lands the state claims to be the author of human rights.

The tragedy of that claim runs through all history and, indeed, dominates our own times. If the state gives rights, it can – and inevitably will – take away those rights.

Without God, there could be no American form of government, nor an American way of life. Recognition of the Supreme Being is the first – the most basic – expression of Americanism. Thus the Founding Fathers saw it, and thus, with God's help, it will continue to be.

Theodore Roosevelt stated October 24, 1903:

> In no other place and at no other time has the experiment of government of THE PEOPLE, by THE PEOPLE, for THE PEOPLE, been tried on so vast a scale as here in our own country ...

> Failure would not only be a dreadful thing for us, but a dreadful thing for all mankind, because it would mean loss of hope for all who believe in the power and the righteousness of liberty.

> Therefore, in thanking God for the mercies extended to us in the past, we beseech Him that He may not withhold them in the future.

John Adams wrote to his wife, Abigail Adams, July 3, 1776, the day after Congress approved Independence:

> You will see in a few days a Declaration setting forth the causes, which have impelled us to this mighty revolution, and the reasons which will justify it in the sight of God and man ...

> The people will have unbounded power ... The new governments we are assuming ... will require a purification from our vices and an augmentation of our virtues or there will be no blessings ...

> The people are extremely addicted to corruption and venality ... I am not without apprehensions from this quarter, but I must submit all my hopes and fears to an overruling Providence.

❧

THE AMERICAN REPUBLIC

Webster's 1828 Dictionary defined "republic"as:

> Exercise of the SOVEREIGN POWER is lodged in representatives elected by THE PEOPLE.

WHO IS THE KING IN AMERICA?

Signer of the Constitution James McHenry noted in a diary entry (published in the *American Historical Review,* 1906), that after Ben Franklin left the Constitutional Convention, he was asked by Mrs. Elizabeth Powel of Philadelphia:

> "Well, Doctor, what have we got, a republic or a monarchy?" Franklin replied, "A republic, if you can keep it."

In other words, a REPUBLIC is where THE PEOPLE are KING, ruling through their representatives.

The Pledge of Allegiance is to the Flag "and to the REPUBLIC for which it stands." When someone dishonors the flag, what they are saying is "I no longer want to be the KING – I want someone else to rule over me."

The founders had, in effect, took the world of kings and flipped it, making the people the king and the politicians the servants.

James Wilson wrote in *Lectures on Law* (1790–1791):

> The sovereign power residing in the people; they may change their constitution and government whenever they please ... In free states, such as ours, the sovereign or supreme power resides in the people.

Justice James Wilson wrote in *Chisholm v. State of Georgia.* (2 U.S. 419, 1793, 453–466):

> Let a state be considered as subordinate to the people ... By a "state," I mean a complete body of free persons united together ...

> I know the government of that state to be republican; and my short definition of such a government is, one constructed on this principle, that the supreme power resides in the body of the people.

Dr. Benjamin Rush explained in *Essays, Literary, Moral, and Philosophical* (1798):

We profess to be republicans, and yet we neglect the only means of establishing and perpetuating our republican forms of government, that is, the universal education of our youth in the principles of Christianity by the means of the Bible.

For this Divine book, above all others, favors that equality among mankind, that respect for just laws, and those sober and frugal virtues, which constitute the soul of republicanism.

President Calvin Coolidge wrote in 1924:

The history of government on this earth has been almost entirely ... rule of force held in the HANDS OF A FEW.

Under our Constitution, America committed itself to power in the HANDS OF THE PEOPLE.

President Donald J. Trump stated January 20, 2017:

For too long, a small group in our nation's Capital has reaped the rewards of government while the people have borne the cost.

Washington flourished – but the people did not share in its wealth. Politicians prospered – but the jobs left, and the factories closed.

The establishment protected itself, but not the citizens ... That all changes – starting right here, and right now ...The United States of America, is your country.

What truly matters is not which party controls our government, but whether our government is controlled by THE PEOPLE.

January 20th 2017, will be remembered as the day THE PEOPLE became the rulers of this nation again.

Daniel Webster stated in a 4th of July Oration, 1802:

The history of the world is before us ...

The civil, the social, the Christian virtues are requisite to render us worthy the continuation of that government which is the freest on earth.

America is a political hybrid. It has representatives – a feature derived from the Roman Republic, which are elected democratically – a feature derived from the Athenian Democracy.

Yet these representatives cannot do anything they want. They are limited by a Constitution – a feature traced back to England's Magna Carta.

All of this is to protect the citizens' God-given rights and guarantee equality before the law – a feature derived from Ancient Israel, a people in covenant under God.

G.K. Chersterton wrote in "What is America" (*What I Saw In America,* 1922):

America is the only nation in the world that is founded on creed. That creed is set forth ... in the Declaration of Independence ... that all men are equal in their claim to justice, that governments exist to give them that justice ...

The Declaration ... certainly does condemn ... atheism, since it clearly names the Creator as the ultimate authority from whom these equal rights are derived.

Daniel Webster stated:

Miracles do not cluster. That which has happened but once in six thousand years, cannot be expected to happen often ...

Hold on, my friends, to the Constitution of your country and the government established under it ...

Such a government, once destroyed, would have a void to be filled, perhaps for centuries, with evolution and tumult, riot and despotism.

U.S. Senator Henry Cabot Lodge stated in 1919:

The United States is THE WORLD'S BEST HOPE ... Beware how you trifle with your marvelous inheritance ... for if we stumble and fall, freedom and civilization everywhere will go down in ruin.

∽

SEEDS ARE PLANTED IN SOIL

Much attention has been given to America's unique form of government – a democratically elected Constitutional Republic. But like a genetically engineered seed, it needed to be planted in soil – it needed to be lived out by people.

Question: Does the quality of the soil have any bearing on the type of harvest the seed will produce?

What if you plant it in a sandy beach, or a gravel parking lot, or in a swamp?

The soil is the "belief system" held by the people. For example, when the Soviet Union fell in 1991, political advisors from America went over to teach them how to set up governments – they planted the seed.

Yet within a few years, it was discovered that those governments basically resorted back to bribes and organized crime.

Political philosophers scratched their heads, asking what is wrong with the seed. The answer is nothing.

It was just planted in a soil that had 70 years of atheism plowed into it, and atheism teaches there is no God, that this life is all there is, so do whatever you can to get ahead.

When Sadam Hussein was overthrown, political advisors from America went over to teach them how to set of governments – they planted the seed.

Yet within one election cycle, the nation was back under Islamic sharia law where women could be beaten

WHO IS THE KING IN AMERICA?

and it was the death penalty to switch religions.

Political philosophers scratched their heads, asking what is wrong with the seed. The answer is nothing.

It was just planted in a soil that had 1,400 year of Islam plowed into it, and Islam has no concept of equality – women are not equal to men, and non-Muslims are not equal to Muslims,

America's founders planted the seed in a soil that was rich in Judeo–Christian beliefs, and the harvest was the freest, most prosperous nation, with more individual liberty, than any nation the world had seen.

Poet Ralph Waldo Emerson wrote:

> America is another name for opportunity. Our whole history appears like a last effort of Divine Providence on behalf of the human race.

∞

WHO ARE COUNSELORS TO THE KING?

If the PEOPLE are the KING in America, who are the COUNSELORS to the KING?

Theodosius was the Emperor of Rome from 379 to 390 AD, and he attended church in Milan, Italy, where the pastor was Bishop St. Ambrose.

A famous painting by artist Anthony van Dyck depicts Ambrose rebuking the Emperor for allowing a massacre in Thessalonica in 390 AD.

What would it be like to be a pastor with the ruler of the nation sitting in your church pews?

Well, that is exactly what exists in America.

The Pew Forum's "Religious Landscape Survey" (2015) reported that 70.6 percent of Americans identify themselves as Christian. This is a majority that could determine the outcome of any election.

Since they are Christian, they would go to church,

either regularly or occasionally, which would make the pastors of America collectively "counselors" to the king.

In the Old Testament, prophets such as Samuel, Nathan, Elijah, Elisha were counselors to the kings.

In America, THE PEOPLE are the KING, and PASTORS are the COUNSELORS to the KING, who is sitting in their pews. Some COUNSELORS lull the KING to SLEEP! Others try to WAKE UP the KING!

In the movie *The Lord of the Rings: The Two Towers* there is a scene where King Theoden's kingdom of Rohan was on the verge of being overrun and destroyed, as he had been asleep – under a spell.

A wicked counselor to the king was the ugly Wormtongue, who whispers in the king's ear to stay asleep, even though his kingdom is being attacked.

Another counselor to the king is Gandalf, who breaks the evil spell, and wakes the king up. King Theodon dramatically comes to his senses, his eyes become clear, and he takes up his sword.

This scene illustrates two different kinds of pastors:

> • one kind are those who whisper in the ears of the "KING–PEOPLE" to stay asleep, shirk responsibility, be negligent and lazy, even though their kingdom faces destruction;

> • the other kind are those who want the "KING–PEOPLE" to wake up and take responsibility to rule – a responsibility for which they will be held accountable to God.

Pastors need to tell their church members that they do not just have the RIGHT TO VOTE, they will be held ACCOUNTABLE TO GOD for what happens!

Ezekiel 3:16–21

> Son of man, I have made thee a watchman

unto the house of Israel ... When I say unto the wicked, Thou shalt surely die; and thou givest him not warning ... to save his life; the same wicked man shall die in his iniquity; but his blood will I require at thine hand.

Pastors have the urgent task of WAKING UP THE KING! The opportunity for Americans to rule themselves is a great blessing, but also a serious responsibility. Pastors are watchmen, responsible to educate their flocks on moral issues facing the nation from a Biblical perspective, and warn their flocks that God will hold them accountable for what happens.

Rev. Martin Luther King, Jr., stated:

The church is the conscience of the state.

Daniel Webster gave a rebuke "if the pulpit be silent" in his address at the Bicentennial of the landing of the Pilgrims at Plymouth Rock, December 22, 1820:

The African slave-trader is a pirate and a felon; and in the sight of Heaven, an offender far beyond the ordinary depth of human guilt ...

If there be ... any participation in this traffic, let us pledge ourselves here, upon the rock of Plymouth, to extirpate [remove completely] and destroy it ...

I invoke the ministers of our religion, that they proclaim its denunciation of these crimes, and add its solemn sanctions to the authority of human laws.

If the pulpit be silent whenever or wherever there may be a sinner bloody with this guilt within the hearing of its voice, the pulpit is false to its trust.

❧

IMAGINE VISITING A KING

Imagine traveling through a kingdom to visit a KING, and on the way, you witness all kinds of fraud, corruption, crime and injustice, even being committed by servants of the king.

As you enter the king's chamber, he reluctantly asks you, "Did you see all the crime and corruption as you came in here ... I wish someone would fix this mess."

You politely tap the KING on shoulder and remind him that HE is the KING, that it is HIS servants who are creating the problems, and that HE is accountable to God to fix the mess.

This is like someone in America watching television, seeing all the corruption and crime, even being committed by politicians, and saying "I wish someone would fix this mess."

A finger should reach through the TV screen and tap the person on the shoulder, reminding them "You, are the KING. You are responsible to fix this mess."

Someone may say, "Well, I need someone to tell me what to do?"

Since when does the KING sit on his throne and ask "Can someone please tell me what I am supposed to do?"

No, it the each person's job to educate themselves on the issues, seek God's will, and then tell their representatives what needs to happen!

Billy Graham stated:

> Bad politicians are elected by good people
> who don't vote.

Not to vote is to abdicate the throne. James Wilson wrote in his *Lectures on Law* (1790–1791):

> In a free country, EVERY CITIZEN forms
> a part of the SOVEREIGN POWER: he
> possesses a VOTE.

Voting is not just a right, but a responsibility for which every American will be held accountable to God.

Sam Adams stated in 1781:

> Let EACH CITIZEN remember at the moment he is offering his VOTE ... that he is executing one of the most solemn trusts in human society for which he is ACCOUNTABLE TO GOD.

It is the difference between the word "subject" and "citizen." Dictators have "subjects" who are subjected to their will. The word "citizen" is from Greece and carries the meaning of "co-regent," "co-ruler," "co-king."

Justice Wilson wrote in *Chisholm v. State of Ga.*, 1793:

> Under that Constitution there are citizens, but no subjects.

Franklin D. Roosevelt stated July 8, 1938:

> Let us never forget that government is ourselves ... The ultimate rulers of our democracy are not a President and Senators and Congressmen and Government officials but the voters of this country.

Some say, don't vote, just trust God. Connecticut Governor Jonathan Trumbull addressed this attitude during the Revolution, August 1776:

> To trust altogether to the justice of our cause, without our utmost exertion, would be tempting Providence.

∽

HOW DO REPUBLICS END?

America's founders studied how to take power from a king and separate it into the hands of the people.

Unfortunately, there have also been ambitious individuals who have studied history to learn how to take the separated power of the people and re-concentrate it back to a king.

As demonstrated earlier, in times of crisis, there is an unconscious, gravitational pull for power to concentrate – like the snapping back of a rubber band.

Economist Milton Friedman stated:

> Concentrated power is not rendered harmless
> by the good intentions of those who create it.

Unscrupulous political philosophers have observed the phenomenon of power concentrating in crisis, and developed strategies to speed it along.

Some notable characters were: Machiavelli, Robespierre, Hegel, Marx, and Alinsky.

∽

MACHIAVELLI

Over 500 years ago, Italy was not Italy. It was number of independent city-states, such as: Venice, Genoa, Sienna, Amalfi, Milan, Corsica, Florence, Pisa, and San Marino. These had armies and navies which fought.

A political philosopher at the time was Machiavelli, who thought if one prince could control all of the Italian city-states, in-fighting would stop and there would be peace. His book, *The Prince* (1513), is credited with promoting the idea "the ends justifies the means."

In other words, the end, of one prince controlling all of Italy, is such a good end, as it would put an end to the in-fighting, any means necessary to achieve this end was justified, including lying, deception, fraud, intimidation, betrayal, murder and the intentional creating of crisis and terror.

A sampling of Machiavelli's statements include:

> The promise given was a necessity of the
> past: the word broken is a necessity of the
> present ...

> A prince never lacks legitimate reasons to
> break his promise ...

> A wise ruler ought never to keep faith when
> by doing so it would be against his interests ...

Politics have no relation to morals.

Following Machiavelli's reasoning, if a prince conquered a city in his quest to unify Italy, the people of that city would hate him.

But if the prince arranged to pay agitators and criminals to kill cows, set barns on fire and create domestic mayhem, then the people would cry out for help. The prince could them come in and dispense with the criminals, and the people would treat him as a hero.

It is good marketing – create the need and fill it. If is the equivalent of going around the back of the house and setting it on fire, then going around the front of the house and selling the residents a fire extinguisher. They will pay anything for it and thank you for being there!

This is called "Machiavellianism" – where one creates or capitalizes on crises in order to consolidate control into the hands of a king!

❧

ROBESPIERRE

The French Revolution resulted in the First French Republic being established in 1792. Without training in virtue, it quickly turned into mob rule.

President Millard Fillmore stated in 1852:

> Our free institutions ... were planted in the free charters of self-government under which the English colonies grew up ...

> European nations have had no such training for self-government, and every effort to establish it by bloody revolutions has been, and must without that preparation continue to be, a failure.

In Paris, agitators stirred the people to riot against King Louis XVI and Marie Antoinette. The mob arrested and beheaded them in 1793.

As mentioned earlier, Maximilien Robespierre then

instituted a Reign of Terror. Leading the "Committee of Public Safety," he gave a speech to the National Assembly titled "The Terror Justified," 1794, stating:

> Lead ... the enemies of the people by terror ... Terror is nothing else than swift, severe, indomitable justice.

Robespierre first accused, then arrested and beheaded:

- first all the royalty;
- then the wealthy;
- then the farmers and businessmen;
- then those hoarding food;
- then the clergy;
- then the former revolutionaries.

Over 40,000 were beheaded in Paris.

He began an intentional campaign to dechristianize French society and replace it with a civic religion of state worship. Not wanting a constitution "Done in the year of the Lord," as the U.S. Constitution was, France retroactively made 1792 the new "Year One."

They did not want a seven day week with a Sabbath day rest, as this was derived from the Bible, so they devised a ten day "decade" week, and ten month year.

French Revolutionary Time divided the day into 10 decimal hours, each consisting of 100 decimal minutes, with each minute made up of 100 decimal seconds.

Every measurement was to be divisible by ten, as ten was considered the number of man with ten fingers and ten toes. This was called " the metric system."

The new secular government proceeded to:

- Forbid crosses as being offensive;
- Religious monuments were destroyed;
- Public & private worship & education outlawed;

- Priests & ministers, along with those who harbored them, were executed on sight;

- Christian graves were desecrated, including that of Ste. Genevieve, the patron saint of Paris who called the city to pray when Attila the Hun was attacking in 451 AD;

- Churches were closed or used for "immoral ... lurid ... licentious ... scandalous ... depravities." The Cathedral of Our Lady of Strasbourg was made into a Temple of Reason.

Yale President Timothy Dwight traced the origin of the radical Jacobin organizers who agitated to overthrow France's government, July 4, 1798:

About the year 1728, Voltaire, so celebrated for his wit and brilliancy and not less distinguished for his hatred of Christianity and his abandonment of principle, formed a systematical design to destroy Christianity and to introduce in its stead a general diffusion of irreligion and atheism ...

With great art and insidiousness the doctrines of ... Christian theology were rendered absurd and ridiculous; and the mind of the reader was insensibly steeled against conviction and duty ...

The overthrow of the religious orders in Catholic countries, a step essentially necessary to the destruction of the religion professed in those countries ...

The appropriation to themselves, and their disciples, of the places and honors of members of the French Academy ...

In this way they designed to hold out themselves ... to dictate all literary opinions to the nation ...

The fabrication of books of all kinds against Christianity, especially such as excite doubt and generate contempt and derision ...

The being of God was denied and ridiculed... The possession of property was pronounced robbery. Chastity and natural affection were declared to be nothing more than groundless prejudices.

Adultery, assassination, poisoning, and other crimes of the like infernal nature, were taught as lawful ... provided the end was good ...

The good ends proposed ... are the overthrow of religion, government, and human society, civil and domestic.

These they pronounce to be so good that murder, butchery, and war, however extended and dreadful, are declared by them to be completely justifiable.

The anti-christian French government sent its army to a rural, very religious Catholic area of western France called the Vendée. Hundreds of thousands who refused to embrace secularism were killed in a what is considered the first modern genocide.

French General Francois Joseph Westermann wrote to the Committee of Public Safety stating:

There is no more Vendée ... According to the orders that you gave me, I crushed the children under the feet of the horses, massacred the women who, at least for these, will not give birth to any more brigands. I do not have a prisoner to reproach me. I have exterminated all.

The young French officer Napoleon pleaded poor health to avoid participating in the slaughter.

In 1799, Alexander Hamilton condemned the French Revolution's attack on Christianity as:

... [depriving] mankind of its best consolations and most animating hopes, and to make a gloomy desert of the universe ...

The praise of a civilized world is justly due

to Christianity; – war, by the influence of the humane principles of that religion, has been stripped of half its horrors.

The French renounce Christianity, and they relapse into barbarism; – war resumes the same hideous and savage form which it wore in the ages of Gothic and Roman violence.

Hamilton wrote further:

Opinions ... have been gradually gaining ground, which threaten the foundations of religion, morality, and society.

An attack was first made upon the Christian revelation, for which natural religion was offered as the substitute.

The Gospel was to be discarded as a gross imposture, but the being and attributes of God, the obligations of piety, even the doctrine of a future state of rewards and punishments, were to be retained and cherished.

Best-selling author Os Guinness stated in an interview with Dr. Albert Mohler, (*Thinking in Public* (6/5/17):

The culture war now at its deepest roots is actually a clash between 1776, what was the American Revolution, and 1789 and heirs of the French Revolution.

During this time, French privateers ignored treaties and by 1798, had seized nearly 300 American ships bound for British ports. Talleyrand, the French Minister of Foreign Affairs, demanded millions of dollars in bribes to leave America's ships alone.

Talleyrand was a master of deceitful political speech called "obfuscation" – intentionally being obscure, speaking out of both sides of his mouth to as convince both sides he supported them. He stated:

We were given speech to hide our thoughts.

Out the chaos in France a dictator arose, Napoleon, who proceeded to conquer across Europe and the Middle East, resulting in 6 million deaths as he invaded the countries of Italy, Austria, Poland, German states, Holland, Denmark, Norway, Spain, Egypt, and Russia.

∽

HEGEL

In 1806, Napoleon conquered the German kingdom of Prussia, forcing its king. Friedrich Wilhelm III, to flee. When Napoleon was finally defeated, the Prussian king decided he needed to strengthen his state.

The philosopher who aided him was Georg Wilhelm Friedrich Hegel. A sampling of Hegel's quotes include:

> The state is god walking on earth ... The state is the march of God through the World ...

> We must worship the state as the manifestation of the divine on Earth ... The state is the Divine Idea as it exists on earth ... State is Objective Spirit ...

> All the worth which the human being possesses – all spiritual reality, he possesses only through the state ...

> The state is the self-certain absolute mind which recognizes no authority but its own, which acknowledges no abstract rules of good and bad, shameful and mean, cunning and deceit ...

> The state is ... the ultimate end which has the highest right against the individual, whose highest duty is to be a member of the state ...

> In considering the idea of the state, one must not think of particular states, nor of particular institutions, but one must contemplate the idea, this actual God, by itself.

> The nation state ... is therefore the absolute power on earth.

> A single person, it hardly needs saying, is

something subordinate, and as such he must dedicate himself to the ethical whole [the nation] ...

True bravery consists in the readiness to give oneself wholly to the service of the state ...

The individual counts but as one among many ... The important aspect lies in self-subordination to the universal cause ...

The origin of a state involves imperious lordship on the one hand, instinctive submission on the other.

Obedience – lordly power, and the fear inspired by a ruler – in itself implies some degree of voluntary connection ...

It is not the isolated will of individuals that prevails; individual pretensions are relinquished, and the general will is the essential bond of political union.

Jean-Jacques Rousseau, considered the Father of the French Revolution, wrote in *The Social Contract* (1762):

The citizen is no longer the judge ... When the prince says to him: "It is expedient for the state that you should die," he ought to die ... because his life is no longer a mere bounty of nature, but a gift made conditionally by the state.

Hegel's method of resolving a contradiction between a proposition and its apparent opposite is termed "Hegelian dialectics." Applied politically, it is a way to concentrate power. It is explained with a triangle:

- where one corner is the THESIS;
- the opposite corner it the ANTITHESIS, and
- the top corner is the SYNTHESIS.

It sounds complicated, but it is not.

Starting at the THESIS–status quo, one creates a problem that is real bad – the ANTITHESIS, then people will be willing to surrender their freedoms for a solution which is only half as bad – the SYNTHESIS.

Each SYNTHESIS becomes the new THESIS, and the process is repeated until all power is voluntarily relinquished by the people into the hands of a dictator.

The practical implementation of Hegel's theory was to identify the tension or fault lines running through a society. Then fan these real or perceived injustices into flames, causing public emotions reach the boiling point.

Once crisis breaks out, everyone is desperate to have the anarchy and random killings stopped. Urgently wanting order restored, they willing relinquish their rights and freedoms to the state.

President Obama's political advisor David Axelrod explained in a NPR interview, April 19, 2010:

> In Chicago, there was an old tradition of throwing a brick through your own campaign office window, and then calling a press conference to say that you've been attacked.

Hegel wrote in *Philosophy of Law* (Section 279):

> When it is contrasted with the sovereignty of the monarch, the phrase "sovereignty of the people" turns out to be merely one of those confused notions which arise from the wild idea of the "people." Without its monarch ... the people are just a formless multitude.

Hegel wrote in *Philosophy of Law* (Loewenberg, ed., *Hegel: Selections,* NY: C. Scribner's Sons, 1929):

> The many ... whom one chooses to call the people, are indeed a collection, but only as a multitude, a formless mass, whose movement and action would be elemental, irrational, savage, and terrible ...
>
> Public opinion deserves ... to be esteemed as much as to be despised ...
>
> The definition of the freedom of the press as freedom to say and write what one pleases ...

such a view belongs to the uneducated crudity and superficiality of naive thinking.

Hegel influenced Darwin, Adolf Hitler and Karl Marx.

∽

MARX & HITLER

Karl Marx was member of the "Young Hegelians" at the University of Berlin. He advocated the communist tactic, which was also used by Nazis, to intentionally fomented domestic unrest and anarchy, and when blood flowed in the streets, the people would allow power to be usurped by a dictator promising to help.

How was domestic unrest created? They would send in agitators, labor organizers, community organizers, agent provocateurs [provoking agents] to create domestic class and race hatred.

Finding those with real or perceived injustices or inequalities, they would promise to champion their cause if the people joined them. Those believing the lies were referred to as "useful idiots."

Forty-five countries fell to communist dictators this way. Marxist communists organized:

- Proletariat (working class) against the Bourgeoisie (business owners);
- Poor against the Rich;
- Blacks against the Whites;
- Catholics against the Protestant;
- Muslims against Christians;
- Hutu's against Tutsi's in Congo & Rwanda.

Communist dictator Joseph Stalin, responsible for over 20,000,000 deaths, stated:

Crisis alone permitted the authorities to demand – and obtain – total submission and all necessary sacrifices from its citizens.

Marxists sent community and labor organizers into countries to create an "antithesis" by organizing those who felt discriminated against, playing upon their lust to have what others have, and stirring them to revolt.

As insecurity spread, citizens became willing to give up their rights and freedoms to have order restored. Adolf Hitler used homosexual activists called Brownshirts to instigate riots, disrupt meetings, and organize boycotts of Jewish businesses, allowing him to seize power.

When the dust settled, a communist dictator had taken over, such as Lenin, Stalin, Castro, Mao Zedong, Pol Pot, Ho Chi Min, Kim Jung Il, and other despots.

❧

ALINSKY

Saul Alinsky rode around Chicago with Al Capone's hitman, Frank Nitti. He saw that if you just killed a few people and smashed a few windows, the whole neighborhood would submit to the mob and pay extortion "protection" money.

Alinsky applied this to politics. It you create a big enough crisis, people will surrender their freedoms to whoever promises to fix it, allowing you to seize power.

Alinsky's political activism influenced American politics. Hillary Clinton wrote her senior thesis at Wellesley College on Saul Alinsky's *Reveille for Radicals* (1946), and Barak Obama taught Alinsky's *Rules for Radicals* (1971), while community organizing in Chicago.

Dr. Ben Carson stated at the RNC, July 19. 2016:

> One of the things that I have learned about Hillary Clinton is that one of her heroes, her mentors, was Saul Alinsky.
>
> Her senior thesis was about Saul Alinsky.

This was someone that she greatly admired and that affected all of her philosophies subsequently.

Now, interestingly enough, let me tell you something about Saul Alinsky. He wrote a book called *Rules For Radicals.* On the dedication page, it acknowledges Lucifer, the original radical who gained his own kingdom.

Now think about that. This is a nation where our founding document, the Declaration of Independence, talks about certain inalienable rights that come from our Creator. This is a nation where our Pledge of Allegiance says we are "one nation, under God."

This is a nation where every coin in our pocket and every bill in our wallet says "In God We Trust." So are we willing to elect someone as president who has as their role model somebody who acknowledges Lucifer? Think about that.

In the front pages of *Rules for Radicals* (1971), Saul Alinsky wrote:

> Lest we forget at least an over-the-shoulder acknowledgment to the very first radical: from all our legends, mythology, and history (and who is to know where mythology leaves off and history begins – or which is which), the first radical known to man who rebelled against the establishment and did it so effectively that he at least won his own kingdom – Lucifer.

> – SAUL ALINSKY.

In *Rules for Radicals,* Saul Alinsky first instructed how to recruit agitators:

> The first step in community organization is community disorganization. The disruption of the present organization is the first step ...

> From the moment the organizer enters a

community he lives, dreams ... only one thing and that is to build the mass power base of what he calls the army.

Until he has developed that mass power base, he confronts no major issues ...

Until he has those means and power instruments, his "tactics" are very different from power tactics ...

Every move revolves around one central point: how many recruits will this bring into the organization, whether by means of local organizations, churches, service groups, labor Unions, corner gangs, or as individuals ...

Once agitators have been recruited, Saul Alinsky laid out the second step of creating chaos:

The organizer must first rub raw the resentments of the people of the community; fan the latent hostilities of many of the people to the point of overt expression ...

Search out controversy and issues, rather than avoid them, for unless there is controversy people are not concerned enough to act ...

The organizer's first job is to create the issues or problems ...

An organizer must stir up dissatisfaction and discontent ...

The organizer ... polarizes the issue ...

The organizer helps to lead his forces into conflict ...

The real arena is corrupt and bloody...

In war the end justifies almost any means.

This is similar to Hitler's Browshirts; or Machiavelli tactics; or Julius Caesar's raiding of the Temple of Saturn to buy supporters to attack Pompey; or Philip II of Macedon using gold to bribe citizens of Athens to betray their city; or Abimelech who took 70 pieces of silver from the temple of Baalberith to hire "vain and worthless persons" to murder the sons of Gideon.

Alinsky's tactics are identified in Proverbs 6:16:

> Six things doth the LORD hate ... A proud look, a lying tongue, hands swift to shedding innocent blood ... he that SOWETH DISCORD among the brethren.

Another translation uses the wording:

> The Lord hates ... a person who stirs up conflict in the community. (NIV)

When one understands this tactic, they can identify agendas at work in response to news headlines:

> •Financial crisis •debt crisis •sub-prime mortgage crisis •911 •Patriot Act •NSA citizen surveillance •Gulf oil spill crisis •border crisis •immigration crisis •AIDS crisis •drug crisis •crime crisis •Avian Flu crisis •Mad Cow Disease crisis •swine flu crisis •global warming crisis •climate change •unemployment crisis •healthcare crisis •Internet virus crisis •computer hacking crisis •terrorism crisis •Occupy Wall Street •"Hands Up Don't Shoot" •BLM (Black Lives Matter) •Confederate statue protest •National Anthem protest •March for Our Lives, etc.

In each case, the media whips the country into a frenzy and Congress is pressured to quickly pass legislation – which conveniently is already written but no one had time to read it – and only afterwards do citizens "find out what is in it."

No matter what the crises are, the answers presented always have something in common – people surrender more of their freedoms.

President Obama's Chief of Staff Rahm Emanuel said:

You never want a serious crisis to go to waste.

Secretary of State Hillary Clinton told the European Parliament in Brussels, March 6, 2009:

The chief of staff for President Obama is an old friend of mine and my husband's ... and he said, you know, never waste a good crisis.

A growing concern is whether America is being set up for another crisis, its own version of an Arab Spring.

Unprecedented numbers of unvetted immigrants have been brought into cities across the nation, with a percentage being fundamentalist members of ISIS or the Muslim Brotherhood who want sharia law.

Race-baiters use inflammatory rhetoric and hire agitators to instigate riots, cause domestic disturbance, and even ambush police, in Ferguson, Baltimore, Charlotte, Milwaukee, Baton Rouge, and Dallas.

News headlines read:

Billionaire George Soros spent $33 million bankrolling Ferguson demonstrators (*DailyMail*); George Soros funds Ferguson protests (*The Washington Times*); Baltimore Riots: A product of the Soros machine (*Activist Post*); Soros group advocates violence against cops in Baltimore (*InfoWars*); Soros behind violent riots at Trump rallies (*DailyCaller*); Father of slain Dallas cop sues Black Lives Matter and George Soros for 550 million (*DailyHeadlines*); George Soros tied to more than 50 "partners" of Anti-Trump Women's March (*Breitbart*); North Dakota wants hired pipeline protesters to pay state income taxes (*The Washington Times*); Look Who Funds The Group Behind The Call To Arms At Milo's Berkeley Event (*DailyCaller*); Leaked memo reveals Soros plan for Federally controlled police (*Breitbart*).

If headlines are true, it would be following Saul Alinsky, Hitler, Marx, Hegel, Robespierre, Machiavelli, Julius Caesar, Philip II of Macedon, and Abimelech:

- Identify racial & class fault lines running through society.

- Fan real or perceived injustices into flames by hiring agitators, community organizers, and agent provocateurs to create riots.

- When tensions erupt into violence, everyone is so desperate to have order restored they relinquish their freedoms to the state.

Once the riots occur, Federal authorities arrive to investigate police departments over accusations of racism; or in other instances, offer departments assistance in fighting increased violence. Either way, local control is usurped and city police departments become, in a sense, a defacto Federal "standing army."

George Washington warned of this in his Farewell Address, September 19, 1796:

And of fatal tendency ... to put, in the place of the delegated will of the Nation, the will of a party; – often a small but artful and enterprising minority ...

They are likely, in the course of time and things, to become potent engines, by which cunning, ambitious, and unprincipled men will be enabled to subvert the Power of the People and to usurp for the themselves the reins of Government; destroying afterwards the very engines which have lifted them to unjust dominion ...

But this leads at length to a more formal and permanent despotism ...

Disorders and miseries, which result, gradually incline the minds of men to seek security and repose in the absolute power of an Individual ... [who] turns this disposition to the purposes of his own elevation, on the ruins of Public Liberty ...

The spirit of encroachment tends to consolidate the powers of all the departments in one, and thus to create, whatever the form of government, a real despotism.

✺

LOVE IS THE ANSWER, NOT HATE

Franklin Roosevelt stated in a radio address for a Birthday Ball for Crippled Children, January 30, 1940:

The answer to class hatred, race hatred, religious hatred ... is the free expression of the love of our fellow men.

Franklin D. Roosevelt stated in a Campaign Address at Brooklyn, NY, November 1, 1940:

We are a nation of many nationalities, many races, many religions – bound together by ... the unity of freedom and equality.

Whoever seeks to set one nationality against another, seeks to degrade all nationalities.

Whoever seeks to set one race against another seeks to enslave all races ...

So-called racial voting blocs are the creation of designing politicians who profess to be able to deliver them on Election Day.

Roosevelt prayed on United Flag Day, June 14, 1942:

Grant us victory over the tyrants who would enslave all free men ... We can make ... a planet ... undivided by senseless distinctions of race.

Rev. Dr. Martin Luther King, Jr., who attended Booker T. Washington High School in Atlanta, Georgia, 1942–1944, warned on August 28, 1963:

In the process of gaining our rightful place we must not be guilty of wrongful deeds.

Let us not seek to satisfy our thirst for freedom by drinking from the cup of bitterness and hatred.

We must forever conduct our struggle on the high plane of dignity and discipline.

We must not allow our creative protest to degenerate into physical violence ...

New militancy which has engulfed the Negro community must not lead us to a distrust of all white people, for many of our white brothers, as evidenced by their presence here today, have come to realize that their destiny is tied up with our destiny and their freedom is inextricably bound to our freedom. We cannot walk alone.

On April 16, 1963, Rev. King warned:

I stand in the middle of two opposing forces in the Negro community.

One is a force of complacency ... The other force is one of bitterness and hatred, and it comes perilously close to advocating violence.

It is expressed in the various black nationalist groups that are springing up across the nation, the largest and best-known being Elijah Muhammad's Muslim movement.

Nourished by the Negro's frustration over the continued existence of racial discrimination, this movement is made up of people who have lost faith in America, who have absolutely repudiated Christianity, and who have concluded that the white man is an incorrigible "devil."

Rev. King continued:

I have tried to stand between these two forces, saying that we need emulate neither the "do-nothingism" of the complacent nor the hatred of the black nationalist.

For there is the more excellent way of love and non-violent protest.

I am grateful to God that, through the influence of the Negro church, the way of nonviolence became an integral part of our struggle ...

If our white brothers dismiss ... those of us who employ nonviolent direct action ... millions of Negroes will, out of frustration and despair, seek solace and security in black nationalist ideologies – a development that would inevitably lead to a frightening racial nightmare.

Booker T. Washington, who founded the Tuskegee Institute in Alabama, wrote in *Up From Slavery* (1901):

I learned this lesson from General Samuel Chapman Armstrong, and resolved that I would permit no man, no matter what his color might be, to narrow and degrade my soul by making me hate him.

With God's help, I believe that I have completely rid myself of any ill feeling toward the Southern white man for any wrong that he may have inflicted upon my race.

I am made to feel just as happy now when I am rendering service to Southern white men as when the service is rendered to a member of my own race.

I pity from the bottom of my heart any individual who is so unfortunate as to get into the habit of holding race prejudice.

Booker T. Washington stated:

In the sight of God there is no color line, and we want to cultivate a spirit that will make us forget that there is such a line anyway ...

I have always had the greatest respect for the work of the Salvation Army especially because I have noted that it draws no color line in religion.

Booker T. Washington wrote:

The man is unwise who does not cultivate in every manly way the friendship and goodwill of his next-door neighbor, whether he be black or white.

Booker T. Washington wrote in *Up From Slavery* :

Great men cultivate love ... Only little men cherish a spirit of hatred.

George Washington Carver was invited by Booker T. Washing to teach at Tuskegee. Carver wrote to Robert Johnson, March 24, 1925:

Thank God I love humanity; complexion doesn't interest me one single bit.

George W. Carver wrote to YMCA official Jack Boyd in Denver, March 1, 1927:

Keep your hand in that of the Master, walk daily by His side, so that you may lead others into the realms of true happiness, where a religion of hate, (which poisons both body and soul) will be unknown, having in its place the "Golden Rule" way, which is the "Jesus Way" of life, will reign supreme.

∽

SPIRITUAL REFLECTION

Franklin Roosevelt stated October 6, 1935:

We cannot read the history of our rise and development as a nation, without reckoning with the place the Bible has occupied in shaping the advances of the Republic ...Where we have been the truest and most consistent in obeying its precepts, we have attained the greatest measure of contentment and prosperity.

President Coolidge stated at the 150th anniversary of the Declaration of Independence, July 5, 1926:

> The Declaration of Independence is a great spiritual document. It is a declaration not of material but of spiritual conceptions. Equality, liberty, popular sovereignty, the rights of man – these are not elements which we can see and touch.
>
> They are ideals. They have their source and their roots in the religious convictions. They belong to the unseen world.
>
> Unless the faith of the American in these religious convictions is to endure, the principles of our Declaration will perish. We cannot continue to enjoy the result if we neglect and abandon the cause ...
>
> If there is any one thing among us that is established beyond question, it is self-government – the right of the people to rule ...
>
> We hold that the duly authorized expression of the will of the people has a divine sanction.
>
> But even in that we come back to the theory of John Wise that "Democracy is Christ's government ..." Ours is a government of the people. It represents their will. Its officers sometimes go astray, but that is not a reason for criticizing the principles of our institutions.
>
> The real heart of the American Government depends upon the heart of the people. It is from that source that we must look for all genuine reform ...
>
> Free government ... must not be permitted to degenerate into the unrestrained authority of a mere majority or the unbridled weight of a mere influential few ...
>
> The things of the spirit come first. Unless we cling to that, all our material prosperity, overwhelming though it may appear, will turn to a barren sceptre in our grasp ... We must not sink into a pagan materialism.

Looking back to ancient Israel as a previous example of a people who ruled themselves under law:

- when they sought the Lord they were blessed;
- when they forsook the Lord, He first sent prophets telling them to repent;
- if they did not repent, He sent judgment by letting people of other nations invade and dominate them. Deuteronomy 28:43: "The foreigners who reside among you will rise above you higher and higher, but you will sink lower and lower."
- when they finally repented, He sent deliverers, such as Gideon, Jephthah, Samson, Deborah, and Samuel.
- When they renewed their covenant with the Lord and were blessed.

In like manner, America honored the Creator, even referring in the Declaration of Independence to:

- Laws of Nature and Nature's God;
- endowed by their Creator;
- appealing to the Supreme Judge of the World; and
- firm reliance on the protection of Divine Providence.

In the early 19th century, America was blessed with unprecedented prosperity and inventions:

- Eli Whitney invented the cotton gin:
- Samuel Morse invented the telegraph;
- Robert Fulton invented the steam boat;
- Cyrus McCormick invented the mechanical reaper;
- Samuel Colt invented the revolver;
- Charles Goodyear invented rubber vulcanization;
- Isaac Singer invented a sewing machine.

But America backslid with the expansion of slavery. Like Old Testament prophets, abolitionist societies called America to repent. When the nation did not repent, judgment came with the Civil War, resulting in over a half a million deaths.

Lincoln declared a Day of Fasting, March 30, 1863:

> The awful calamity of civil war ... may be but a punishment inflicted upon us for our presumptuous sins to the needful end of our national reformation as a whole people ...

> We have forgotten God ... We have vainly imagined, in the deceitfulness of our hearts, that all these blessings were produced by some superior wisdom and virtue of our own.

> Intoxicated with unbroken success, we have become ... too proud to pray to the God that made us! It behooves us then to humble ourselves before the offended Power, to confess our national sins.

Lincoln warned in his Inaugural, March 4, 1865:

> The Almighty has His own purposes. "Woe unto the world because of offenses; for it must needs be that offenses come, but woe to that man by whom the offense cometh."

> If we shall suppose that American slavery is one of those offenses which, in the providence of God, must needs come, but which, having continued through His appointed time, He now wills to remove,

> and that He gives to both North and South this terrible war as the woe due to those by whom the offense came, shall we discern therein any departure from those divine attributes which the believers in a living God always ascribe to Him?

> Fondly do we hope, fervently do we pray, that this mighty scourge of war may speedily pass away.

WHO IS THE KING IN AMERICA?

Yet, if God wills that it continue until all the wealth piled by the bondsman's two hundred and fifty years of unrequited toil shall be sunk, and until every drop of blood drawn with the lash shall be paid by another drawn with the sword, as was said three thousand years ago, so still it must be said "the judgments of the Lord are true and righteous altogether."

The Civil War ended and the country survived, renewing the covenant with God by putting "In God We Trust" on the National coins and declaring a National Day of Thanksgiving.

With the challenges facing America today, there is a renewed call for those of Judeo–Christian beliefs to once again follow Lincoln's admonition.

Jeremiah 18:7–8

At what instant I shall speak concerning a nation, and concerning a kingdom, to pluck up, and to pull down, and to destroy it;

If that nation, against whom I have pronounced, turn from their evil, I will repent of the evil that I thought to do unto them.

Persecution is increasing. Christianity is the world's largest religion, estimated at 33 percent of the earth's population. An estimated 80,000 people convert each day. Christianity is also the most persecuted religion, with an estimated 500 being martyred each day.

Anti-Christian attitudes have increased in Western countries through the aggressive advance of the LGBT agenda and fundamental Islam.

As crises appear, it is important to be reminded that, from a Biblical perspective, two things happen at these times:

- In CRISIS people turn to CHRIST!
- In CRISIS leaders are raised up!

The most popular stories in the Scriptures are when God's people are in a hopeless situation, then He raises up little nobodies, who are small in their own eyes but big in faith and courage, to save His people.

Such were the examples of Moses, David, Gideon, Deborah, and now you!

∽

FOR THE SAKE OF POSTERITY

For a Christian, the MOST important thing is to bring people to Christ, but the SECOND MOST important thing is to preserve the freedom to do the MOST important thing!

For any responsible citizen, the concern is for one's posterity. Proverbs 13:22 states:

> A good man leaves an inheritance to his children's children.

At the beginning of the Revolution, Dr. Joseph Warren, who died in the Battle of Bunker Hill, had written in the Suffolk Resolves, September of 1774:

> That it is an indispensable duty which we owe to God, our country, ourselves and posterity, by all lawful ways and means in our power to maintain, defend and preserve those civil and religious rights and liberties, for which many of our fathers fought, bled and died, and to hand them down entire to future generations.

The Preamble of the U.S. Constitution, 1787, states:

> We the people of the United States, in order to ... secure the blessings of liberty to ourselves and our posterity, do ordain and establish this Constitution.

George Washington wrote on July 2, 1776:

> The fate of unborn millions will now depend, under God, on the courage and conduct of this army.

Our cruel and unrelenting enemy leaves us
no choice but a brave resistance, or the most
abject submission. We have, therefore to
resolve to conquer or die.

Colonel William Prescott fought at the Battle of
Bunker Hill. In the face of overwhelming odds, he
repeated General Israel Putnam's order, "Don't shoot
until you see the whites of their eyes."

When British General Gage saw Prescott through
his telescope, he asked a local if Prescott had enough
courage to fight, to which came the reply:

Prescott is an old soldier, he will fight as
long as a drop of blood is in his veins.

In August of 1774, leading men from the town of
Pepperell in delivering loads of rye to the starving
citizens in Boston, William Prescott admonished:

Our forefathers passed the vast Atlantic,
spent their blood and treasure, that they might
enjoy their liberties, both civil and religious,
and transmit them to their posterity ...

Now if we should give them up, can our
children rise up and call us blessed?...

Let us all be of one heart, and stand fast in
the liberty wherewith Christ has made us free;
and may He, of His infinite mercy grant us
deliverance out of all our troubles.

Theodore Roosevelt stated March 4, 1905:

If we fail, the cause of free self-government
throughout the world will rock to its foundations,
and therefore our responsibility is heavy, to
ourselves, to the world as it is today, and to
the generations yet unborn.